NOCHE BUENA

NOCHE BUENA

Hispanic American Christmas Stories

Edited by

NICOLÁS KANELLOS

OXFORD
UNIVERSITY PRESS

2000

OXFORD
UNIVERSITY PRESS

Oxford   New York

Athens   Auckland   Bangkok   Bogatá   Buenos Aires   Calcutta
Cape Town   Chennai   Dar es Salaam   Delhi   Florence   Hong Kong   Istanbul
Karachi   Kuala Lumpur   Madrid   Melbourne   Mexico City   Mumbai
Nairobi   Paris   São Paulo   Singapore   Taipei   Tokyo   Toronto   Warsaw

and associated companies in

Berlin   Ibadan

Copyright © 2000 by Oxford University Press, Inc.

Published by Oxford University Press, Inc.
198 Madison Avenue, New York, New York 10016

Oxford is a registered trademark of Oxford University Press

Noche buena : Hispanic American Christmas stories
/ edited by Nicolás Kanellos.
p. cm. Includes bibliographical references.
Prose in English, some translated from Spanish; poetry in English and Spanish.
ISBN 0–19–513527–X — ISBN 0–19–513528–8 (pbk.)
1. Christmas—United States—Literary collections.
2. American literature—Hispanic American authors.
3. Hispanic American literature (Spanish)—Translations into English.
4. Hispanic Americans—Literary collections. I. Kanellos, Nicolás.
PS509.C56 N63   2000   810.8'0334—dc21   00–26116

Book design by
Carla Bolte

1 3 5 7 9 8 6 4 2
Printed in the United States of America
on acid-free paper

Para Crissy y Miguel y toda la familia—

Feliz Navidad

Special thanks to Alejandra Balestra, coordinator, and all the research assistants of the Recovering the U.S. Hispanic Literary Heritage Project for helping me find the historical materials for this anthology.

Un fuerte abrazo

Contents

II. Puerto Rico and New York

◀ NOCHE BUENA ▶

Introduction

Hispanic American Christmas
in the United States

Nicolás Kanellos

O ther than the piñata and the occasional Christmas carol sung in Spanish, few Hispanic Christmas practices have found their way into the American customs associated with celebrating Christ's birth. That may change as the Hispanic population of the United States becomes larger and more integrated into everyday American life. It is to be expected that both Hispanic and U.S. mainstream customs will change and evolve, because the history of both the American and Hispanic cultural mosaics has been characterized by adaptation to new peoples and places as well as adoption and borrowing from their diverse cultural baggage. When it comes to Christmas, Hispanic traditions have always been at the crossroads of religious and cultural conflict and can thus serve as an indication of cultural change over time.

The stories, poems, and songs in *Noche Buena: Hispanic American Christmas Stories* are a sample of narrative and lyric literature that depicts both original Christmas celebrations and beliefs among Hispanics and those that have been adopted or adapted from Anglo-American traditions. Somehow, throughout centuries of colonialism, cultural mixing, and roots stemming from three continents, Hispanics have preserved a uniqueness in character and worldview that can be appreciated in our Christmas literature. Each literary piece included here, even the earliest, which evinces no Anglo-American influence, is truly mestizo in nature; for mixing and blending has been part of Hispanic identity since the centuries of conquests in Spain itself, before the inevitable bringing together of peoples of the Americas and Africa. The process continues today with the bilingualism and biculturalism of Hispanics in the United States.

Christmas traditions in the development of Hispanics within the United States have been at the crossroads of religious and cultural conflict as well. They also indicate the level of accommodation and comfort that Hispanics have negotiated for themselves within the United States since the days of U.S. geographic and political expansion southward and westward. As Catholic Hispanics confronted migration of predominantly Protestant "pioneers" into the lands previously owned by Spain and Mexico, sentiments held since the Counter-Reformation in Spain became inflamed. In addition to being forced to adapt to a new language and new legal, political, and educational systems, Hispanics had to get used to new Anglo-American customs at the heart of public belief and behavior. And Christmas was the greatest national holiday. At first, adapting the new Christmas customs was akin to betraying one's religion, national identity and even family. But as the twentieth century rolled on, Hispanics more and more embraced the most public elements of Christmas celebration, and some Hispanics even became Protestants.

Christmas traditions in the Hispanic world have been consistently and predominantly related to Catholic religious practices, for Hispanics the world over are predominantly Catholic in their faith and tradition. As Hispanic civilization spread around the world, its culture changed as many of the cultural practices of the colonized peoples eventually found their way into mainstream Hispanic life—even in the mother country of Spain. While the Spanish language, for the most part, has historically resisted change, the culture of Spain has certainly blended with the indigenous cultures of the Americas. In Mexico and the Andean republics of South America, where Amerindian populations have remained substantial, distinctly national cultures have emerged that anthropologists consider to be *mestizo*, or mixed Spanish-Indian. Likewise, in the Caribbean, where the population of African peoples has remained high, mulatto cultures have emerged. In Mexico and the Caribbean—where lie the cultural roots of most Hispanics in the United States—the native religions of the Amerindians and Africans often combined with Catholicism in noninstitutional and informal ways, as well as in officially sanctioned religious practices. There have even developed syncretic or hybrid religions, such as santería, that maintain their own separate institutions and practices but rely heavily on the pairing of African or Amerindian rituals and deities or saints with Catholic ones.

As the American republic expanded during the nineteenth century, it incorporated lands through conquest and purchase that were inhabited predominantly by Hispanics. At one time or another, the territory from the present states of Georgia and Florida all the way to the Pacific Coast and north to Oregon belonged to the Spanish crown. After 1821, the year of Mexico's independence from Spain, the present states of the Southwest, plus parts of Oklahoma, Utah, and Nevada, belonged to Mexico. Cuba, the Dominican Republic, Panama and Puerto Rico have all been under U.S. colonial rule well into the twentieth century; Puerto Rico to this day is still a colony of the United States. At the present turn into the twenty-first century, the peoples of these formerly Hispanic lands in and outside the United States have had two centuries of contact, exchange, and reaction to Anglo-American culture.

American political and economic dominance in this hemisphere has resulted in the export of many cultural practices, including everything from Santa Claus to rock and roll. On a more substantive level, the growth of Protestantism among Hispanics in and outside of the United States has been especially marked since World War II. The variety of cultural practices maintained by Hispanics is often a reflection of the historical and economic forces that have determined their relationship with Anglo-America. The economic and political success of the United States today has been accompanied by the acceptance abroad of many of its cultural products. Thus, a number of American Christmas traditions have been adopted in Mexico, Puerto Rico, Santo Domingo, Cuba, and elsewhere; Santa, his reindeer, Christmas trees, and the quaint traditions associated with much colder climates and snow have now become commonplace.

Mexico and the Southwestern United States

What has come to be considered the traditional literature of Christmas in Mexico and elsewhere in the Spanish-speaking Americas is really the product of Spanish missionary attempts to evangelize the Amerindians by schooling them in the mysteries and dogma of the Catholic faith. The early missionaries in the Caribbean, the Floridas, and Mexico immediately recognized the importance to the American Indian nations of musical, poetic, narrative, dramatic, and dance rituals in sustaining and passing on the beliefs and histories of their peoples. These missionaries, first the Franciscans and later the Jesuits, studiously set about utilizing these cultural forms as tools for converting the Indians to Catholicism. They took particular advantage of native dance-drama and song, replacing the content of the rituals while often preserving the indigenous music, costumes, flower and feather decorations, and even masks. First, they learned the languages of the Amerindian groups and translated the New Testament and the catechisms into those languages. These translations were soon followed by translations of the religious songs and miracle plays of the friars, staged in outdoor patios adjacent to the early missions. As the Indians became more Hispanicized, this hybrid religious ritual and literature was presented, learned, and passed on in Spanish, and the indigenous languages and many of the indigenous performance elements were forgotten. Nevertheless, these hybrid or mestizo songs and performances have become some of the most widespread and longest lasting folklore in the New World, surviving in some cases even today in parts of New Mexico, Texas, Mexico, and the Caribbean.

In 1531, the evangelization of the Amerindians accelerated with the miraculous appearance of the Holy Virgin to a humble mission Indian, Juan Diego, on a site that had been traditionally used for Aztec and Toltec religious ceremonies, the Tepeyac mound just outside Mexico City. The appearance of the Virgin of Guadalupe as an Amerindian herself, with bronze skin and high cheekbones, and the miraculous impression of her image surrounded by roses onto Juan Diego's serape became the symbol of acceptance of the Catholic faith and its saints by the Amerindians throughout the hemisphere. The Virgin of Guadalupe has since then been considered the patron saint of the Americas, as well as the patron saint of Mexico.

The Christmas season in Mexico runs from nine days before Christmas, shortly after the feast day of Our Lady of Guadalupe, on December 12, until Three Kings' Day, on January 6. In addition to dramatic reenactments of Our Lady's apparition to Juan Diego, the season is characterized by two Christmas pageants of communal nature: *Las Posadas* and *La Pastorela*. The first of these shares the European roots of caroling door-to-door. The community or neighborhood groups march in procession and solemnly sing the antiquated syntax of the seventeenth-century lyrics of "Las Posadas" as they reenact the flight and search for shelter of Joseph and Mary requesting *posada* or lodging on a stormy night in Bethlehem. The Posadas are reenacted nightly, with the procession visiting different homes until Christmas Eve. The procession is finally admitted into the ninth home each evening, where the pilgrims place the statuettes of Mary and Joseph that they have been bearing and partake of special food and refreshments. The traditional food usually includes tamales, a food that the women of the family ritualistically gather together to prepare for Christmas feasts. Except for the pork, the tamale is almost entirely a Native American corn-based dish of pre-Colombian origin. While the ritualistic procession certainly originated in Europe, much of the music, dress, decorations, and food served reveals the influence of the Amerindians, whose own dance processions were displaced during colonial times.

Las Posadas continue until Christmas Eve, which is decidedly more important than Christmas Day. Midnight mass or *misa de gallo* is attended, after which families return home to party and, in many Mexican homes, eat *menudo*, a chili-pepper-and-hominy-laden beef tripe stew that is considered to have many healing qualities. Christmas gift-giving occurs when the arrival and gifts of the Magi are celebrated on January 6, Three Kings' Day, which, as in Spain, is accompanied by the ritual of lining a box with straw for the Magi's camels; the children awake early on the sixth to find gifts where the straw had been placed. As can be seen, the tradition of Wise Men riding camels is more appropriate for Hispanics living in warm climates, where they can hardly imagine Santa's reindeer prancing in snowflakes or a rotund Santa, in a fur-lined coat, letting himself down a chimney.

Los Pastores, commonly called *La Pastorela*—*pastor* means shepherd in Spanish—is a miracle play with roots in medieval Spain, where the church fathers hosted dramatizations of the

birth of Christ in the church itself during the Christmas festivities. The Franciscan and Jesuit missionaries in the Americas
imported these miracle plays and adapted them to the culture
of the Amerindians to act out and learn the central mysteries
of the faith: God becoming man and sacrificing himself for
man's salvation. The basic plot of the *pastorela* involves the
shepherds' following a star to Bethlehem to find and adore the
Christ Child. Among the hazards of the journey to Bethlehem
are the legions of demons, led by Lucifer, who try to dissuade
and otherwise detour the shepherds from their pilgrimage. In
the end, the shepherds join the Three Wise Men in adoring the
Christ Child in the manger. Even before these miracle plays
traveled across the Atlantic to the New World, some of the
shepherds, such as Bartolo, became comic characters, and, along
with his humor, a certain frolicking and bawdiness entered the
performances staged by villagers. This led to numerous prohi-
bitions of the miracle plays by church authorities. Ironically,
prohibiting these plays may have resulted in the birth of secular
theater in Spain: the folk persisted in their performances outside
of officially sanctioned church practices.

Likewise in Mexico, the *pastorela* performances, which over
the years had incorporated comic motifs and indigenous
non-Catholic religious elements, were outlawed from church
grounds on and off beginning in the late seventeenth century.
The banishment of such a popular enterprise among the common folk ensured that the *pastorelas* would live on as folk drama,
especially in the outlying provinces and on the frontier. Much
religious practice on the northern frontier running from Texas
to California during the eighteenth and nineteenth centuries
was informal and folk-based; in fact, the first settlers of New
Mexico have been documented as performing a *pastorela* in 1598
(María y Campos, 32). Many memoirs written during colonial
times and even under U.S. rule in the nineteenth century doc-

ument the performance of *pastorelas* during the Christmas season
by country folk touring the large ranches or by the Amerindian
workers in the missions. Throughout the nineteenth and early
twentieth centuries entire towns in these areas participated in
their staging as part of or in addition to the church's Christmas
festivities. Then, too, in New Mexico during the same period,
amateur players from rural areas hired themselves out to perform the play in town churches and plazas. All that was needed
in most of these cases was a hand-copied (copied many times
through the years) version of the play, complete with its
seventeenth-century diction and poetics, or, at least, the un-
failing memory of the town's folk poet, whose job it was to
memorize all of the roles and teach them to the new actors each
year. Many of the plays and performance styles were kept within
the same families for generations, and these families would assume the cultural-spiritual leadership of the town or region
each Christmas with the preparation of the *pastorela*. An early-
twentieth-century eyewitness account of the tradition in New
Mexico came from Jennie M. González, writing in a civil rights
organization magazine, *LULAC News* (4 December 1937):

> *Los Pastores*, a sixteenth century dramatization, of the birth of
> Christ, is to be presented. In each village there is a copy of the
> *Pastorela*. It has been handed down from father to son and the
> proud possessor is by virtue of his possession the director. A
> committee is made up of men from the village who ask the
> director in the name of the Infant Jesus to offer his services that
> the play may be presented. An Infant Jesus is borrowed from a
> housewife to be carried by this committee. It is considered a
> great honor to lend the statue for this occasion consequently
> that must be attended to immediately. When this has been
> settled the committee starts out with the statue to visit the
> director's house and says "In the name of the Infant Jesus we

have come to solicit your help in presenting Los Pastores for
the Nativity." Because the director has been asked in His name
he cannot refuse. That having been accomplished the committee
proceeds from house to house until the cast has been completed.
Each one is designated his part by the committee. From year
to year the same people take the same role with the exception
of St. Michael who according to New Mexican tradition must
be a boy about fourteen years old. A very young girl takes the
part of the Virgin and she is changed after a couple of performances due also to her age. The only other female character is
Jila who accompanies the shepherds to the manger. She is also
a very small child usually about eight years old. The other
members of the cast know their parts, have saved their para-
phernalia and are ready to play their parts in very short notice.

Everything is symbolic. The shepherds carry crooks that are
elaborately decorated with tinsel, shiny decorations and sweet
sounding bells. Each shepherd carries a pack made of white silk,
strapped with white ribbons over his shoulders. These packs are
very small say about 12 inches in diameter and about 14 inches
long. On this pack is embroidered the name of the character
which he plays. Five characters are not dressed symbolically—
St. Michael who wears an armor over his flowing white robe;
the hermit who is dressed in a brown robe resembling a monk's
habit; and the devil who is dressed in red with a long tail and
ferocious horns. Jila is dressed in white (modern dress) and
wears a veil and artificial flower wreath on her head. The Virgin
is dressed in the traditional garb.

The setting is very simple. Usually an altar is used for a
background in front of which is set the statue of the Infant
Jesus with Mary sitting on one side and Joseph on the other.
The performance takes place in front of the manger. The play
is long and monotonous because of the many verses in the
hymns and the long speeches made without any gestures or

intonations. The monotony is broken by the antics of the hermit and the devil or Bartolo who is so lazy that when the other shepherds tell him that he will glimpse a bit of heaven by going to see the Infant Jesus he answers that if heaven wants to be seen heaven should come to him.

The motivation for the players was often not just spiritual, as they toured and performed for modest fees. What is distinctive about the *pastorelas* of the Southwest is the homemade costumes and masks, revealing Amerindian influences, as well as the prominent roles taken on by the Hermit, the comic shepherd Bartolo, and Gila, the virginal shepherdess. So important have these characters become that a modern dramatist, Luis Valdez, has featured Gila as the protagonist in the stage and film versions of his updated *La Pastorela*, loosely based on the *pastorela* script that belonged to the San Juan Bautista Mission in California.

In *Noche Buena: Hispanic American Christmas Stories*, as a matter of fixing origins, we have included a sample Los Pastores, translated in 1907 from a Rio Grande City, Texas, version that was hand-copied in 1891 by a cobbler who owned the manuscript and would use it yearly to dictate the parts to the actors. Besides representing an important historical text, the extraliterary circumstances of the dictation and memorizing make clear how immense an undertaking it was for semiliterate, rural folk to learn the antiquated diction and baroque poetry that has survived in this script for this community pageant. In addition to the *pastorela*, in this collection are a series of nineteenth- and early-twentieth-century poems that also exhibit the traditional elements associated with a Mexican and Hispanic Christmas, in general: the birth of Christ, the shepherds' journey to Bethlehem, the coming of the Three Magi. But running throughout these poems and much Christmas literature are the subthemes of the eternal cycles of the dying year and rebirth, as in José María Bustillos's "Christmas Carols," and the inequalities of wealth and class in society, as in "Christmas Night," by Jesús María Flores. Newspaper editors and cultural leaders, always concerned with preserving traditions, often published materials from Spain that would serve as models for Mexicans in the Southwest; such was the case of the reprinting of Spaniard Manuel Reina's famous poem "Christmas Eve" in El Paso's *Las Noticias* in 1899. All of these selections in this collection exhibit the religious faith and cultural foundation on which later practices would evolve.

In the early twentieth century, native Mexican Americans of the Southwest realized that the old ways had passed, having been displaced by the new language and traditions of the recently arrived northeasterners and Europeans, who were convinced their ways were superior to whatever previously existed in that southwestern landscape. The native New Mexican writers and intellectuals, as overwhelmed as were their communities by the massive migrations, struggled to remember and retain times past and to take control of their own history and identity. In so doing, they discovered that writing was a form of cultural preservation, even writing in the English language, the language of the newcomer and of the state. Perhaps their short-run and poorly distributed publications did not make it east as testimony of their people's surviving worldview, but the writers had made heroic efforts at recording for future generations life as it was once, or at least as it was in their nostalgia and their dreams and idealizations. Christmas traditions, at the crossroads of religious and cultural conflict, were a common indication of the shifts in culture that had transpired in the making of Mexican Americans out of Mexicans.

San Antonio's Adina de Zavala, the granddaughter of the first vice president of the Texas Republic, researched the history

and legends of central Texas in her efforts to preserve a balanced
Texas mythology, one that included the Amerindian, Spanish,
and Mexican historical records, in her effort to stave off the
current and popular Texas history defined by proponents of
Manifest Destiny. She sought to save her "Legend of the First
Christmas at the Alamo," just as she fought to save the building
itself from destruction. As well, Jovita González, writing in the
1930s, sought to retain the lore and history of South Texas
prior to the coming of the Anglos in her recollection, "The
Good Eve." Essayists and memoirists Nina Otero and Cleofas
Jaramillo emphasized the old Spanish roots of New Mexican
culture in an effort to elevate the status of their southwestern
culture by identifying it with European civilization and down-
playing the Native American background. If Manifest Destiny
and the culture of the Northeast affirmed that white was right
and Anglo-Americans were superior because of their high culture derived from Europe, then New Mexicans could also point
to the achievements of the Spanish Empire in introducing civilization and religion to the Americas, specifically in what became the southwestern United States. Even a Mexican immigrant writer such as Adolfo Carrillo found a rich history and
romance in the Hispanic Southwest of missionary days in his
recasting of the Don Juan legend in the "Los Espectros de San
Luis Rey." All of these writers looked to the past for their
identities and cultural validation. Christmas and its traditions
was a distinct marker of what made their culture unique and
valuable.

On the other hand, cultural change was already evident by
the late 1920s, when Protestant writers such as J. N. De los
Santos and S. R. Acevedo, both of Texas, were publishing their
songs and scripts for children's Christmas pageants in the local
religious newspapers. The world of *Las Posadas* and *Los Pastores*
had definitely been replaced by more formal church perform-

ances and Protestant hymns in Spanish translation. Then, too, "Samuel's Christmas Eve," by New Mexican Herminia Chacón, not only captures the spirit of Santa Claus as early as 1923 but seems to have been heavily influenced by such American writers as O. Henry. While in many parts of rural New Mexico the *pastorelas* were still being performed, E. Luján wrote in the Albuquerque newspaper *La Bandera Americana* (The American Flag) on December 28, 1923, that "many homes are even grander with the magnificence of the Christmas tree. Never as much in this season are gifts and giving so desired and expected; the wishes of an entire year are all granted by that kind old gentleman Santa Claus. The child, the teenager, the mature and the aged, all follow their visits with the multiple and changing colors of the gifts hanging from the tree, lost amid the beautiful prisms of light that like a shower of diamonds that sparkle and twinkle midst the sheen of the frost and gold leaf of the ornaments. In each countenance is sketched a wish, the desire for a gift." The growing acceptance of the Christmas traditions of Anglo-America in these works was no longer seen as a novelty but as a permanent part of the annual celebration.

It was not a novelty either for many Mexican-American writers emerging after World War II, who began to examine realistically the life and culture of their communities as American ethnic minorities. Their works show a glaring awareness of the expectations of U.S. consumer society, within which Mexican American poverty and marginalization had become so obvious. In their stories, the privation and injustice suffered by the poor is heightened during the Christmas season, when parents struggle and sacrifice to buy toys for their children. Often the children have nothing but the Virgin of Guadalupe and God himself to hang onto, as in Américo Paredes's "A Cold Night," or a sack of oranges and nuts is their gift instead of toys in Tomás Rivera's "The Night before Christmas." In Rivera's story, the parents emphasize Three Kings' Day as a means of getting the children to forget about Santa Claus and Christmas because they have no money to buy the children toys, and maybe by Three Kings Day the children will forget about Santa. And Saint Nick, in Rolando Hinojosa's "The Gulf Oil Can Santa Claus," has finally become the totem, the signifier of triumphant Americanization, the symbol in the story that represents the most Americanizing period in Mexican American history: World War II and the Korean War. After these types of tales, Diane de Anda's "The Christmas Spirit Tree" treats all the traditional Anglo-American symbols of Christmas as Mexican American as well: matter-of-fact, completely assimilated traditions, part of their national identity. Today, a "Hispanic" Christmas in the Southwest or Mexico is something for children's literature, something to be taught to them as exotic practices from lands far away and quaint, as in Pat Mora and Charles Ramírez Berg's "The Legend of the Poinsettia," where *Las Posadas* and gifts to the Christ Child are perhaps rituals that grandparents once performed but now must be communicated in a special type of bicultural artifact: the children's picture book.

Puerto Rico and New York

In Puerto Rico, as in much of the Hispanic world, the sacred festivities of Christmas have traditionally centered on a Christmas Eve feast, midnight mass, and the gift-giving on Three Kings' Day, as described above. What is specific to Puerto Rico, however, is the two-to-three weeks of festivity that is characterized by singing Christmas songs and dancing out in public and in private homes, all of which is done to Puerto Rico's particular blend of Afro-Caribbean music. Also, groups of *jíbaros* were known to descend from their mountain homes to sing their soulful highland *décimas*, with intricate ten-line stanzas that are improvised by these rural minstrels. In a ritual loosely equivalent to Mexico's *Las Posadas*, families and neighbors join together to sing *aguinaldos*, or traditional Christmas songs, accompanied by guitars, maracas and *güiros* (a ridged gourd for scraping), as they go from house to house in their *parrandas* (similar to caroling), pleading to be invited in to partake of such sweets as Spanish marzipan, rum drinks, and traditional Christmas foods, which include roast suckling pig, rice with pigeon peas and bits of pork, and *pasteles* (a tuber and meat pie wrapped in banana leaves, influenced by indigenous, Spanish, and African foods). All of these foods figure prominently into the traditional songs, quite often more than any references to the sacredness of the holiday. A sampling of these songs is included here. But in this traditional oral literature, when the religious meaning of Christmas is addressed, the emphasis remains on the coming of the Three Magi, which can be seen in the song "The Three Wise Men," also included in this collection.

The whole gamut of these traditional Christmas practices comes into conflict with Anglo-American traditions in a battle that resembles Puerto Rico's struggle to preserve its own particular cultural identity and heritage while existing as a colony of the United States. After being sought by the United States as a spoil of the Spanish American War in 1898 and after Puerto Ricans became citizens of the United States in 1917, the island continued under military rule and under governors appointed by U.S. presidents until 1949. For more than half a century the United States imposed its own laws and institutions upon the natives and for more than thirty years attempted to implement English as the official language of public education in Puerto Rico. One of the officials in charge of the Americanization of public education in Puerto Rico was Juan B. Huyke, the Commissioner of Public Instruction in Puerto Rico in the early 1920s, when he wrote "A Story of Santa Claus." An author of textbooks and children's literature, Huyke intended that his Santa story not only be read in homes but at school. To adapt his endearing Santa to the Puerto Rican climate and environment, the jolly bearded one travels in a coach from outer space to Earth, rather than from the North Pole in a sled pulled by reindeer. And so as not to conflict with Catholic teachings, while Santa descends to Earth, he witnesses the souls of deceased children rising up to Heaven.

Throughout the twentieth century, the vast majority of writers in Puerto Rico and on the mainland have longed for the self-determination of their island nation. For many, while political and economic independence have not been seen as possible, they nevertheless have struggled for cultural independence and national identity. To do this, they insist on the purity of the Spanish language in their works and identify themselves more with the writers and cultures of Central and South America than with the United States. When creating their national literature, they base their works on roots deeply planted in the culture and traditions of the *jíbaro* highlander or the Afro-Puerto Rican coastal dweller. In 1947, Abelardo Díaz Alfaro figuratively sent Santa Claus to the guillotine in his story set in the fictive highland town of La Cuchilla (literally guillotine). Díaz Alfaro's satirical tale involves a young teacher and his supervisor, both very much convinced of the superiority of American ways, like Juan B. Huyke himself, who attempt to teach English and American traditions to the children of simple sharecroppers and farmers of La Cuchilla. An out-and-out duel between traditions ensues at the school's Christmas celebration when the new teacher tries to displace the traditional songs and festivities with Santa Claus, a Christmas tree, and all the other accoutrements of the American celebration.

A recent story, "The Day We Went to See the Snow" by Alfredo Villanueva-Collado, is based on the magic realism in everyday life in the tropics: the Mayor of San Juan in the 1950s, Felisa Rincón de Gautier, actually made a Christmas gift of snow flown in from the Northeast to the children of San Juan. Villanueva-Collado and many other cultural commentators suspected that this effort was like so many others that pointed to Puerto Ricans' cultural deficiency: the children would be deprived by not experiencing snow firsthand. As in "Santa Claus Goes to La Cuchilla," Villanueva's tale points to the folly of the Americanizing enterprise.

The result of this cultural conflict, of course, has been a blending, a merging of traditions that can be seen in Nicholasa Mohr's "Christmas Was a Time of Plenty," in which the author reminisces about the traditional foods eaten at her family's celebrations in New York City, and of the expectations of the children for new toys under the Christmas tree, even during the Depression. For Piri Thomas, reminiscing about the same period of time in "Those with Less Shared More," the answer was accepting both traditions and being doubly enriched: both Christmas tree–Santa Claus on December 25 and the Three Magi on January 6. But as the Mexican American writers mentioned above, both Mohr and Thomas dwell on the poverty experienced by Puerto Ricans in New York, who were also confronted by the materialistic expectations of American consumer society. Thomas's comment is poignant, that most people at a party would leave the room "if anyone was uncouth enough to play 'I'm Dreaming of a White Christmas.' Considering the constant lack of heat in apartments in winter time, you could hardly expect the singing of 'White Christmas' to be a big hit." Thomas's story is also significant in that it also shows a merging of Protestant faith and practices—Seventh Day Adventist and

Pentecostal—with Puerto Rican traditions. Christmas *asaltos* and traditional *aguinaldos* come together with Dickens's Tiny Tim in these bilingual, bicultural people.

A Hispanic Immigrant Christmas

Immigration has been part of Hispanic culture in the United States since the seventeenth-century Sephardic Jewish communities were established in New England and on New Spain's northern frontiers. Throughout the nineteenth century, political and economic refugees from the Hispanic world joined already long-standing communities in the southwestern and northeastern United States. Spanish Americans from throughout the hemisphere flooded the booming San Francisco area during the Gold Rush. The first Mexican laborers were imported for agricultural work during the American Civil War. To this date, disparity between the economic and educational opportunities in the U.S. and Spanish America, American interventions in the Spanish American republics, the need for manpower in times of war and economic expansion—all these and many other reasons account for the steady stream of Hispanic immigrants who continue to settle here and become part of the American mosaic.

The Christmas literature of the immigrants and their children reveal the same familiar themes as the rest of immigrant literature: nostalgia for the homeland and its culture, struggles in adapting to the United States, an ultimate acceptance and blending with American ways. "Christmas Eve," a narrative poem by a Mexican immigrant poet, Aurelio Luis Gallardo, nostalgically evoked in 1852 what a Christmas Eve celebration was like in his native Guadalajara. The long narrative reproduces the splendor and hubbub of Christmas in the big city and contrasts it with the humble and wholesome Christmas of the country folk, a wholesomeness that would surely lead the predominantly male immigrant society of San Francisco to long for the homeland.

While not waxing nostalgic for the homeland, the offspring of immigrants often fondly remember the culture in the immigrant enclaves where they themselves became the bridges from their parent's traditions to those of the larger society as they left the enclave behind. In "La Nochebuena: The Best of Nights," New Yorker Jose Yglesias recalls how his family and community succeeded in secularizing the sacred feast day, transforming it from the celebration of the "good night" (or holiest night) to the the celebration of the "good life," possibly in honor of the modest success in providing for their families as cigar factory workers in Ybor City, Florida. He recounts how the holiday back in the 1920s and 1930s was laden with traditions that were practiced perhaps out of racial memory and how it was central to the identification and consolidation of family and friends into one proud community of "the privileged of the earth"—despite their struggles for survival during the Depression and their blue-collar status and uprootedness from Cuba and Spain.

Generations of immigrants, on the other hand, have told their stories of adaptation and blending. Cuban immigrant writer Roberto G. Fernández has penned a number of books satirically documenting the quirks and maladjustments of the Cuban community in Miami. His "The Good Night" is a humorous sketch of how a particular family attempts to reproduce the type of middle-class Christmas celebration they were accustomed to back in Havana, only now in a foreign land and with more modest means. In Gustavo Pérez Firmat's memoir, he describes how he is torn between the two cultures and their folkways, particularly during Christmastime, in "Nochebuena Good Night." In an excerpt from her young adult novel, *Loves*

Me, Loves Me Not, Anilú Bernardo recreates the uncertainty of a teenage girl's first experience with an Anglo-American Christmas dinner. Her home culture and that of her hosts come into strong contrast not only because of the differing traditions but also because of the uprootedness of her family of modest means. The Christmas described in Elías Miguel Muñoz's novel *Brand New Memory* revolves around a thoroughly assimilated Cuban American Princess living in Southern California; thus, apparently, ends the distinctiveness of the Hispanic immigrant's traditions during that most traditional of religious feasts: Christmas.

Conclusion

An Hispanic American Christmas in the United States can be many different things, depending on the native or immigrant status of the celebrating family or community. What is evident throughout this illustrated collection of customs and practices is that Christmas in life and lore, history and literature, is a key to Hispanic identity and its relationship to other peoples and societies. Christmas may mark a crossroads of cultural and religious conflict or adaptation for Hispanics, but their richly diverse literature reflects the unity and wholeness of their experience while living bilingual-bicultural lives. It is the individual, the family, and the community that attribute meaning to life's experiences and rituals. And it is the writer's job to record and affirm their choice, their identity. In each of these life-affirming poems, stories, and dramas, the individual and community are celebrating their survival and flourishing, even under the threat of political and cultural extinction. The birth of the new god, the new cycle of existence, is an affirmation of Hispanic culture's ability to constantly renew itself across time and geography.

A Note on the Sources for
Noche Buena

Many of the stories, poems, and songs and the play included in *Noche Buena* represent the first fruits of a ten-year national project, Recovering the U.S. Hispanic Literary Heritage, centered at the University of Houston, to reconstitute the literary traditions of Hispanics in the United States. Many of the selections have been chosen from the writings recovered from Spanish-language newspapers published in the Southwest during the nineteenth and early twentieth centuries. These works by mostly unknown authors have captured the Christmas sentiments of their communities at the time; they exhibit both the nostalgia for tradition and the new embrace of the all-pervasive American national culture. A number of poems have been drawn from religious newspapers published in Texas, during the time that Texas was the publishing center for Hispanic Protestants not only in the United States but throughout the hemisphere. The works reveal the new religious literature that was displacing traditionally Catholic interpretations of Christmas in the Southwest and, to some extent, in the rest of the Hispanic hemisphere. Other works, such as those of Salvador Calderón, Aurelio Luis Gallardo, and the contemporary Cuban authors, were selected from books published in the United States by their immigrant authors and represent the first scholarly recognition of a body of Hispanic immigrant literature created and published in the United States from the nineteenth century to the present. *Los Pastores* and a number of songs have been drawn directly from the folklore that is still very much alive among Hispanics in the United States; these works of oral literature are artifacts dating back some three hundred years. Finally, *Noche Buena* includes works by contemporary Hispanic authors who reflect the latest blending of Hispanic and Anglo-American interpretations of Christmas in a new syncretism that very much responds to a bilingual and bicultural reality.

Except for the translation of *Los Pastores* and that of Tomás Rivera's "The Night before Christmas," all translations have been provided by me, without any pretense to artistry or poetic imagination. I offer them humbly for their meaning, as it is practically impossible to render their true cultural and poetic value.

I

Mexico and the Southwest

Noche Buena and Religious Dramas

Cleofas M. Jaramillo

Cleofas M. Jaramillo's (1878–1956) attempts to preserve the culture of her native New Mexico extended to her founding the Folkloric Society of Santa Fe and her untiring attempts to research and document the cultural practices of Hispanics in the region before the coming of the Anglo-American. To further this historic preservation, she not only wrote down the history and lore of New Mexico but also its culinary recipes and other folkways. Thanks to the documentation in passages such as the following from her Shadows of the Past, *details about Christmas customs have come down to us.*

Further reading: Cleofas M. Jaramillo, *Shadows of the Past (Sombras del Pasado)* (Santa Fe: Seton Village, 1941); Cleofas M. Jaramillo, *The Genuine New Mexico Tasty Recipes: Potajes Sabrosos* (Santa Fe: Ancient City, 1981); Ramón Sánchez, "Cleofas M. Jaramillo," *Dictionary of Literary Biography*, Vol. 122 (Detroit: Gale Research Inc, 1992), 154–58.

Noche Buena and Religious Dramas

> "Let the luminarias leap high
> As the night grows long,
> And the shadows dance
> To the caroler's song."

On the twenty-fourth of December the snow lay heavily on the deep valley, half burying the silent little villages nestling among the white hills. As the last rays of the setting sun turned the highest snow-capped peaks into gold and rose, the men and boys of the three villages busied themselves clearing the snow from the front yards in every house. They were preparing the ground for the *luminarias*, which later in the evening they built of *ocote*—pitch wood sticks, placed by fours in log cabin fashion. Rows of these *luminarias* outlined the towns and *cordilleras*.

As the deepening shadows of night spread over the valley, the brown adobe houses were brightened with the red glow of their fire, which warmed the groups of men and boys standing around them. The fires built in front of my house were kept burning brightly until midnight by an occasional addition of an empty kerosene barrel, which had been saved in the store for that purpose.

Inside the house there was great activity in the kitchen. The children warmed the *piñones* and shelled them by rubbing them between two boards. These nuts were used in the mince meat for the *empanaditas* (little fried pies). An extra hired woman beat the white corn dough until it was so light that a small piece dropped into a cup of water floated on top. It was then ready for the *tamales*, which were made and steamed, to be served with hot coffee after the midnight chapel services. Lupe and her helpers were kept busy until almost midnight, frying the *empanaditas* and *buñuelos* for the *Oremos* boys, who came to the door singing:

Orémos, Orémos,	*Oration, Oration,*
Del cielo venimos,	*From heaven we come,*
Angelitos somos,	*Angels we are,*
Si nó nós dán Orémos,	*If you won't give us gifts,*
Ya no volverémos.	*Alas, we won't return.*
A lás señoras caséras,	*From the housekeepers,*
Aguinaldos pedimos,	*New Year's gifts we ask.*
Con mucha alegría,	*With great joy,*
Con mucho conténto,	*With great contentment,*
Vamos celebrándo,	*Let's celebrate this birth.*
Este nacimiento.	*Give us here, if you will give,*

Dénos aquí, si nos han de dar,   *For the night is long,*
  La noche es larga,   *And we have lots to walk.*
Y hay mucho qué andar.

A large pan of fried dainties was passed to these *Oremos* boys at the kitchen door, and they ate them, sitting around the bonfires.

Santa Claus was still unknown in those days. The *abuelo* (bug-a-boo man) took his place, although he was a stern old man dreaded by the children. Dressed in an old, shabby, patched suit and shabby hat, the *abuelo* went around the *luminarias* cracking his long whip, sending the boys home on the run. He followed some of them into their homes and made them kneel down and say their prayers. If they did not know their prayers, he gave them a good scolding and told them to stay home and learn them, but no sooner was the *abuelo* out of sight than the boys were out again, hopping, running and jumping over the bonfires, for the Spirit of the Christ Child filled their innocent hearts and fear could not remain long in them.

Down in the village the group that was to take part in the performance of the play of *Los Pastores* was going from house to house making *Las Posadas*. They represented Mary and Joseph going through the streets of Bethlehem seeking shelter for the night.

In earlier times, for nine days before Christmas groups of children led by a couple representing Mary and Joseph went through the village to nine houses. The group was refused entrance until they came to the ninth house, where they were admitted and refreshments passed to them. Here the hermit held up his cross at the door, trying to prevent *el diablo* from entering, but the shrewd evil one watched his chance and entered while the hermit was busy eating the refreshments spread

before them. Satan played his pranks, helped himself to anything he liked, rattled his long nails, wrote in his book the
names of the girls and women who smiled at him when he
asked them if they wanted to come with him.

At the end of the village the group came to the chapel where
the wake of *el Santo Niño* was taking place. Here the group gave
the play of *Los Pastores*, the religious drama of the shepherds.

When making *Las Posadas*, Joseph knocked at the door of
each house singing:

Quién le da posada	*Who will give lodging*
A estos peregrinos,	*To these travelers*
Que vienen cansados	*Who come weary*
De andar los caminos?	*From traveling long roads?*

A voice from within answered:

Quién da golpes a la puerta,	*Who bangs at the door?*
Que de imprudente hace alárde,	*The imprudent makes a commotion,*
Sin reflejar que ya es tarde	*Without noticing that it's late,*
Y a los de cása despíerta?	*And the household he awakes.*

Joseph:

Señor os implóro,	*O Lord, I implore Thee,*
Que en vuestra caridad,	*That in Thy mercy*
Le des posáda a ésta dáma.	*Thou wilt give shelter to this damsel.*

Voice from within:

Para él qué tiene dinéro	*For him who has money,*
Mí casa está lista,	*My house is ready,*

Para él qué no tiene,	For him who has nothing,
Díos lo asista.	May God assist him.

Into a stable door they retired, where an ox and a mule were their only companions.

A BRIEF SYNOPSIS OF THE DRAMA *LOS PASTORES.* There were twelve shepherds in the original play of *Los Pastores*, but at the time of which I write only six took part:

Characters

Shepherds—	Tubal	Gila
	Belicio	San Miguel
	Lipido	El Ermitaño
	Barto	La Estrella Oriental
	Lizardo	Bartolo
	Tebano	El Diablo

In earlier reproductions of this play, there was another female character—Dora, wife of Barto, one of the shepherds.

A shrine had been arranged with white sheets and a table at the head of the *oratorio* chapel. A double row of pine trees formed an aisle from the shrine to the middle of the room, through which the shepherds marched in double file, carrying flowery staffs with dingling little bells. A bundle slung over one shoulder suggested the bedding of the shepherds.

Ahead of them walked Hila, a serious-looking little girl, dressed in white, wearing over the veil on her head a tinfoil covered crown. She carried a small baby statue in a basket filled with snow.

Bartolo, the lazy shepherd, walked behind the other shepherds, carrying a sheepskin, which he spread under a tree and then lay upon.

The shepherds tramped up and down the aisle singing verses

about the heavy snow and their flocks sleeping down in the valley.

Shepherd Song

Cielos soberános,	Sovereign heavens,
Tenednos piedad	Have pity on us
Que ya no sufrímos,	For we cannot longer endure
La Nieve qué cae.	The snow that falls.
Suspénde tus íras	Suspend Thy rage
Y tanto quebránto,	So many damages,
Qué ya están poblados,	For the valleys
De Nieve lós cámpos.	Are already covered with snow.
Las estréllas brillan,	The stars shine brightly,
Y luego se apágan	Then get dim
Absortas se quédan	Amazed to see
De ver tal neváda.	Such a heavy snow.
Que cópas de nieve,	What large snowflakes
Caen sobré el ganádo,	Fall over the flock,
Aunque entre el monte	Although resting
Está reclínado.	Under the forest.

Belicio suggested stopping a while, to let the flocks rest, saying:

Pues hermanos míos,	Well, my brethren,
Ya que el cielo nos ha permitido,	Since heaven has permitted
Traernos con grán dicha,	Bringing us with great happiness
A estos valles dé Egipto,	To this valley of Egypt,
Si les parecíere bien,	If it seems right to you,
Parémos aquí un poquíto,	Let's stop here a while
Que descansen los ganádos.	To rest the flocks.

The rest of this drama will be found in my book of translated Spanish dramas.

EL DIA DE LOS INOCENTES (HOLY INNOCENTS DAY). I do not know why this day was celebrated on the twenty-eighth of December instead of after the Kings' visit to the Manger, for it commemorates the day on which King Herod put the children of Judea to death by the sword. On this day one had to be very careful about lending things; and if you loaned something, you must not forget to say, *"Se la empresto, pero no por inocente."* Anyone who forgot to say this had to pay a penalty.

On one occasion my aunt, who lived close by, sent her maid to ask my mother to let her have my baby brother for a little while. My mother, forgetting the day, let the girl take the baby. A few minutes later the maid returned with a tiny broom made of a few straws tied with red floss and wrapped in a little note with the words, *"Barrete la inocencia paga la pena."* Mother at once set to work baking a cake which she sent to my aunt to *desempeñar* (redeem) the baby; he was sent back with the same cake bearer.

DIA DE ANO NUEVO (NEW YEAR'S DAY). Instead of the birthday, the Spanish celebrate the Saint's name day. New Year's day is the day of los Manueles, and the women and men called by this name were serenaded on this day.

One year my brother, who was visiting at my home during the holidays, thought he would play a joke on my husband. He slipped quietly out of the house at four o'clock in the morning and rounded up the musicians who were going around the town *dando los dias a los Manueles* (serenading).

We awakened with the sound of music and singing at our front door; my husband in bathrobe and bedroom slippers opened the door and was greeted by the usual verse:

> *"Por aqui caigo, por aqui levanto,*
> *A darle los buenos dias,*
> *Pues hoy es dia de su santo."*

He politely invited the serenaders to enter; and they made themselves at home, while he ransacked my pantry for refreshments. My brother sat among them, with a broad smile, quite pleased with the success of his joke.

My husband's grandmother's name was Manuelita; and not wishing to disturb her so early in the morning, my brother had them come to our house to give the serenade in her honor.

————

Gifts were exchanged on the sixth of January, celebrating the arrival of the Three Kings at the Manger in Bethlehem to offer their gifts to the newborn Babe.

On New Year's day Grandma Melita started counting *"Las Cabañuelas"* for twelve days. Each day of the month represented one of the months of the year, and as the weather showed on each day so would the month be fair, stormy or cold. If January the second was fair and mild, so would the month of February be. The third was counted as March, and so on through each succeeding month. On the thirteenth, *Las Cabañuelas* were reversed and counted backwards, beginning with the month of December. This count was said to come out more true. The definition given for the word *"cabañuelas"* is *"Festival of the Jews of Toledo,"* so this custom must be originally from Spain.

This marked the end of the Christmas ceremonies.

RELIGIOUS DRAMAS. As the dramatization of Bible stories was an old Spanish type of entertainment, it has been assumed that the Spanish *conquistadores* brought the religious drama to Mexico, and that from there the Spanish missionaries introduced it into New Mexico in their efforts to convert the Indians to Christianity. There are four Christmas plays that come in a cycle—in this order: *El Coloquio de San José ; El Auto del Niño Dios*, or *Pastorela*, now called *Los Pastores* with several versions; *Los Reyes Magos*; and *El Auto del Niño Perdido.*

El Coloquio de San José begins with a summons from Simeon to all the males to appear at the temple with a reed in hand, for the purpose of choosing a husband for Mary, one of the Virgins in the Temple.

When Feliciano, the herald, comes to Joseph, he voices the wishes of his master, saying:

Vós patriarca escuchad.	*Patriarch, thou listen.*
Pues ya sabeis que Simeón,	*Well thou knowest that Simeon,*
Cabéza de éstas comárcas,	*Head of this territory,*
Manda púes qué los patríarcas	*Commands that all the patriarchs*
En sú real generación,	*In his royal generation,*
Hoy al templo soberano	*Today at the sacred temple*
Sean obligados a llevar,	*Are obliged to appear*
Una vara en sú máno	*With a reed in their hand,*
Y de parte de Simeón	*And I, for Simeon,*
He venido a tí avisar.	*Have come to inform you.*

Joseph, because of his poverty, is reluctant to go into the temple, and he sits in the portico. Suddenly his reed sprouts forth a lily, and he is chosen to espouse Mary.

After the Annunciation, several months elapse; and Joseph and Mary are on their way to Bethlehem. On reaching the town, they go from house to house seeking lodging for the night. This part of the action is represented by *Las Posadas*, which is an introduction to the play of *El Niño Dios*, or *Los Pastores*, the second drama of the cycle.

Then comes the third drama, *Los Reyes Magos*. The three kings, noticing the new star in the East, decide to go to Bethlehem and offer gifts to the Christ Child. They stop at the palace of King Herod, who gives them welcome and asks them to stop again on their return. The kings reach the manger and present their gifts. After they leave, an angel appears and bids

Joseph to take Mary and the Infant and flee into Egypt. On the way the Holy Family meets a number of shepherds, who recognize them.

The fourth drama of the series is called *El Niño Perdido*. Christ, being separated from His parents comes, in his wanderings, to a rich man's palace. The rich man is seated at a banquet table when the Child arrives. He tries to confuse the Child with his questions, but is given wise answers. At the end, the Child arrives at the temple, and the Doctors of the temple gather around to question Him, while Mary and Joseph are looking for Him. *The script of this play is given in my book of Spanish dramas.*

Christmas Eve

Manuel Reina

The Spanish modernist poet Manuel Reina's (1856–1905) works were often reprinted in the newspapers of the Southwest. Reprinted in the December 23, 1899, edition of El Paso's Las Noticias, *"Christmas Eve" reinforced the Hispanic themes of the contrasts of wealth and class seen during the holiday season.*

Further reading: Manuel Reina, *Manuel Reina: sus mejores versos* (Madrid, 1928); Manuel Reina, *La vida inquieta*, ed. Richard Andrew Cardwell (Exeter, England: University of Exeter, 1978.)

Christmas Eve

Fun and laughter, a golden altar,
A family seated round the fireplace
Singing and making merry;
A sprightly waltz played with grace.

Hear the beat of a valiant heart
Of a soldier recalling his hometown,
A shining goblet of champagne,
with crystalline foam crowned.

Those poor unfortunates out in the cold;
An abandoned child so sad and chilled;
The deepest depth of an ocean filled
With its bellowing howl, angry and bold,
And the ferrous peal of a lily-shaped bell,
Seems first a cheer, then a mournful yell.

Noche Buena

Risas, placeres, el altar dorado,
La familia que canta y se recrea
En torno de la blanca chimenea
El walz alegre, rítmico y alado.

El corazón valiente del soldado,
Henchido del recuerdo de su aldea,
Y el champagne que en la copa centellea,
De cristalina espuma coronado.

Los infelices, la tormenta, el frío;
El niño abondonado que suspira
Triste y glacial; la voz atronadora
Del hondo mar colérico y bravío,
Y la campana, que cual férrea lira,
Ya parece que canta, ya que llora.

Christmas Carols

José María Bustillos

The Mexican man of letters José María Bustillos (1866–1899) had his poems and essays published widely in Mexico. In San Antonio, Texas, readers anticipated his Christmas poems for promoting the spirit of the season. But in "Christmas Carols"—reprinted in the December 23, 1928, edition of El Heraldo Mexicano—*the poet sounds a note similar to that in other poems in* Hispanic American Christmas: *the narrator will die before the next Christmas rolls around.*

Further reading: José María Bustillos, *Versos (1884–1898)* (Toluca, 1900).

Christmas Carols

Oh dreamy Christmas night!
Oh holy Christmas night!
Each one of your carols
is a sweet piece of my soul.
You arrive amid everyone's emotion,
all then arise in their devotion,
each accent sung by them a hymn
and their every look a kiss
and each breast a honeycomb
of sweet memories and of hopes.
Oh Christmas, oh flower of winter,
poem whose immortal strophes
withering time carries on its wings:
your story is a legend,
your drama a play in the soul,

Cantares de Navidad

¡Navidad noche de ensueños!
¡Navidad noche sagrada!
cada uno de tus cantares
ea un pedazo del alma!
Tú llegas, y todo el mundo
se conmueve: se levanta,
y es un himno cada acento
y un beso cada mirada
y cada pecho un nectario
de recuerdos y esperanzas.
Navidad, flor del invierno,
poema cuyas estancias,
conduce, de siglo en siglo,
el tiempo, mustio, en sus alas:
tu argumento es la leyenda,
tu escenario está en las almas,

and all people are your poets
and with their lutes to you do sing!
It's midnight already! Oh Christmas! . . .
You are already gone! . . . Here comes the dawn! . . .
Perhaps when you return, *ay*,
you'll ne'er again hear my song!

December brings death to the fields,
and the abandoned plains are desolate,
that hoary winter season
strikes cold the lilies with its frost.
The city and all its fine palaces
seems like a nest of herons grey,
and the humble homes of humble people
are like white roses all in a bunch . . .
The sun goes off afar . . . the evening
lets loose her nacred hair,
and all heaven above is a canopy
by bright carnations all bedecked.
As the moon poses languidly
upon its azure swing,
the cold rises to the hills
and in the city all is still! . . .
Then, as in a conjuration,
oh Christmas you appear,
weaving into your fair curls
strands of hay and Easter lilies,
gathering resins from the woods,
pine trees from the thicket,
you dress yourself in thin garb
all adorned in deep green
to prance with grace across the plain,
lightly tapping your tambourine,

y tu poeta es el pueblo
que en sus vihuelas te canta!
¡Navidad . . . ! ¡ya son las doce!
Ya te vas . . . ! ¡ya viene el alba . . . !
¡Tal vez !ay¡ cuando regreses,
ya no escuches mi guitarra!

En diciembre muere el campo;
y en la llanura abismada,
el invierno tembloroso
esparce lirios de escarcha.
La ciudad, con sus palacios,
parece un nido de garzas;
y las casitas del pueblo
un puño de rosas blancas. . . .
Y el sol se aleja. . . . La tarde
suelta el cabello de nácar,
y el espacio es una tienda
con claveles adornada.
La luna, lánguidamente,
se yergue en su azul hamaca;
y en la sierra crece el frío;
y en la ciudad. . . . todo calla . . . !
Y entonces, como a un conjuro,
Navidad, tú te levantas:
entretejes tus cabellos
con heno y flores de pascua;
juntas resinas del monte,
cortas pino en la cañada,
te ciñes el tenue traje
formado de verde lama,
y atravesando graciosa,
la llanura solitaria,
sacudes tu pandereta,

to rend a *piñata* into shreds,
and fan us with your mossy wings.
On hearing you the people cry,
they kneel to you and vocalize . . .
Christmas! . . . God bless Christmas!
Long live winter, Hosannah!
Perhaps when you return, *ay*,
you'll ne'er again hear me sing!

Progress, oh God of the era,
through your sovereign touch,
has laid rails to mountain tops
and crossed the seas with wires.
As reason has conquered all,
the faithful abandon now the plow
and Jesus Savior no lilies finds
on the steps of his sanctuary!
Only you remain alive,
Christmas, you never change;
it's that you give us light
to brighten the winter wake.
It's that you regale us with a kiss
a remembrance of past happiness.
You fight the snowy bull of winter,
you nestle in our very soul! . . .
It's already one in the morning, Christmas!
Spread your wings and be on your way.
Perhaps, perhaps next year, *ay*,
my song you shall not hear!

Oh Christmas, have you forgotten?
In my childhood days I was happy,
happy was I in joyful play

despedazas tu piñata,
refrescas los corazones
con el musgo de tus alas,
y llora el pueblo al oírte,
y so arrodilla y te canta. . . . !
¡Navidad. . . . ! ¡Bendita seas!
Reina el invierno ¡hosanna, . . . !
¡Tal vez ¡ay! cuando retornes.
ya no escuchas mi guitarra!

El progroso—dios del siglo—
con su mano soberana,
tiende ríeles en las cumbres,
tiende alambres en las aguas.
El pensamiento, conquista;
los fieles dejan el ara,
y Jesús no tiene lirios
de su santuario en las gradas!
Sólo tú, sigues viviendo,
Navidad, tú nunca cambias;
y que tú nos prestas lumbre
para la invernal velada,
¡es que tú nos das un beso
de las dichas ya pasadas!
¡es que tú, torcaz de nieve,
tienes tu nido en el alma . . . !
Navidad. . . . ! ya dió la una. . . .
Vete ya. . . . tiende tus alas . . .
¡Tal vez ¡ay! el año que entra,
ya no escuches mi guitarra!

Navidad, ¿se te ha olvidado?
En los años de mi infancia,
fui feliz jugando mucho

with all your flowers incarnadine.
Today I am young but oh so sad
without hope, without love,
my meadowlarks all flown off! . . .
Have you knowledge if next year
my fevered brow'll be frozen here?
Ay, then, forget me not,
Christmas, be not ungrateful;
cover my tomb of blanched stone
with strands of hay and moss,
hang a tiny branch of pine
on my withered and forgotten cross . . .
And strum a song of mourning
with your breath o'er my guitar!

con tus flores encarnadas.
Y hoy soy joven y estoy triste,
sin amor, sin esperanzas,
y ya todas mis alondras
se fueron a la montaña. . . . !
¿Sabes tú si el año que entra
estará mi frente helada?
¡Ay! entonces, no me olvides;
Navidad, no seas ingrata:
adorna con heno y musgo
mi tumba de piedra blanca,
cuelga ramitos de pino
en mi cruz abandonada. . . .
¡Has que lloren con tu aliento
las cuerdas de mi guitarra. . . . !

The New Year Is A-Comin'

Anonymous

The following is a verse of folk poetry, repeated and passed on orally as the old year expires. The somewhat macabre celebration of death is a traditional theme in New Year's literature in Spanish.

The New Year is a-comin'
The New Year is a-goin'
We too shall be leavin'
A-comin' back no more.

El año nuevo se viene,
El año nuevo se va,
Y nosotros nos iremos
Y no volveremos más.

Christmas Night

Jesús María Flores

Nothing is known of Jesús María Flores other than that he published
"Christmas Night" and other poetry in El Paso's Las Noticias *news-*
paper on December 23, 1899. In his poem, the author explores the
traditional contrast of the wealthy and poor that is a subtheme of
Christmas literature.

Christmas Night

In front of a hall so bright,
A happy band plays into the night,
All is joy and all is light,
There is where the rich delight.

Before this scene passes a loving mother
In the poorest of threads she's dressed,
She covers over the small bare head
of a child of her loins in rags bedecked.

As the child spies such a splendid sight
Where the happy band plays into the night,
"How grand it is there, my dear mother,
even on this hardest of all nights so dour!"

On spying this unusual pair,
A tiny child from within does stare:
"Oh, Dear Mother of Our Newborn God,
How awful is this Grandest of All Nights!"

Noche de Navidad

Frente á la brillante sala
Donde suena alegre orquesta,
Donde todo es luz y fiesta,
Donde el rico se regala

Una madre con cariño
Vestida con pobres trapos,
Abriga entre sus harapos
De sus entrañas á un hijo.

El cual mirando á la sala
Donde alegre orquesta suena.
—¡Madre! dice, ¡allí cuán buena
Debe ser noche tan mala!

En tanto mira esta escena
Desde dentro un pequeñuelo
Y dice: ¡Madre del cielo,
Cuán mala es la noche buena!

The Star of Bethlehem

J. N. de los Santos

The Reverend J. N. de los Santos was a Presbyterian minister and frequent contributor to the Kingsville, Texas, El Eco. Published in the December 1938 issue, the following recital piece for seven children must have served him well in the religious instruction of the church members' children.

Further reading: Anthony S. Arroyo and Gilbert Cadena, eds., *Old Masks, New Faces: Religion and Latino Identities*, 3 vols. (New York: City University of New York, Bildner Center, 1995).

The Star of Bethlehem

[Recital for seven children. They enter in step to march music.]

I

After so many years
Of doubts and fears
Of desires and frustrations,
Of ill will and disdain:
Dark disillusionment
Was lifted like a veil
And today in our sky is shining
The Star of Bethlehem.

II

The beauteous firmament
Is lined with glory,

El Astro de Belén

[*Recital para siete niños y niñas. Entran marchando al son de una marcha*]

I

Después de tantos años,
De dudas y temores,
De afán y sinsabores,
De males y desdén:
Los negros desengaños
Pasaron como un velo
Y hoy brilla en nuestro cielo
El Astro de Belén.

II

El bello firmamento
De gloria tiene rastros,

Lighted by the stars
And by the earth sustained;
And all of these omens
Of sun and of glory
Not a single one equals
The Star of Bethlehem.

III

The humble shepherds
Who were all reposing
By the calm waters of fonts
Saw its white reflection;
They leaped with joy
And headed for high ground
As light circled them all around
Of the Star of Bethlehem.

IV

The beautiful avian creatures
Quieted their chirping discourse,
The rivers and the winds
Quieted their rumors too;
The flowers and the roses
Also withheld their colors
On seeing the resplendence
Of the Star of Bethlehem.

V

Why is all this silence,
So grave and so profound,
Spreading the world around
With a mystic anticipation?
Why only below that blanket

Su luz le dan los astros
Y el mundo su sostén;
Y en todo ese portento
De soles y de gala,
Ni uno solo iguala
Al Astro de Belén.

III

Los tímidos pastores
Paciendo en las corrientes
Tranquilas de las fuentes
Su blanca imagen ven;
Y saltan placenteros
Buscando la montaña
Mientras la luz los baña
Del Astro de Belén.

IV

Las aves primorosas
Callaron sus acentos,
Los ríos y los vientos
Calláronse también:
Las flores y las rosas
No dieron sus colores
Al ver los resplandores
Del Astro de Belén.

V

¿Por qué silencio tanto,
Tan grave, tan profundo
Está llenando al mundo
De místico vaivén?
¿Por qué bajo ese manto

Descending from on high
Is it shedding its light
The Star of Bethlehem?

VI

Only to these shepherds
Was this prize revealed
And for their enjoyment
This mysterious good:
Angels all a-singing
Descended down to them
All bathed in the light
Of the Star of Bethlehem.

VII

The news they were announcing
Said, "Behold He is born
Jesus the One promised
in Eden by Our God;
Now that the holy prophesies
Have all come to bear,
Search ye all for the Messiah
The Star of Bethlehem."

VIII

They all approached the Child
Without a doubt in their faith,
And what did they find but Christ
In his crib, in all His Goodness;
They gave him all their love,
They returned home following
The shining light above
Of the star of Bethlehem.

Que viene de la cumbre
Tan sólo da su lumbre
El Astro de Belén?

VI

Tan sólo a los pastores
El goce les fué dado
Y a ellos revelado
El misterioso bien:
Pues ángeles cantores
Vinieron hasta ellos
Cubiertos con destellos
Del Astro de Belén.

VII

Las nuevas que les dieron
Decían: "Ha nacido
Jesús el Prometido
Por Dios en el Edén;
Pues ya cumplidas fueron
Las santas profecías,
Buscad, pues, al Mesías
El Astro de Belén."

VIII

Y fueron con el Niño
Con fe sin duda alguna,
Y hallaron en la cuna
A Cristo nuestro Bien;
Le dieron su cariño,
Volvieron después ellos
Bajo los gratos destellos
Del Astro de Belén.

IX

For this the rivers and the breeze
Suddenly stilled their activity,
Even the birds in the trees
Were stilled mutely;
For they all could feel
The joy and happiness
Of Jesus' nativity
'Neath the Star of Bethlehem.

[*In unison:*]

2–Today like yesterday
3–Happy Nature sings.
4–Humanity has risen
5–Singing of goodwill
6–Joining their trophies
7–With voices of victory
8–To sing the glory

[*Everyone:*]

Of the Star of Bethlehem.

IX

Por esto enmudecieron
Los ríos y los vientos,
Detuvo sus acentos
El pájaro también;
Porque también sintieron
El gozo y la alegría
Cuando Jesús nacía
Bajo El Astro de Belén.

[*Al unísono:*]

2—Ahora como entonces
3—Feliz Natura canta,
4—La humanidad levanta
5—Canción de parabién;
6—Uniendo con los bronces
7—Sus voces de victoria
8—Para cantar la gloria

[*Todos:*]

Del Astro de Belén.

New Year's Eve

Anonymous

*The following poem was published anonymously in the January 1940
installment of San Antonio's Baptist magazine,* El Bautista Mexicano. *In the poem, a common undercurrent to much Christmas and
New Year's literature in the Spanish language is fully developed: the
cycle of life and death and rebirth, which is a cycle central to Christianity itself.*

New Year's Eve

Wake me up early, very early, mother dear.
I want to greet the birth of this New Year.
This may be the last New Year I see
And you'll forget, when I die, all about me.

Today when the sun sank amid such peace
My soulful memories also sank into the sea.
No, dear mother, I'll not another year see
Nor a bud nor a flower on the sloe tree.

Under the white hawthorn and its faint shadow,
In May a crown kissed my brow of snow.
Around the maypole in the thicket we danced nigh
Until Osa Major's cart rose high in the sky.

No more flowers, ice on the pane shines bright.
Let me see once again the fragile bell flower

Víspera Del Año Nuevo

Despiértame temprano, temprano, madre mía.
Del Año Nuevo quiero mirar nacer el día.
Quizás este Año Nuevo veré por vez postrera,
Después—después tu olvido cuando muera.

Hoy cuando el sol poniente hundióse en plan calma.
Llevóse mis recuerdos, llevó la paz de mi alma,
Y no veré ya, madre, del próximo Año Nuevo,
La flor en los endrinos, del arbol el renuevo.

De los espinos blancos, bajo la sombra leve,
En Mayo, una corona besó mi sién de nieve,
Bailamos junto al poste, bajo la selva humbrosa.
Hasta que alzarse vimos el carro de la Osa.

No hay flor; en los cristales, el hielo, esplende y brilla,
Quisiera ver de nuevo la frágil campanilla.

Or upon this orb the sun shine its light
Or at least a flower . . . any kind before I expire.

High on the elm a crow's loud appeal
And a puffin sings as he leaves the field.
The dark swallows return all to their nest . . .
But in a dark tomb my stiff corpse will rest.

To my tomb, through a golden gate
The sun rays will bring on a new day.
Before the rooster crows in the nearby town
You too, my mother, in peace will lie down.

At the dawning hour, when sprout the new flowers
You'll no longer see me mid hill and dale,
Not even with the wind tearing down the vale
Nor moaning mid rushes, nor whistling in bowers.

Lay me down, mother, 'neath the hawthorn tree,
and come visit my tomb, oh mother, occasionally.
You'll see that your image in my mind will not pass . . .
I'll feel your feet stepping above me on the soft grass!

Forgive me, dear mother, my capriciousness.
Just one kiss, one kiss to die in happiness.
Do not cry, oh please, don't let my absence bother.
For remember, sweet mother, your other daughter.

I shall not leave my grave, oh my loving mother.
Even when you see me not, your image I'll see,
Without us speaking, your voice I'll perceive,
And when your thoughts turn to me, I will return to thee.

When, dear mother, you hear my eternal farewell,
And carried out upon shoulders I exit this cell,

Del sol los rayos de oro por la celeste esfera.
O alguna flor . . . alguna, para antes que me muera.

So los copudos olmos graznará la corneja,
Cantará el frailecillo que la campiña deja,
La obscura golondrina retornará a su nido . . .
Mas dormirá en la tumba mi cuerpo entumecido.

Sobre el cancel dorado, sobre la tumba mía,
Del sol darán los rayos al despuntar el día,
Antes que cante el gallo de la cercana aldea
Y duermas tú, mi madre, y el mundo quieto sea.

A la hora del crepúsculo, cuando haya nuevas flores,
No me verás ya nunca vagar por los alcores;
Ni cuando el viento sople por la campiña obscura,
O gima entre los juncos, o silve en la llanura.

Bajo un espino quiero dormir cuando sucumba,
E irás, Oh madre! a veces a visitar mi tumba;
Verás como en mi mente tu imagen se conserva.
¡Yo sentiré tus pasos sobre la blanda yerba!

Perdóname, mi madre, he sido caprichosa;
Un beso quiero, un beso, para partir gozosa,
No llores . . . ¡oh! no llores; mi ausencia no te aflija;
Recuerda, dulce madre, que tienes otra hija . . .

No dejaré si puedo, mi tumba, madre amante,
Aun cuando no me mires veré yo tu semblante;
Aun cuando no te hable escucharé tu acento,
Y siempre que en mí pienses retornaré al momento.

Cuando te dé ¡oh madre! mi eterna despedida,
Y veas que me llevan en hombros suspendida,

Promise you'll keep from my grave Ethelinda, the belle.
Whose beauty makes flowers all wither in Hell.

Should she tend to my garden with care,
Give her my tools, I keep by the granary there.
And she tend to my roses I planted myself
and the seeding carnation up on the shelf.

Until tomorrow, come by early, mother dear.
I'll lay awake the night, at dawn to sleep.
I want to greet the birth of this New Year.
Wake me up early, very early, mother dear.

No dejes que a mi tumba vaya Ethelinda bella
Hasta que no haya flores; verás cuán buena es ella.

Si mi jardín quisiera cultivar con esmero,
Mis utensilios dale que están en el granero.
Que aquel rosal que puse yo misma en la ventana.
Lo cuide mucho, y cuide mi clavellina grana.

Mi madre, hasta mañana; vendrás a buena hora,
La noche paso en vela más duermo con la aurora,
Del Año Nuevo quiero mirar nacer el día;
Despiértame por eso temprano, madre mía.

Little Christmas Candles

S. R. de Acevedo

All that is know of S. R. is that she was the wife of the Reverend C. C. Acevedo and occasionally published religious poetry in the Kingsville, Texas, Presbyterian magazine El Eco, *which was directed by her husband. This dramatization for little children, printed in the November 1939 edition, assigns traditionally structured four-line couplets to each for recitation. The verse form is the backbone of Spanish folk poetry and has been adopted here for a Protestant religious ceremony.*

Further reading: Anthony S. Arroyo and Gilbert Cadena, eds., *Old Masks, New Faces: Religion and Latino Identities*, 3 vols. (New York: City University of New York, Bildner Center, 1995).

Little Christmas Candles

[*A children's presentation: each of ten children comes on stage carrying a small candle; a little girl follows them all, and with her lighted candle lights each child's candle as he or she recites.*]

1. The light of this little candle
   Speaks to us with clarity
   Of that story so sublime
   Brought to us at Christmas time.

2. This is what my candle means:
   Christ in Bethlehem was born
   And by Magi and the shepherds
   the Christ child was adored.

Velitas de Navidad

[Ejercicio para pequeños: cada uno lleva una velita; al estar todos en la plataforma, entra una niñita con su vela encendida quien irá encendiendo cada velita a medida que cada niño recita.]

1. La luz de esta velita.
   Nos habla con claridad
   De la historia tan sublime
   Que nos trajo Navidad.

2. Mi velita significa
   Que Cristo nació en Belén,
   Que los magos le adoraron,
   Y los pastores también.

3. This little bitty light
   Shining so brilliantly
   Teaches us the humility
   All of us must learn.

4. My little candle shines
   Rays of holy peace
   So all the world can see
   All must love each other.

5. This little light so slight
   Is a symbol of love so bright
   That all the children of the world
   Must give unto Our Lord.

6. I hope my little candle
   Brings the light of faith,
   Which is the lens so mighty
   It brings Christ into sight.

7. My candle brings expectation
   Of goodness and redemption;
   It will always nourish the heart
   Of the tired and worn-out.

8. If there are shadows in your way
   And you are lost in obscurity,
   The rays of my candle will display
   The right path with beauteous clarity.

9. My little candle's not a star,
   But it lights you where you are,
   And with undaunted desire
   It will always shine its little fire.

3. La lucesita pequeña
   Que mi vela puede dar.
   La humildad nos enseña
   Que debemos imitar.

4. Mi velita siempre alumbra
   Con rayos de santa paz,
   Ahora que todo el mundo
   Debiera de amarse más.

5. Esta luz tan pequeñita
   Es el símbolo de amor
   Que los niños y las niñas
   Deben dar a su Señor.

6. Yo espero que mi velita
   Traiga la luz de la fe,
   Es el lente poderoso
   Con que a Cristo se ve.

7. Mi vela trae esperanza
   De bien y de redención;
   Alimenta de continuo
   Al cansado corazón.

8. Si tu senda tiene sombras
   Y te llega oscuridad,
   Mi velita tiene rayos
   De una bella claridad.

9. Mi velita no es estrella
   Pero alumbra su lugar;
   Con anhelo se propone
   Constantemente brillar.

10. On a Happy Christmas Eve
    My little candle shows the way,
    Every ray a little beacon
    on the path to Bethlehem.

    Let us all now take our candles
    To the manger at the inn,
    Where we'll all sing in praise
    and sincerest adoration.

10. En alegre Noche Buena
    Mi velita enseña el bien;
    Con sus rayos nos alumbra
    El sendero de Belén.

    Todos-Llevaremos las velitas
    Al pesebre del mesón,
    Allí demos alabanza
    Y sincera adoración.

Christmas

Felipe Maximiliano Chacón

Editor and publisher of Albuquerque's La Bandera Americana *newspaper, Felipe Maximiliano Chacón (1873–?) was the son of a newspaper publisher, Urbano Chacón, and part of a family of New Mexican men and women of letters. Chacón was a patriot and a champion of all things American, but in his poem "Christmas," published on December 23, 1923, in his newspaper, there is no Santa Claus novelty, only an evocation of the spiritual and religious meaning of the feast day.*

Further reading: Felipe Maximiliano Chacón, *Obras de Maximiliano Chacón, "el cantor nuevomexicano": prosa y poesía* (Albuquerque, 1924); Meyer, Doris, *Speaking for Themselves: Neomexicano Cultural Identity and the Spanish-Language Press, 1880–1920* (Albuquerque: University of New Mexico Press, 1996).

Christmas

The night was so full of peace
and the heavens so clear and bright
what finally arrived at midnight
was the Christ that for mankind
on Christmas had brought his light.

Beneath a beautiful shining sky,
an angel spreading glorious light,
announced to the shepherds' delight,
"I bring good and joyful news
that in Judea the Christ is born!"

La Navidad

Era la noche de calma plena
mostraba el cielo su claridad,
y a media noche de gloria llena
dábase al hombre la enhorabuena
por ser del Cristo la Navidad.

Baja del cielo, diáfano, hermoso,
vertiendo un ángel gloriosa luz
y a los pastores, con alborozo
dice les traigo nuevas de gozo,
¡que hoy en Judea nace Jesus!

Up above sang a heavenly choir
a dulcet and celestial symphony
GLORIA IN EXCELSIS! sweet harmony
with myriad golden notes echoing
throughout the terrestrial community.

Moved by joy, hope and faith,
to Beth'lem shepherds' paths were traced.
There prostrate in adoration
grateful for their great fortune,
they welcomed the Messiah and his grace.

Caesar Augustus was fast forgotten
overshadowed by the chaste shepherd:
He who is exalted becomes humbled
and the humble exalted do become
through this Herald of the Redemptor!

Fly off, oh angelic melody,
take the message of joy and peace,
to all those nations in war embraced
spilling rivers of blood and disgrace,
in a world of ruin and arrogant fury.

May this clear and glorious day
serve them as shining inspiration.
Exchange that horrid conflagration
for sweet canticles of joy,
dignity and angelic benediction.

Let us in holy exaltation
spread among men good will;
today, let us forget our petty battles
and join the angels in healing the ill
with love and goodness forever.

Canta en seguida del cielo un coro
su dulce antífona celestial,
¡GLORIA IN EXCELSIS . . . ! eco sonoro
que se difunde con notas de oro
por todo el ámbito terrenal . . .

Llenos de dicha, fe y esperanza
van los pastores hasta Belén,
y allí postrados en alabanza
píos contemplan su bienandanza
dando al Mesías el parabién.

César Augusto vése ignorado
y distinguido el casto pastor:
¡el que se exalta se vé humillado
el que se humilla se vé exaltado
por el heraldo del Redentor!

Vuelen las notas angelicales
de aquel mensaje de amor y paz,
a las naciones que hoy en fatales
lides derraman rojos raudales
de sangre y ruina con furia audaz.

Séales este glorioso día
fulgido foco de inspiración;
¡truéquese la hórrida lid impía
en dulces cantigas de alegría
digna y angélica bendición!

En santo júbilo estimulemos
entre los hombres el buen humor;
nuestras rencillas hoy olvidemos,
y con los ángeles prodiguemos
al desvalido bondad y amor.

Samuel's Christmas Eve

Herminia Chacón

From the noted family of New Mexico (later El Paso) journalists and writers — we have included a poem by her father Felipe Maximiliano Chacón in this collection — Herminia Chacón began her literary career publishing poetry and short stories in her father's Albuquerque newspaper La Bandera Americana. *The December 21, 1923, issue contained this well-wrought Christmas tale that, except for its having been written in Spanish, could have appeared in just about any English-language newspaper or magazine in the country.*

Further reading: A. Gabriel Meléndez, *So That All Is Not Lost: The Poetics of Print in Nuevomexicano Communities, 1834–1958* (Albuquerque: University of New Mexico Press, 1997).

Samuel's Christmas Eve

It was December 24, and it seemed that each and every soul on earth was busy and content. Except, that is, for Samuel. He just could not find a job, and he was so tired of roaming the streets, suffering hunger and freezing from the cold.

What's worse, the landlady running the boardinghouse where he rented a room—who always charged him on time and to the penny—at last announced that he either pay up or get out. Samuel answered that he'd be leaving, he just did have a penny to his name. Just one favor was all he asked her: that she let him stay one more night, that being Christmas Eve. But the landlady was not in the mood for charity. She needed money, and it was hard for her to earn it, too. The poor woman had been abandoned for a time by her beloved husband, who had taken off all of a sudden and was not to be found. So, poor Samuel left the house with all his earthly possessions tied up in a red silk neckerchief.

As he passed a large toy store, a boy called out for him to enter. There Samuel found the owner: a short and fat but greedy man.

"Would you like to earn five *pesos?*" he asked Samuel. "Yes? Well, I need a Santa Claus. That boy, there, will give you a suit and you'll go outside with a sack of toys and do all you can to get people to come into the store. You understand?"

Samuel did not understand him all that well, but he nevertheless followed the boy, who helped him dress up.

After awhile, Samuel appeared in the happy garb of good old St. Nick. He picked up his sack of toys and a bell, went out and started calling for passersby to enter the store. As the day was quite cold and Samuel was shivering and coughing, prospects did not look too good. Children surrounded him, laughing and shouting, "That's not Santa Claus!" All that noise and carrying on at last caught the attention of the store owner, who came out and yelled at Samuel in a furor: "Take your five *pesos* and get out of here. You're nothing but a laughingstock!"

Samuel took the five *pesos* and, forgetting to take off his Santa suit and leave the sack of toys, he headed down through some of the poorest neighborhoods in town.

Samuel walked as if in a dream. He headed for the boardinghouse he had left behind that morning and went in. He stopped for a moment to rest at the foot of the stairway, when all of a sudden he was surrounded by poor children from the neighborhood. For these miserable and needy children, Samuel was not an object of ridicule but St. Nicholas himself.

Among the joyous shouts of "Saint Nicholas" and "Santa Claus," Samuel gave out the gifts to all of the children, even to the landlady's kids.

"God bless you," she told Samuel. "If it weren't for you, my poor children would have had a very sad Christmas Eve. But, come on in, my husband is here too."

Samuel entered the house to the greetings of a tall, strong-looking man. "Are you Samuel?" he asked. "Well, cheer up, I have work for the both of us in a new factory."

Samuel was so choked up, he couldn't speak. He had five pesos in his pocket, and outside children were shouting, "Hurrah for Santa Claus!" and "Wow, that was Santa Claus!" And now, his friend was telling him that there was work for the both of them!

Samuel was happy. It was Christmas Eve and church bells were ringing: "Peace on earth, goodwill to men."

Christmas Eve

E. Luján

Virtually nothing is known today about E. Luján, other than that he lived in Velarde, New Mexico, and published articles in La Bandera Americana, *an Albuquerque Spanish-language newspaper. For him, as for many of the readers of this issue that celebrated American culture, "Christmas Eve" (December 28, 1923) was now a space where the cultural practices inherited from the Anglo-Americans could be celebrated.*

Further reading: A. Gabriel Meléndez, *So All Is Not Lost: The Poetics of Print in Nuevomexicano Communities, 1834–1958* (Albuquerque: University of New Mexico Press, 1997).

Christmas Eve

> *Night full of delight!*
> *Oh, fortunate night!*
> *Happy night! Lovely night!*
> *Holy night! Christmas Eve!*
>
> *Let's forget our pains,*
> *Children, youths and aged!*
> *Singing joyfully and proud,*
> *This for sure is Christmas Eve!*

Who is it that, amid the vicissitudes of life, does not recall with pleasure the beautiful moments enjoyed at home on a cold but lovely Christmas night, a happy Christmas Eve? Who is that generous and foresighted person, spirited and feeling the emotion of the season, who does not associate the name of his good friends with delight and contentedness?

Lovely night of wonderful poetry that lets us trade our ills for the enjoyment of children's glee, infecting both the youthful and the aged, men and women who, at the sound of guitars and tambourines sing earth's tender refrains. The family is in want of nothing, as the home is full of joy and satisfaction.

In the middle of all this enthusiasm many homes are even grander with the magnificence of the Christmas tree. Never as much in this season are gifts and giving so desired and expected; the wishes of an entire year are all granted by that kind old gentleman Santa Claus. The child, the teenager, the mature and the aged, all follow their visits with the multiple and changing colors of the gifts hanging from the tree, lost amid the beautiful prisms of light that like a shower of diamonds that sparkle and twinkle midst the sheen of the frost and gold leaf of the ornaments. In each countenance is sketched a wish, the desire for a gift.

This year has been particularly prosperous; there has been work for whomever has sought it. Everyone has made money, and we hope that next year the luck and abundance will continue. We must give thanks for these benefits we receive, we must toast the outgoing year and celebrate the incoming year.

We should not hesitate any further during this season in which sadness is fleeing in shame and suffering, when the palace on the hill as well as the humble hovel are dressed up and resplendent. You, too, must prepare yourself to enter into that universal accord and celebrate the coming of the Messiah as did the shepherds in Bethlehem.

The Good Eve

Jovita González

An advanced student of folklore, under the mentorship of Texas's J. Frank Dobie, Jovita González (1904–1983) was an assiduous collector and interpreter of the life and lore of the Lower Rio Grand Valley. It was her particular concern that the historical record and common folks' memories forever preserve the rich legacy of her ancestors and her childhood on Texas-Mexican ranches. Part of that effort was the writing of two novels that were never published during her lifetime; after her inability to have her novels published or to find employment as a college teacher, she spent most of her years as a public high school Spanish teacher in Corpus Christi, Texas. "The Good Eve" is a selection from her novel, Dew on the Thorn, *which was edited by José Limón. The footnotes are his.*

Further reading: Jovita González, *Caballero: An Historical Novel*, ed. José Limón and María Cotera (College Station: Texas A & M University Press, 1996); Jovita González, *Dew on the Thorn*, ed. José Limón (Houston: Arte Público Press, 1997).

The Good Eve

Chapter VII*

It was evening in the pasture. The clear, cold air had the crispness and sharpness of a Texas norther on a December night.

*This chapter of the manuscript was stored separately and was in very poor condition—pages missing, heavy handwritten editing by González and unnumbered pages. It has called for more editing on my part than the rest of the manuscript in order to connect disparate fragments, but I believe that this result is more than less true to González's intentions.

The stars, like diamonds against a tapestry of black velvet, shone more brilliantly than ever for they were awaiting the coming of *El Niño Dios*, the God-child so tender and sweet. Tío Patricio and Cristóbal kept watch with the stars and sheep. The beauty of the night and the thought of Day kept them quiet. All of a sudden from a distance by the *cañada* came a soft murmur, a mournful, melancholy sound almost like a sob. "Listen, little one, do you hear that?" "Yes, Tío, what is it? It seems to say, 'Coo-coo, shepherd,' " "Tomorrow is Noche Buena, the Good Eve, Little Mouse," the old shepherd continued, "and we shall not be here to watch and wait for the coming of the little Jesus."

"But we shall be at Don Francisco's, we shall see the Crib and hear the singers on the *nacimiento*."

"But it is not like being under the stars, waiting for the angels to sing, Little Mouse. I like to watch here in the pasture until midnight on the Good Eve. The sky becomes silvery then and the stars shine as they have never shone before. Everything hushes and if you listen closely you may even hear faintly but distinctly the singing of the angels in Heaven."

"Do you think they will sing this Christmas?" Cristóbal asked in an awed whisper.

"I cannot tell. Only those who are pure in mind and heart or who grieve have that great joy."

"And did you ever hear them, Tío?"

"Only once, little one, many years ago. Not because I was good but because I had a grief in my heart. I was a young shepherd then. The winter had been a trying one and very cold. The coyotes had carried away many of the master's sheep. To make matters worse, *El Inocente* had died in a most horrible manner. That was a long time ago, even before your mother was born."

"And who was *El Inocente*? Won't you tell me about him?"

"Yes, since it was his death that made me hear the angels sing. Juanito, as *El Inocente* was called, was born without a mind. It had remained in heaven waiting for him. Perhaps the same angel that brought him carried his mother back; it was she, no doubt, who had taken his mind back to her Creator, not wishing her son to realize the sufferings of this world. Because he was lacking all understanding, he came to be known as *El Inocente*, The Innocent. His father, a good soul, better than holy bread and as harmless as a new-born lamb, soon followed his wife to join Juanito's mind in heaven. And the unhappy creature was left to the mercy of the good people of the ranch.

No one seemed to assume the responsibility, but Juanito, himself, solved the situation to his liking. One morning, much to the surprise of the whole family, the Master's wife found him sitting on the steps as she opened the kitchen door.

"*Pobrecito angel de Dios*, poor Angel of God," she said to herself. "He has come himself to shame us for our neglect." From that time, *El Inocente* became her property. He grew. His thin arms and legs filled, but mentally he remained the same, just a big boy with the mind of a baby. At the age of thirteen he was a big boy. It was about this time that in the same manner he had chosen a home, he decided to become a shepherd. One day he followed a sheep dog to the pasture and there he remained all day, caring for the sheep only to come home at night. After this, every morning he called his dog and went to join the bleating herd and in the evening when the sun, pale like the smile of an old woman, went to rest, Juanito returned to the ranch.

But one day the flock returned without him. His companion, the faithful shepherd dog came alone, his back and face all torn and bleeding from the bites of some wild animal. He barked and yelped to attract the attention of those around him. However, so preoccupied were they with Juanito's absence that no one paid any attention to him. Finally in desperation he jumped upon the Master Don Ramón, pulled him by the trousers, looked at him, and started running in the direction of the pasture. We followed for a mile or so. Under a mesquite we found *El Inocente* bleeding and unconscious. By his side was a dead coyote. Juanito had strangled it, but in doing so had been horribly mangled. Two days later *El Inocente* and his mind were reunited in heaven from where he often helps me."

"But how can he help you if he is dead?"

"Not he, my child, but his spirit. Sometimes when I cannot gather the flock together, I think of him and say, 'Spirit of *El Inocente*, help me,' and I have never known it to fail, the flock comes together as if by enchantment."

"And when did you hear the angels sing?"

"Oh yes, my heart was sad and I thought of poor Juanito. He had been a better shepherd than I was; he had given his life for the sheep. And I also thought of the Good Shepherd as I have seen him in a picture at the Master's house, carrying a stray lamb on his shoulders. And here I was, poor miserable sinner that I am, failing in my duty. I wept for shame and despair. All of a sudden the sky was filled with a radiance never seen until then and I heard the most beautiful singing. I could not understand the words, but I did make out the words, 'Gloria, Gloria.' I realized then I was listening to God's holy angels and I fell on my knees in adoration. It was beautiful and I felt my soul become like the soul of an angel. Had I died then I would have gone straight to heaven, no doubt."

"Could we hear them if we stay here tonight?"

"Tonight I shall take the part of the holy Joseph and you will be home once more. Listen, do you hear the roosters crowing at the ranch?"

"Not at the ranch, Tío, isn't it too far?"

"Ordinarily yes, but during the Christmas season they crow

louder and clearer. It is like a clarion call announcing the coming of a great event. Morning is not far off," continued the old shepherd. "The turtle-dove is singing. Do you hear it?"

'Coo, coo, Christ is born.'

"Why, Tío, you told me before that it mourned for her lover."

"So I did. But on Christmas Eve she weeps because she, of all the birds, did not see the Christ Child."

"And how did that happen, Tío?"

"She was so humble, so unassuming, no one thought of telling her the wonderful news. All nature, the stars of the heavens, the beasts of the forest, and the birds of the air had been told that the Messiah was to be born. And when the Angel announced the birth of the Savior, all the creatures came to worship Him, all but one—the dove. Yet the sign that brought the birds and the beasts to the Manger itself was the form of a fluttering dove—assumed by the Holy Spirit. But the dove herself never saw the Christ Child and that is why her song is a sob at Christmastime.

"The morning star is descending and the sun will be coming up, but late as usual. That lazy vagabond is like city people; he likes to sleep late. Lobo, Lobo, time to get the flock together and go; we must be at the ranch by noon."

———

Christmas Eve, the Good Eve, was the time for the patriarchal feast at the Olivareño. It was the time when all the friends and relatives gathered there for the annual Posadas* and Tamalada.† Old feuds and enmities were forgotten and people who were irreconcilable enemies during the year met as friends, at least

*The Posadas is a ceremony described later in this chapter.
†Tamalada—A supper of tamales and coffee.

while they remained under that hospitable roof. Even Don Ramón, forgetting his grievance towards Don Francisco, because of his attitude towards Carlos, had come.

Christmas in the border ranches would not be Christmas without the traditional *tamales** and baked turkey. A hog had been butchered and dressed turkeys, hanging from the beams of the *portal*, exposed their fat, naked bodies to the wind. The living room, which had been decorated by Rosita and Nana Chita with garlands of cedar and rosemary, was filled with fragrance and brought happy memories to the old nurse's heart.

"When your father was born," she reminisced, "the first garment he wore was warmed with rosemary fumes to keep him from all evil and bring him happiness. I never smell this good plant without thinking of him as a child. My mother's words, may she be in Heaven, come to me, 'Chita,' she used to say, 'if you want children to follow in the footsteps of the good Jesus, you must always keep rosemary bush in your garden.' And I always have. It is said," Nana Chita continued, "that the Virgin had a big rosemary plant growing by the door of her humble home in Nazareth. In the spring the swallows made their nest on the side of the house, where it grew, hiding it from the bad boys that might rob the birds of their eggs. In the summer the nightingales serenaded her and the good Saint Joseph with their sweet voices. The good priest says that when the little Jesus was born, the whole world was covered with snow and when the Blessed Family returned from Bethlehem, the little Babe, even though he was God, got the colic like all babies do when they get cold. The Blessed Mother was beside herself with anxiety and did not know what to do. All mothers are that way with their firstborn. That's the way I felt about my Pedro, bless

---

*A Mexican dish made of corn meal rolls seasoned with chile and stuffed with highly seasoned pork meat.

him. She must have a fire, and right away too. I can imagine she was even a little cross with her patient husband, Joseph, for not having any wood in the house. The good Joseph, not daring to leave her and the baby alone while gathering the wood for the fire, decided to cut some branches from the bush growing by the door. The room was soon filled with the sweet smell and warmth, and the little Jesus began to coo and gurgle with contentment. The bush became useful in many other ways too; when the Virgin washed the Baby's clothes, she hung them on the branches to dry; when the bad soldiers were killing all the 'Innocents,' the branches of the rosemary bush, of their own accord, covered the door. And when they passed by and saw the gray-looking bush covering the entrance to the house they did not enter there thinking the house deserted. And because the rosemary protected Him, Our Lord blessed the plant and made it holy."

Rosita had lost no time during the old woman's recital. While listening, she made *El Nacimiento* (the crib) with figures of clay. Mary and Joseph stood in the Manger before the Holy Child and shepherds were kneeling in adoration. Around them had been placed all the flora and fauna of the earth, growing and living together regardless of climatic differences and natural tendencies; pines beside palm trees; tropical fruits growing on ice-covered steppes; macaws beside ptarmigans; flocks of sheep peacefully feeding by the side of ravenous wolves. The Three Wise Men, one white, one yellow, and one black, brought their gifts of gold, frankincense, and myrrh. And surmounting all, the Star of Bethlehem shone with brilliancy and paper angels on invisible wires fluttered around on paper wings.

The *piñata*, an earthen pot filled with candy and nuts, patted its enormous belly foolishly as it hung from one beam of the *sala*. From its dizzy elevation it swayed and bowed much to the delight of the children. In a corner of the room stood its executioner, a big, heavy stick with streamers of paper and tinsel which in the hands of blindfolded children would convert its glory into a mass of debris and waste.

After a collation* of *buñuelos*† and coffee, the guests gathered in the *sala* to sing *Las Posadas*. Christmas Eve being the day of fast, the Christmas supper would not be served until after Midnight Mass.

The custom of singing *Las Posadas*, introduced from Mexico by Don Francisco, had become very popular on the border. There was a feeling of joy and expectation as the master led Tío Patricio into the room. The brown-robed, turbaned old shepherd, a very realistic Joseph, walked to the center of the room leaning on his staff. Radiant of face, and voice which vibrated with emotion, the shepherd explained the meaning of *Las Posadas*. It is, he said, the most beautiful and the most solemn service of the Christmas season, a service which those who are still Christians and speak God's language hold every year in remembrance of the wanderings of the Holy Family in Bethlehem, that cold night so many years ago.

"Tonight," he said, "they are to be given lodging in this house and the Angels will no doubt sing in unison to announce the coming of *El Niño Dios*, the God-child."

The guests divided themselves in groups, each representing a house in Bethlehem. The group nearest the Crib was the Inn. The young people, carrying musical instruments, guitars and mandolins, followed Tío Patricio to the *patio* where Rosita,

---

*Collation, in the original sense of the word, was a reading from some edifying book at a gathering of monks in a monastery at the close of the day. During fast days the monks were permitted, if tired, to drink just before the reading. In this way the collation came to be accompanied by light refreshments; hence any slight meal allowed during a fast day came to be known as *collation*. This expression is still used in the same sense in the Texas-Mexican frontier.

†*Buñuelos*—Crisp, fried cakes sprinkled with sugar and cinnamon.

wearing the white robe and blue mantle of the Virgin, was waiting.

In spite of the merriment, there was a certain subdued solemnity as the Holy Pilgrims began their weary journey asking for lodging from door to door,

> *"In the name of Heaven*
> *We ask for lodging*
> *My beloved wife*
> *Can no longer walk," sang Joseph.*

Weary and foot-sore the Pilgrims made the rounds only to be rebuffed brusquely, even with threats of a beating. Finally Joseph made his last appeal,

> *"My wife Mary*
> *Is the Queen of Heaven*
> *For she is to be the Mother*
> *Of the Child Divine."*

The group at the *Nacimiento*, rejoicing at the wonderful news, sang joyfully,

> *"Is that you, Joseph?*
> *Is that you, Mary?*
> *Enter Holy pilgrims*
> *We knew not who you were."*

The Pilgrims and the guests, kneeling in adoration before the Crib, continued singing while two children, taking the image of the Christ Child from the Manger, rocked it in swaddling clothes to the tune of a lullaby,

> *"Good news to you, Oh shepherds!*
> *A virgin just gave birth*

To a Child so beautiful
As the light of day."

The *Posada* ended, the children were given whistles and ser-
pentines and amidst much noise and merriment, the *piñata* was
broken. At the first strains of the orchestra, the *sala* was cleared
for dancing.

No sooner were the first chords of *Sobre las Olas**preluded
when Don Francisco offered his arm to his wife. "Let's show
these slow-minded, slow-moving boys how a waltz is danced."
They whirled and glided across the room amidst the cheering
and clapping of their friends.

"Bravo, bravo, Francisco," cried Don Ramón who had been
watching him. "You shame the girls, Margarita. I often say that
things are getting worse instead of better since our time. No
offense to you, young Ladies," he continued turning to the
group of giggling girls, "but your mothers were better-looking
and better dancers than you are."

"Bless my soul, there is old Alejo with his fiddle," exclaimed
Don Francisco seeing the old man peeping into the room.
"Come in, my good Alejo." The old man entered holding the
fiddle under his chin precluding a polka, and bowing to the
company gathered there. When he finished, he bowed again in
all directions not wishing to leave anyone out. Then clearing
his throat and wiping his wrinkled forehead he repeated his
customary Christmas greeting,

"Praised be the Lord, forever be He praised. Goodnight, I
bid you all assembled here tonight. Perhaps someone will think
I am a drunken Indian. But whoever thinks that of me may
his spine be shriveled forever. I am that good Alejo of whom
you have heard. I am not an Indian beggar, but have some
Spanish blood. On my father's side I am humble; of him I dare

Sobre las Olas—A favorite Mexican waltz composed by Juventino Rosas.

not say much, for although a man of honor, I understand he was hanged. Of myself, I do not speak; you see me here before you, whether good or whether bad that's for you to judge. I am somewhat of a student; I can sing a requiem Mass and play a good quadrille. Praised be the Lord and may you have your wish!"

Not waiting for an answer, old Alejo began playing a quadrille and started tapping his foot on the floor.

"Ay, ah! Alejo, you want the old people to dance." But the descendant of Spaniards did not deign to answer. He merely nodded his head in assent and continued playing.

"*Bien*, Alejo, you call the dance and we will follow you." And as old Alejo played, fathers and mothers, portly grandfathers and . . .*

*Here, the concluding pages to "The Good Eve" are missing. Again, these pages may have continued the story of Carlos and Rosita.

The Phantoms at San Luis Rey

Adolfo Carrillo

A political refugee from persecution by the government of Mexican dictator Porfirio Díaz, Adolfo Carrillo (1865–1926) settled in San Francisco, California, where he continued working in his profession as a journalist for Spanish-language newspapers. Besides working as a newspaperman, Carrillo also ran his own printing establishment and wrote books. His book Cuentos californianos, *first published in the early 1920s, indicates the degree to which he identified with the Hispanic background of California and the Southwest. In his story from that book, "The Phantoms at San Luis Rey," Carrillo creates a Don Juan–type libertine whose sins are even more egregious because they are committed during the sacred season of Christmas.*

Further reading: Adolfo Carrillo, *Cuentos californianos* (San Antonio: Lozano, 192?).

The Phantoms at San Luis Rey

I

Friar Pedro Somera, Prior of the San Luis Rey Mission, was leaving the Refectory, where he had just enjoyed a large breakfast, and proceeded to make his way along the broad arches that bordered the vegetable garden. With one hand, he held his Breviary, and with the other, he patted his belly, as if to tell it, "Look how stuffed you are! If you keep that up, we'll have to roll around instead of walk." Later, feeling tired, he stretched out in his favorite hammock, drawing in great whiffs of the fragrant air that wafted through the flower gardens. As he began to read his Breviary, the vibrating ring of the large bell in the squat tower announced its presence: One! Two! Three!

"Holy Mother of God!" murmured Friar Somera, hopping up from his swing all at once. "Someone needs Communion urgently! Is it possible that Doña Claudina is still sick?"

At that moment, Gervasio, the neophyte, appeared. After kissing the Prior's hand reverently, he said that Don Cirilo Zárate's wife was in agony and was begging for his presence at her deathbed.

"I have a saddled horse outside awaiting your Reverence. It is tame, but fast, and we'll arrive in Encinitas within a half hour."

This transpired one morning in June, 1815. After a half hour of riding their horses at a loping trot, the Prior and his aide were crossing the Estero Valley, which was thickly vegetated around sand dunes and white oaks, and inhabited by meadow larks and aquatic fowl. In the distance, Lake Piedras Blancas appeared in a silvery ribbon which reflected on its surface the branches of the weeping willows along its banks. It was an enthrallingly beautiful day, with the chiaroscuro of woods and mountains and reds and blues in the distance.

"Finally, we're here!" Friar Somera exclaimed with impatience upon seeing the estate house of the large Encinitas Ranch, with its white walls, wide portals and reddish roofs.

Don Cirilo came out running to greet the illustrious prelate who, after dismounting, made his way to the patio between two rows of servants competing with each other for the honor of kissing his habit. He followed the hacienda owner into a large living room whose windows faced the threatening outline of the San Isidro Hills.

II

In a room of feudal dimensions, with natural light entering in golden cascades, could be seen a generously proportioned bed in whose center lay the emaciated figure of Doña Claudina, almost lost amid quilts of purple silk. On the wall over the bed hung a tormented ivory crucifix inclining its divine head, radiating from its wounded body sublime hope and spiritual motivation. In one of the corners was erected a small alter lighted by candles and covered with flowers. On seeing the priest, the sick woman extended a hand glittering with precious stones.

"Glory be to God!" she murmured.

She gestured for her husband to leave them, and was soon left alone with her conscience and the missionary. After her husband had exited and the door closed, the agonizing woman gave a tender glance at the crucifix and moved her lips in silent prayer. Then she turned from the altar and, propping herself up on pillows, began to speak.

"Did your Reverence ever meet Juan José de la Serna, who was prior of San Luis Rey for many years? When he arrived in California from Spain, I was a young woman of marrying age considered to be very beautiful. My father, Don Juan Regil, was the owner of Rancho Escondido, about a league from the mission. Of course, I would come into contact with José . . . I mean, Friar Serna . . ."

"Continue, Doña Claudina, continue. As sinners, we are all the same, even at the time of death!" interjected Somera, kissing the golden cross that hung from his gray habit.

The dying woman continued: "Serna was a young, gallant-looking man, with shining dark eyes, and his Franciscan habit fit him beautifully. What happened was that he fell in love with me and I with him. And, with my eyes wide open, I fell head over heels, right into his arms . . . We would see each other every night in the basement of the mission, only able to see each other in the dim light shed by a lantern. The fruit of that sacrilegious love affair was a little girl . . ."

"How can this be possible, Doña Claudina? Isn't what you've said the product of feverish hallucinations?" asked the priest, growing pale.

"Father, I am confessing what I did, and not what I imagine I did!" the sick woman blurted out, lowering herself into the bed sheets.

Slowly and painfully, the confession grew, passing from the idyllic to the dramatic, from the dramatic to the tragic. Before wedding Don Cirilo, Claudina was already the mother of two little children, both of whom had been entombed by Friar Serna in fear that his secret and that of his lover would be discovered. Crazy and furious on the very same day of her wedding, attired in her shimmering wedding gown, Claudina lifted her veil and, before the entire devout wedding assembly, cursed the Prior with these infamous words:

"May God grant that your black blood stain the steps of this altar! May the heavens ordain that you die the agony of the damned and that your unburied cadaver be food for buzzards and wolves!"

Seeing that the penitent woman was failing as she gripped her bed sheets, Friar Somera prostrated himself by the bed and with a sympathetic and solemn voice said, "In the name of the Father, the son and The Holy Ghost, I absolve you and bless you."

And turning his saddened face toward the ivory crucifix, which seemed to move its angelic blue eyes, he began singing the "Veni Creator Spiritus" hymn in a vibrant voice.

III

In 1816, Prior Serna had been transferred from San Luis Rey to San Juan Capistrano, and in 1818, he was still there scandalizing the region with his binges and loud orgies. It was at this time that he was interrupted by the sudden invasion of that ferocious pirate René Buochard, who had been commissioned as a corsair by one of the nascent Spanish-American republics involved in a war to the death with Spain and its possessions in the Americas.

Bouchard was about thirty years old, a giant of a man with Herculean strength. It is said that he could kill a man with just one blow of his fist and that he could bend a horseshoe with just two fingers. On the night before Christmas Eve of that same year, 1818, Bouchard disembarked in San Diego, followed by three hundred of his men, all armed to the teeth, each one with a cutlass, two pistols and a combat knife. Captain Buochard wore a short red jacket, short pants of the same color and knee-high boots. A skull cap covered his unruly black mane and from his waste hung a cutlass with a silver hilt, a knife with a gold handle and dragoon pistols. His face was fiery red with a condor's eyes, a curved nose, a large black, twisted mustache that reached back to his ears. When his boats had been spied along the Pacific Coast, flying the skull and crossbones, all the fearful people headed for the hills, leaving behind their homes and possessions. Bouchard would drink the strongest liquor without ever getting drunk, as he entertained himself sacking, killing and raping virgins, many of whom he would pass on to his soulless crewmen after he had had first rights.

Bouchard disembarked as evening fell, and without wasting time headed straight for Vista Linda, crossing through La Luz Ranch and San Onofre Ranch, setting them on fire as he went by. The owner of the latter got it into his head to mount a horse and gallop off to San Juan Capistrano Mission in order to warn the missionaries and save the holy reliquaries housed there.

While this was happening in the countryside, where everything was ablaze, lighting up the landscape with an infernal glow, the prior of San Juan Capistrano was using the pretext of Christmas to host a feast of imperial proportions, so much so that the large oak table was squeaking from the weight of the wines and exquisite cuts of meat it had to support. Half a dozen women of the night brought from Monterey, which was at that time a nest of smugglers, were attending to the erotic desires of the missionaries, many of them perched on the ample laps of the friars.

Friar Serna poured one cup after another of amontillado sherry, and from time to time, he rolled up his habit to dance, singing verses so profane that they made the statues of the Virgin tremble in their niches.

Suddenly, there was a furious knocking at the door, and Don Serafín Roquena entered with a distorted look on his face. He had witnessed the advance of the pirate hordes of Bouchard.

"Save the holy relics and, if possible, yourselves as well! In less than fifteen minutes, the enemies of the King and of God will arrive at Capistrano!"

And, without answering all the questions that were flying at him from every direction, he remounted his horse and headed for Los Angeles.

With the scare, the drunkenness evaporated in a second; the fallen women cried while grabbing on to the Franciscans' habits, and Serna, taking advantage of all the confusion, ran out to the stables, bridled a mare and balanced himself on its back. But it was too late! The pirates had surrounded the mission and were already sacking and pillaging it. Captain Bouchard, who without a doubt had heard of Prior Serna, ordered that the reverend be brought to him.

Facing the prior, Bouchard stated, "So you're the one who walled up and killed your own children? Ah, this Ferdinand VII has created the best disciples! But he cannot beat me in devilry. By killing I serve God better than he does praying."

What followed that night was a saturnalia. The mission cellar was emptied of all its wines, the orgy lasting until four in the morning, when the pirates decided to head for the San Luis Rey Mission. They arrived there as the first rays of the morning sun shone on the Coyuco Hills. Prior Serna, who had been tied to a mule, with his habit stained with blood and wine, was taken by the pirates to a place called Aguaje. Swearing and laughing the whole time, they strung him up to the branches of a stout birch tree, which still exists today and the campesinos call the "Friar's Tree." They say that every bird that perches on its branches immediately falls dead as if struck by lightning. And every time they try to burn it down, it grows back even stronger. And they say that on moonlit nights, you can see the silhouette of a lynched man swinging in the nocturnal breeze, causing the coyotes foraging in that deserted thicket to howl.

IV

One winter night, some travelers were warming themselves by the stove of the Grant Hotel in the city of San. . . . Among the guests, mostly Americans, there was a Hollywood photographer who had been searching for phantasmagoric images, that is, images of specters and ghosts for one of Ibsen's dramas that was being produced.

"My camera lenses," he was saying to the group, "were

ground in Berlin by the famous lens maker, Dr. Urbach. Nothing escapes those lenses, not even intangible and invisible objects. I've heard that at the San Luis Rey Mission there are apparitions, and this very night I'm going to see if that's true or not. Can any of you give me any details?"

After a few seconds of silence, a corpulent old-timer, a Californio from his appearance and diction, responded in a slow and even tone, "Well, they've been telling you true. Night after night, ghosts are seen at the mission. First there are two girls who appear dressed in white; then, there's a young woman; and lastly, there's a missionary priest who is really terrifying. I've seen them myself on various occasions."

The listeners were so interested in the conversation that they crowded around the young photographer and the old Californio.

After a minute, the photographer broke the silence and said, "Very well, would you accompany me there? If what you say is true, I'll give you a check for one thousand dollars. But if it's a lie, you'll have to pay the bill." Then, addressing everyone at once and nobody in particular, he exclaimed, "Gentlemen, would you all like to accompany me?"

So, some out of curiosity and others out of love for art, left the hotel and headed for San Luis Rey.

It was raining on and off, and a threatening sky cloaked the evening. Mr. Link, the Hollywood photographer, loaded his camera and prepared his lenses on arriving. He told his companions to keep silent and to keep searching through the ruins. How many hours did they spend in their vigil? No one knows. But all of a sudden from the cracked walls of the mission appeared two girls dressed in white, one holding the hand of the other, both shadowy profiles in the halo of light. Click, click! went the photographer's camera, and the apparition disappeared among the crumbling colonnades.

By the light of an electric bulb Mr. Link examined the negative and shouted in excitement, "Gentlemen, the world of the spirits is an undeniable reality! Wonderful! Let's continue!"

Fifteen minutes later, lightning erupted in the countryside and bathed the colonnades with a livid radiance. A woman dressed in mourning was wandering through the ruins, bending over here and there in search of something or someone. On the click-clicking of the camera, the mysterious silhouette was swallowed by the shadows, leaving the impression among the observers that it had not been anything but an optical illusion caused by the midnight shadows.

The proud and sharp voice of the Hollywood artist soon was heard to remove their doubt, as he held up another negative and exclaimed, "By jingo, splendid! We have stolen heaven's secret!"

Later, he looked at his timepiece and, guided by the old Californio, he started walking to the southeast of San Luis Rey, while pushing his equipment on wheels. It was about two in the morning; the thick drizzle had ceased and a thick fog had come in from the nearby ocean. His companions followed Mr. Link to the banks of a small stream in whose curve the white oak tree was standing, a grey skeleton profiled against the pulsing clouds. The group stopped in front of the tree and crowded around the camera. During a few moments, the hooting of owls and croaking of swamp frogs were the only beats to be heard in the dead of night. But then the click-click of the camera was heard again and, on raising their eyes, not without fear, they perceived the figure of a lynched man swinging in the tree while trying to untie with fleshless hands the knot and the hangman's noose. As the apparition extinguished itself, flocks of carrion flew back and forth like blind bats in search of their lairs. The illusion had completely disappeared!

V

The next day by breakfast time, Mr. Link had developed his negatives. There they were, without the shadow of a doubt, the details of the somber drama, the phantasmagoric transformed into positive images, suffering souls surprised by science, dramatic episodes right out of Aeschylus, emerging briefly in life as a weird phenomenon.

"And why not?" Mr. Link was saying on being congratulated by his friends. "In England, the modern camera has captured the silhouettes of King Lear and Banquo entering the banquette hall, thus demonstrating that the Bard of Avon's creations were reality and not fantasy.

"Ladies and gentlemen," concluded the quicksilver photographer as he put on his coat and tied up his suitcase with a nervous hand, "the train for Los Angeles leaves in ten minutes. Very soon people will applaud the showing on screen of the tragedy without music that you have just witnessed. So long!"

And in two hops he was at the station, improvising a way to take a slug of liquor from a whiskey flask without being seen, because the spirited enjoy the privilege of communicating with spirits.

The Márgil Vine

Nina Otero

During the early twentieth century, a group of Hispanic women from distinguished families set about recovering the history and lore of the Southwest prior to the coming of the Anglo-Americans. Nina Otero (1882–1965) was one of the folkorists who collected oral lore and then created literary versions of them. Her "The Márgil Vine" is a version of the practice and lore of the children bringing modest gifts to the Christ Child during the Christmas season.

Further reading: Nina Otero, *Old Spain in Our Southwest* (New York: Harcourt, Brace and Company, 1936).

The Márgil Vine

It was Christmas Eve!

In the year 1718 there came to the little Mission Church of San Antonio de Valero, a visiting priest, Antonio Márgil. The Patron Saint of the village was San Antonio; so Father Márgil, or Padre Antonio as the people always called him, came not only to assist in the celebration of the great Fiesta of Christmas, but also to do honor to the Saint, his patron.

A kindly man was the Mission Priest, who traveled over mountain passes, crossed desert sands, to give help to those in distress. But this was a happy day, *La Fiesta de los Niños*—so thought the Padre, as he strolled in the small plaza which was always the center of community activities.

Preparations were under way for the annual performance of the "Posada," or search for lodging, representing the wanderings of Joseph and Mary to find a place to spend the night. After the decree of Caesar that all the world should be taxed, Joseph and Mary had left their home in Nazareth to go to the city of Bethlehem to be enrolled for taxation; but they were poor people, and no one had room for them. For eight days they had traveled, asking lodging without avail, until on the ninth day they took shelter in a stable in *Belén* where, at midnight, the Christ-Child was born.

Father Antonio watched the preparations for the enactment of this scene with a deep religious sympathy.

That evening the little mountain village was illuminated by small fires of cedar wood which crackled and blazed high, lighting up groups of people taking the part of Mary and Joseph with their followers.

As Father Antonio watched the simple procession, he noticed a little boy of eight years who wandered around following the performers, always keeping close to those taking the part of the Holy Family. *"El Niño Perdido,"* mused the Priest, thinking of the folk-play that tells of Christ's visitation to the Jewish temple.

After being refused lodging by several families at whose door the "Holy Family" knocked, they approached the church. At the door the priest met them and accompanied them inside. The church was lighted by wax candles in tin sconces on its whitewashed walls and many more candles before the altar. At the foot of the altar, before the Crib, Mary took from under her shawl a small figure of the Christ-Child, which she placed in the little manger-crib, made ready by the people of the mountains to receive their Saviour.

Christmas Day many gifts were brought to the Christ-Child and laid at His feet. Not of gold, frankincense and myrrh, such as the Wise Men brought, but such gifts as the poor shepherds offered. A hand-woven bedspread was placed around the table to hide its crude carpentry; colored beads glistened as the flame from the candles was reflected on the red and blue glass; colored stones of gypsum and of flint; paper flowers of red and pink and yellow; an assortment of gifts and of color which reflected the gay and child-like nature of the Spanish people, and which awakened a corresponding emotion in the beholders.

As he walked outside the church to watch the people bringing their gifts, Father Antonio encountered the child he had observed the night before. Laying his hand on the child's head, he said:

"Why do you cry, little one?"

"Because," answered the child, "I have nothing to give the Holy Child. I saved a piece of my *tortilla* from my breakfast and as I was bringing it my little dog took it out of my hand and ate it."

"Oh," said Father Antonio, "you have much to offer the Christ-Child. Come with me and we will visit Him. Give Him your heart and your thoughts."

"No," answered the boy, "I will not go in that church again without something to give. I can't give Him my heart, He can't see it. I want something real."

"Run to your house and find a jar, one that your mother is not using for cooking. We will find something to put in it and make the Divine Infant a real gift that you and He can see."

The child, delighted, ran home and soon returned with an earthern jar, black and covered with ashes from recent use.

As they walked along the dry ditch, they found a trailing vine, brown and dry. "Here," said the Padre, "let us dig this vine and place it in your jar! It will make a lovely gift to the new-born Saviour."

"It is not pretty," exclaimed the child. "It does not shine as those pretty beads on His altar do."

But the child was persuaded, and together they returned to

the church, the child carefully holding his precious gift. Straight to the Crib they went, past kneeling women, quiet children, men whose heads were bowed in prayer and resignation. Father Antonio Márgil lifted the child and his gift, holding him until the vine was entwined around the Crib by his small hands.

"There, dear little Jesus," said the small boy as the priest put him down on the adobe floor. "There is my gift to you. I wanted red beads, but Father Antonio said you would like the little vine."

So saying, he joined the priest on his knees before the Crib. Neither of them was conscious that the entire village had entered the church; neither of them heard the words, though the music of the chant moved through them:

> *Vamos todos á Belén*
> *Con amor y gozo,*
> *Adoraremos al Señor*
> *Nuestro Redentor.*

Excitedly then the child pulled at the sleeve of Father Antonio's coat:

"Father, dear Father!" cried the child. "See, my vine is green, the leaves reach upward! Jesus is smiling at me. He tells me something! Oh, Padre, listen, can't you hear Him?"

"What is it, little son, what did He say to you?"

Eagerly, the child answered: "Jesus said, 'Thank you.' "

Legend of the First
Christmas at the Alamo

Adina de Zavala

*Adina de Zavala (1861–1955) was a crusader for Texas history
and culture. The granddaughter of the first vice president of the Texas
republic, Lorenzo de Zavala, she was ever vigilant that the legacy and
contributions of the Amerindians, Spanish, and Mexicans not be forgotten in the official history of the state and the region. Thanks to
Zavala and the movement she started, the Alamo has been preserved
as a shrine of Texas history for posterity. Thanks to her as well, this
and many other legends and historical facts have also been preserved
as part of the foundation for present and future constructions of cultural
identity.*

Further reading: Adina de Zavala, *History and Legends of the Alamo and Other Missions
in and around San Antonio* (Houston: Arte Público Press, 1996).

Legend of the First
Christmas at the Alamo

The Márgil Vine

At the first Christmas season celebrated at Mission San Antonio
de Valero (The Alamo), in 1718, the good padres made the
Crib of Bethlehem as realistic as possible, and the Indian children and neophytes were taking part in adorning the crib and
bringing gifts to the Christ-Child.

Some brought beads and hung them where the lights would
make them glisten; others, pretty colored stones or pebbles;

others, bits of bright Indian blankets—everything and anything that to the crude Indian mind seemed beautiful. And the
padres did not chide them, for their intention was to honor the
Christ-Child. One afternoon as the Venerable Anthony Márgil
was re-entering the Mission from a visit to a sick Indian not
far away, he came upon a wee Indian boy sobbing. "What has
made you sorrowful, little Shavano, at this happy time of the
coming visit of the little Christ-Child?" "That is the very trouble," answered little Shavano, "all the rest have a gift for Him,
and I can find nothing." "O, never mind that, little Shavano.
The Christ sees into your heart and mind; you wish to love,
obey and serve Him, do you not?" "Indeed I do!" replied the
boy. "Give Him then your heart and service; tell Him this, and
that will be the grandest gift." But little Shavano would not
be satisfied; he sought the tangible gift, and the good padre,
touched by his grief and sympathizing with his aspirations, said
to him: "Bring a wide-mouthed olla, Shavano, and I shall help
you find a gift." The wee Indian lad did as he was bid, and not
far outside the Mission gate, on the acequia, was found a vine
with triform green leaves and dark green berries. "We will take
this to the little Christ-Child," said the Venerable Anthony
Márgil. "It is not very pretty," said little Shavano. "Never mind,
it will be pretty to the Christ-Child; He will make it pretty,"
replied the padre. And so consoled, little Shavano helped to dig
the vine and planted it in the olla. They carried it to the crib,
and setting the olla on one side, twined and festooned the vine
over the front of the crib. Little Shavano decided that it was
better than nothing, and asked the Christ-Child to be satisfied
with the best he could do, and promised to do all in his power
during the coming year to serve Him faithfully. The next morning as he renewed his promises to the Christ-Child, he was
gazing on the vine, wishing that his gift had been pretty like
some of the others, when lo! the dark leaves began to glisten,

and the green berries turned to a beautiful scarlet, and festooned as they were about the front of the crib, delighted the boy beyond measure. He ran for the padre, excitedly exclaiming, "The Christ-Child did make my gift beautiful! Come and see it!"

The Venerable Anthony Márgil, who was in one sense only a visitor at this mission, took the happy little Indian boy by the hand, and together they joined the procession just then winding through the arcaded galleries surrounding the patio, leading to the chapel, and which followed acolytes with lighted candles. The joyous paean of the Adeste Fideles was borne upward as they moved forward, and these two, the venerable, noted and learned man and the wee Indian boy, with grateful hearts united their voices with the chorus of praise chanting:

> *"With hearts truly grateful,*
> *Come all ye faithful,*
> *To Jesus, to Jesus, in Bethlehem.*
> *See Christ your Saviour,*
> *Heaven's greatest favor,*
> *Let's hasten to adore Him;*
> *Let's hasten to adore Him;*
> *Let's hasten to adore Him,*
> *Our Lord and King.*
>
> *The Splendor Immortal,*
> *Son of God Eternal;*
> *Concealed in mortal flesh our eyes shall view.*
> *See there the Infant*
> *The swaddling clothes enfold Him.*
> *Let's hasten, etc.*
>
> *Angels now praise Him,*
> *Loud their voices raising,*

The heavenly mansions with joy now ring.
Praise, honor, glory,
To Him who is most holy.
Let's hasten, etc.

To Jesus, born this day,
Grateful homage repay;
To Him who all heavenly gifts doth bring,
Word uncreated,
To our flesh united.
Let's hasten, etc.

This vine is still of spontaneous growth around San Antonio and is called by those of the old days the "Márgil Vine." From that early time its bright red berries come to do honor to the season of the Christ-Child.

The Legend of the Poinsettia

Pat Mora and Charles Ramírez Berg

*Part and parcel of celebrating Christmas is keeping tradition alive.
For many Hispanics in the United States, their parents' and grandparents' customs seem like exotic rituals, long forgotten. Children's authors Pat Mora (1942–) and Charles Ramírez Berg (1947–), both
of El Paso, Texas, have researched and resuscitated the very Mexican
legends that give the world the poinsettia flower and sustain the practice
of Las Posadas.*

Further reading: Sylvia Cavazos Peña, ed. *Tun-Ta-Ca-Tun: More Stories and Poems in
English and Spanish for Children* (Houston: Arte Público Press, 1986); Pat Mora,
Nepantla: Essays from the Land of the Middle (Albuquerque: University of New
Mexico Press, 1993).

The Legend of the Poinsettia

Long ago, in the little Mexican town of San Bernardo, there
lived a boy named Carlos.

One cool night Carlos opened the heavy wooden door of his
small home and peeked out. It was quiet. Chimney smoke
danced from the roof of each adobe home. Carlos knew why
families were eating early. Tonight was the first night of the
posadas.

"Chico, come and look at the stars," Carlos said to his playful
brown dog. "See how they glimmer. Even the heavens know
the celebration begins tonight."

Carlos shut the door and looked at his aunt, Nina, who
was roasting green chiles. Her hair was white and she moved

slowly. She was Carlos' whole family and she was enough. They sang, they danced, they played, they talked. Their home was small and bare, but full of warm love that made the air sweet.

Carlos carefully put Chico's food next to the fireplace. Chico licked Carlos' face and put his paws on Carlos' shoulders. "No, Chico, no time to wrestle tonight."

Chico tried to push Carlos over. Carlos laughed, took Chico's head in his hands and put his face close to Chico's.

"Oh, little dog," said Carlos. "You know how I have waited for this night. All year Nina has been telling me about the nine nights before Christmas. This is my first year to join the *posadas*. I can't be late. Come. Eat."

Carlos combed his hair and went and stood before Nina. She looked at him and smiled her Nina smile.

"Carlos, when you are out under the stars, sing with your heart. When you return, I will make you hot chocolate, and you can tell me all you saw. You are my eyes tonight, Carlos. See everything. Here is your candle."

Outside Carlos took a deep breath and straightened his shoulders. He looked in the window of his home and saw Chico and Nina warming themselves by the fire. He felt happy knowing he would return to share his adventure with his two friends.

Carlos joined a group of people gathered before a home that seemed to glow. There were candles in all the windows. Soon four men arrived carrying a large wooden tray on their shoulders. Carlos stood on tiptoes to see the statues of Joseph and of Mary riding the donkey.

A tall man spoke. "Time to start," he said. "Tonight we begin our journey. We are travelers seeking room in the inn, the *posada*, just as Mary and Joseph did. Each night for nine nights we will meet and carry the statues to the next house on our trip. We will knock and ask for shelter for the night. This special time is a time of preparing our hearts for Christmas, of deciding what gift each of us can offer the Infant Jesus."

Carlos looked at the people around him. Most wore better clothes and newer shoes, but tonight they all held hands.

The tall man knocked on the door and the group sang:

Who will give them shelter?
Who will help these two?

The family inside the house answered:

> *What if they are thieves?*
> *What are we to do?*

It is Mary and Joseph.
They need a place to rest.

> *Open all the doors*
> *For our very special guests!*

Slowly the door of the house opened. Carlos' eyes grew wide as he saw the mounds of food and the sparkling decorations. Nina had been right. The birth of Jesus was the best reason for a party.

The group knelt and prayed. Carlos squeezed his eyes shut and thought. A frown wrinkled his little face. On Christmas Eve he would go with the other children of San Bernardo to the church. Each child would place a special gift at the manger for the Baby Jesus. He had no money, neither did Nina. What gift could he give that would be special?

The prayer was over.

With a cheer the children hurried to the other side of the room to play the games and enjoy the food. The lady of the house said, "Come, Carlos. You play and eat too. Enjoy the *posada.*"

"How much I will have to tell Nina and Chico," thought Carlos. "So that my story will not be too long, each night I will tell them about one little part of the *posada*. Tonight I will tell them of the statues, the songs, the prayers."

And so it was.

"Tonight it rained candy," said Carlos when he came home on the second night. Nina smiled. "Ah, a *piñata*," she said.

"Oh, Nina, it was so beautiful," Carlos said. "A star made of colored paper hanging from the ceiling. Whack! Whack! Whack! went the stick as one by one we tried to break the *piñata*. Finally a strong girl did break it and candy, delicious candy, poured out of it covering the floor. We all scrambled to grab some. Here, Nina," said Carlos, holding out his hand. "I brought us each a piece."

Then Carlos held up a bit of homemade candy for Chico. Chico yelped, then jumped and snapped it from Carlos' hand. There they sat chewing their Christmas candy. They stared into the fire, imagining the *piñata* swinging back and forth, back and forth.

On the third night Carlos returned carrying a small bundle. "Tonight I will tell you of a table like the tables in my dreams. There were mountains of steaming *tamales*, a huge pot of beans, plates of cookies, and a tower of thin, crisp, round *buñuelos* sparkling with sugar."

Carlos unwrapped his bundle and smiled at the look on Nina's face as she saw all the treats that had been sent to her. "Help me eat all this," she said. Carlos held up a bit of sweet *tamal* for Chico and Chico jumped and picked it from his hand and ate it. Even Chico enjoyed the food from the *posada*.

"What do you have there?" asked Nina when Carlos entered his home on the fourth night. His hand was closed in a tight fist.

"You'll see," he said with a wide grin. Carlos sat down and began his story with Chico's head in his lap. "Tonight I will tell you about my favorite game at the *posada*. The lady of the house gave the children special egg shells filled with confetti. We all ran about cracking eggs on heads but trying not to get hit. We laughed and laughed."

Carlos then held up one of the eggs to show Nina, but Chico thought it was another treat and jumped to bite it. The egg exploded and suddenly there was confetti everywhere in the air. All three of them were covered with tiny bits of red, yellow, green and blue paper.

Carlos placed a soft kiss on Nina's head. "You look pretty with paper jewels in your hair," he said.

"And you!" said Nina, pointing at him and laughing.

"And Chico!" they said together and laughed.

The following night Carlos went to bed early after the *posada*. Nina tucked him in his snug bed. She knew something was troubling Carlos. But she said nothing.

After Nina went to sleep, Chico began to lick Carlos' face. Carlos scratched Chico behind the ears and whispered, "My friend, what shall I do? I can bring Nina candy and *buñuelos* and confetti, but what can I take to Baby Jesus on Christmas Eve? These are magic nights. I want my gift to Jesus to glow like a jewel." Chico put his head on Carlos' shoulder.

On the sixth night Carlos walked home humming the carols he had sung. The stars were so bright that he sat on his favorite round rock to stare at them.

"I wish a star would drop into my hand," he thought. "I would carry it home and surprise Nina and Chico with the beautiful light. I would take it to the church Christmas Eve. I would set it before the manger."

Now that would be a gift to be proud of.

But no star fell. Carlos walked home and tried to sound cheerful when he sang carols to Nina.

"Look what the lady at this house gave me," Carlos said as he entered the house on the seventh night. He held two colored paper lanterns. "They are to make our town glow on Christmas Eve. They will light the way for the Christ child. On Christmas Eve we will light the lanterns. They will be in trees, on roofs, around the church. And this year, Nina, we too will have our own to hang outside our door. Oh, Nina, what a special night this Christmas Eve will be."

On the eighth night after the prayers and refreshments, the children were told that the Indians from the nearby hills would be coming to join the procession to the church.

Again the tall man spoke:

"On Christmas Eve the Indians will be like the shepherds at Bethlehem. After you children place your gifts before the manger, they will dance outside the church. They will chant. That will be their gift."

That night Carlos asked, "Tomorrow will you go with me, Nina? And Chico will guard our home. First we will light our lanterns. Then we will go carrying our candles to the last house of the *posada*. We will take the statues of Mary and Joseph and place them in the manger at the church. Their journey will be over."

Carlos became quiet.

"And then," said Nina, "you and the other children will each place a small gift before the manager."

Carlos said nothing.

"I know," said Nina, "we have not talked of your gift. I know you have been thinking of it. Does it make you so unhappy that we have no shiny coins or beautiful flowers to give?"

Carlos said nothing.

"Jesus was not a rich boy either, Carlos. He loved to run and play in the hills by his town just as you do. Go out tomorrow and collect the small plant that grows wild near the rock you watch the stars from. That will be your gift."

Carlos wanted to obey Nina's words but it would be hard. These nights of the *posadas* had made him so happy. He wanted his gift to show that happiness. He wanted his gift to shine. How could he give a king only a common plant, a simple weed people stepped over and ignored because it was everywhere?

"The Infant Jesus will understand," said Nina. "Love makes small gifts special."

———

Finally it was Christmas Eve. Carlos lit two candles and placed them in the paper lanterns. He hung them on either side of the door. He left Chico at the doorway. The lanterns swayed in the wind.

Carlos then took Nina's arm to escort her to join the *posada*. In his other hand he carried his gift, his small plant. The air was warmer, sweeter. The whole town of San Bernardo was aglow. The Indians quietly walked with the others to the church.

Carlos stood in line holding his little plant. Some of the children carried roses, fruit; others carried bread or cheese. Tears of shame slipped down Carlos' face. Such a small gift.

Then something happened. One of Carlos' tears fell on the plant and where it touched the green leaf it made a red dot. A bright, beautiful, spreading red. Carlos looked at Nina. When he looked back at the plant in his hand, another tear fell away from his eye. His tears were making the whole leaf red. He looked up at Nina again; she smiled.

When it was his turn, Carlos carefully placed his plant before the manger. Now the entire top of the plant had turned red. It was the most beautiful gift.

Outside Carlos looked at his town of San Bernardo. He saw the colored lanterns dancing in the trees. Tonight in his little town in Mexico he saw that all the small plants like the one he had given had changed color. They were like bright red stars. They too would light the way for the Christ child.

The Indians began their slow dance beating the rhythm by shaking gourds filled with seeds. As Carlos watched, he squeezed Nina's hand. She had been right again.

Love is magic.

Love does make small gifts special.

The Christmas Spirit Tree

Diane de Anda

Hispanic authors today are examining the nature of bicultural existence in the United States. In "The Christmas Spirit Tree," children's author De Anda (1943–) reveals how singing carols in Spanish easily combines with cultivating and continuing the traditions of Christmas trees and Santa Claus, which now belong to everyone. De Anda is a professor of education in Southern California, a mother, and the author of numerous stories for middle readers.

Further Reading: Diane de Anda, *The Ice Dove and Other Stories* (Houston: Arte Público Press, 1997).

The Christmas Spirit Tree

Friday afternoon trilled with the high-pitched sounds of children rushing out of Ninth Avenue Elementary School into the beginning of Christmas vacation. Children stood in wiggling rows, weaving into their big yellow buses with shiny red and green Christmas projects tucked under their arms and into backpacks empty of their usual books and binders.

Marika, Tonia and Roberto snaked their way together through the lines of buzzing, ever-moving children to the street corner. There Mrs. Sánchez, the crossing guard, greeted them with a smile. As she nodded her head toward them, the bell on the top of the Santa's hat she wore that day gave a cheery ring.

"*Buenas tardes, niños** And what are all those pretty things you're carrying?" she called to them.

Marika, the youngest of the three, pressed forward with her shiny red foil ball. She stood on tiptoe and held it up for Mrs. Sánchez to see.

"It's for our tree. I'm going to put it up real high so the sun will make it shine," the excited seven-year-old said in rapid-fire speed.

"Yes, it's beautiful, Marika. I always look for your Christmas tree each year when I drive down the street."

Marika, Tonia and Roberto responded with a chorus of smiles. Their Christmas tree was a family tradition that they were proud had now become an annual event for the neighborhood as well. A twelve-foot-tall pine with branches that swung out in perfect, even, deep green arcs stood in the middle of their front yard. On the Saturday before Christmas, their father took the big carton full of Christmas bulbs and lights and glittering gold garlands out of the garage. Papá would make the strings of bulbs flow in beautiful rings of light around the tree.

Then it was their turn. Mamá would balance delicately on the ladder as the children handed her the green and gold and red bulbs and pointed to the branch where they wanted her to place them. Sometimes Papá would lift them up or let them sit on his shoulders to put some of the decorations high on the tree.

But mostly, the bottom half of the tree was theirs. They packed the bottom half with bulbs, foil balls, decorated pie tins and other decorations they made until it burst with color. Then everyone would step back as Papá threw the switch. Suddenly

---

*Buenas tardes, means "good afternoon" in Spanish.

there was a rush of color as the tree lights went on to the cheers of the three children.

The three Pérez children crossed the street, waved good-bye to Mrs. Sánchez, and continued down the half block to their house. Marika couldn't keep the slow, steady pace of her brother and sister. She was too excited to walk in an everyday way. She sailed ahead in a long leaping skip, her shoulder-length dark hair bouncing about her face and head.

Marika didn't stop until she reached the tree. She dropped her backpack onto the grass and walked up to the tree with the red foil ball in her hand. Marika stood on her tiptoes and leaned up into the tree. She held onto a heavy lower branch to balance herself as she hooked her red foil ball as far above her head as she could reach. She fell back onto her flat feet and tilted her head to watch the sunlight play on the ornament's shiny surface.

"Hey, it's not time to decorate yet," Roberto insisted as he entered the yard.

"I know, I know," replied Marika. "I'm just practicing. Papá will help me put it higher tomorrow."

Eleven-year-old Roberto might have argued with Marika last year, but he was a sixth-grader now and was not about to argue with a second-grader over a big wad of aluminum foil. He just shook his head and walked in the front door.

Marika reached out and grasped two green sprigs on a lower branch. One in each hand, she rocked back and forth singing, *"Feliz Navidad, Feliz Navidad** . . . I want to wish you a Merry Christmas. I want to wish you a Merry Christmas." She hummed the melody as the song Mamá played on her stereo trailed out of her memory.

**Feliz Navidad, Feliz Navidad*, means "Merry Christmas" in Spanish.

When Tonia passed by, Marika called out, "Come on, Tonia, come and dance with me. There's plenty of room."

Tonia laughed. "This is crazy," she replied as Marika reached out to pull her into the celebration. The two girls locked fingers then leapt on tiptoe around the tree, laughing together at their silliness as they danced their way into Christmas vacation.

On their second trip around the tree, they spotted their father coming through the gate. The girls broke their rhythm and dashed to the gate to meet him. Before he could greet them, they grabbed onto the sleeves of his jacket, jumping up and down, asking when they could decorate the tree.

Mr. Peréz smiled. This playful pleading was part of their family tradition. They would beg and wheedle for the decorations a day early, but he would remind them that Saturday morning was the traditional decorating day. By the time they reached the porch, the girls had accepted that the decorating would have to wait until tomorrow.

That evening Tonia and Marika rushed through dinner so they could prepare for the following morning. They set the table at top speed. When dinner was served, they scooped heaping spoonfuls of food into their mouths so they could excuse themselves and dash to the work table in their bedroom.

In the bedroom, Tonia pulled out a cardboard box filled with paints and other art supplies: pieces of colored paper, cellophane and red, green and gold foil. As soon as she placed the box on the table, their fingers played through the contents, plucking out the pieces that sparked ideas for new ornaments for the tree. Tonia carefully traced the outline of a bell across a piece of heavy gold foil. Marika admired how easily Tonia outlined and cut its perfect shape. Tonia smiled at Marika's admiring glance.

"Come on. I'll help you cut out your decorations," Tonia encouraged, and leaned across to cut round and diamond and oblong shapes into the sheets of foil Marika had spread across the table.

When their mother knocked on the door at nine o'clock to say good night, Marika and Tonia had a table filled with foil ornaments. Each one was painted in bright colors with a different design.

"They're wonderful!" Mamá exclaimed as she looked at the glimmering lines of color across the table.

Marika and Tonia were happy it was bedtime. They quickly changed, brushed their teeth, exchanged family good night wishes and hugs and leapt into bed. They knew the sooner they slept, the sooner tomorrow would come.

———

The morning sunlight stole into the girls' bedroom, tickling them across their eyelashes to wake up. Marika blinked, opened her eyes briefly, then closed her eyes and started to pull the blankets over her head to block out the morning sun and lull herself back to sleep. But then she remembered: It was Saturday. It was time to decorate the tree. She bolted into a sitting position and gave a great yawning stretch. Then she shook her sister.

"Wake up, Tonia. Wake up. It's morning. Come on, let's get our box of decorations and start now."

Tonia made soft grumbling sounds at Marika and buried her face in her pillow.

"Okay, okay," responded Marika. "I'll do it myself."

She bounded from the bed and walked over to pick up the box of decorations they had made last night. With careful steps, delicately balancing the awkward, bulky box, she moved down the hall toward the front door. In the still and quiet morning, she could hear every footstep down the long hallway as she passed the other family members enjoying their Saturday morning rest. Marika parted with her precious box for only a moment when she placed it on a table to free her hands to unlock and open the front door.

She balanced the box down the front steps, blinking at the bright sunlight that poured over her. At the bottom of the steps, she began to take larger, more bounding steps as her eagerness to begin the decorating grew.

She had taken only three steps when she came to an abrupt halt. Marika stood frozen, her mouth wide open. For a minute she remained motionless, staring in disbelief. There, where the tree had always been, was a stump, broken and jagged with a few small branches and pine needles scattered around it. Suddenly she broke free from her trance. Without thinking, she let the box drop from her arms and ran yelling into the house.

"Mamá, Papá, help, help, it's gone, it's gone." She kept repeating this as she tore into the house and down the hallway to her parents' bedroom and leapt onto their bed. Her startled parents sat up, confused and anxious, seeing Marika shouting at the foot of their bed.

Suddenly, Marika began to cry. She covered her face, shouting between sobs, "It's gone. It's gone."

By this time, her parents were very concerned. Her mother quickly moved toward the foot of the bed, took Marika into her arms and gently rocked her and stroked her hair. Her father got out of bed and came over to the edge of the bed.

"*¿Qué pasó m'ija?* What happened, Marika? Why are you so upset?" he asked.

Marika held her breath a moment and clenched her jaw to

stop her crying. Between sobs she blurted out, "The tree is gone. Somebody took the tree. It's gone!"

"You must have had a bad dream," her father replied, gently wiping the streaks of tears from her cheeks.

"No, no, it's really true. Come, come with me and see."

Marika leapt from her mother's arms and beckoned her parents to follow her. By this time the noise had also awakened Roberto and Tonia, so all four followed Marika down the hallway and out the front door.

Mamá gasped; Tonia sighed, "No," and buried her teary face in her mother's robe.

Papá yelled, "*Dios Mío*, My God," and walked up to the stump with a dazed Roberto close behind. Roberto felt the tears well in his eyes as he looked at the maimed and broken stump.

"Who could have done this, Papá? Why?" Roberto pleaded.

"Who can understand why someone would do such a thing?" Papá replied.

"How could someone steal a Christmas tree? How could someone celebrate Christmas around a stolen tree?" Mamá added.

"They probably took it to sell it," replied Papá. "Let's see if they left a trail."

Papa followed lines of fallen needles and a few small pieces of branch across the lawn and sidewalk to the curb.

"Looks like they loaded it into a car or truck here," he said at the end of the trail. He looked down into the street. There alongside the curb was the red foil ball Marika had left on the tree the day before. He picked it up and shook off some dust, then slowly walked over to Marika with it.

"Here, *m'ija,*" he said, putting it into her hands. "At least we have your beautiful decoration."

Marika pressed her lips into as much of a smile as she could manage.

Tonia finally moved forward and surveyed the empty lawn. "What are we going to do, Papá?" she asked.

"I'm not sure yet, but I think it's important that we don't let the person who stole the tree also steal our Christmas spirit away. Let's get on with our day and discuss it at dinner time."

"And let's start with a good breakfast," Mamá added. "Remember, we're going to the mall to see Santa today."

The three children managed weak smiles and huddled around their mother as they all went in to eat and get ready to finish their Christmas shopping.

Papá stayed out surveying the yard. Then he walked up and down the block, talking to the neighbors about what had happened. He hoped to find some leads or some explanation, but no one had seen or heard anything. Dogs had barked a few times during the night, but they always barked at cats or strays and no one ever paid much attention. Everyone was not only shocked and sad for the Pérez family, but felt they had lost an important part of their own Christmas as well.

Tonia, Roberto and Marika looked different from the other children in the line to talk to Santa. The other children talked in quick, excited voices to each other or their parents. The three Pérez children stood silently looking at the floor or sightlessly ahead. They had all written and practiced their lists. They knew exactly what they were going to say. But now, they didn't feel the same anticipation of good things to come that they had other years. Tonia and Roberto gave polite smiles, recited their lists, took their candy canes and scooted off the stage.

A wry smile came over Marika as she approached Santa. Unable to contain herself, she ran up to Santa, grabbed his sleeve and blurted out, "You can get it back for us, Santa, can't you? Please bring back our tree for Christmas."

Santa gave a puzzled look towards Mrs. Pérez, who stood behind Marika.

"I'm sorry, Santa. Marika doesn't understand. Someone cut down and stole the Christmas tree that has been growing in front of our house for as long as we've lived there. That's the tree she wants back."

Santa's face looked sad and serious as he turned toward Marika. "I'll see what I can do to help, but even Santa can't make things just like they were before. But I promise you something special will happen this Christmas that will make you feel happy again."

Marika said thank you with a broad and hopeful smile as she took her mother's hand and walked off stage. She ran up to Tonia and Roberto and declared, "Santa said we're going to get our tree back."

"That's not exactly what he said," her mother interrupted.

"I know," she continued, "but he promised to make everything okay—right, Mamá?"

"Well, I guess he did. We'll just have to believe and wait and see," replied Mrs. Pérez with a worried look on her face.

"No one can fix a cut-up tree," added Roberto, trying to sound very logical and grown-up.

"You'll see," said Marika. "You'll see."

When they arrived home, their father met them at the door with a big smile on his face.

"Hurry up, come on in. I've got a surprise for all of you."

The children and Mrs. Pérez rushed in the door and dropped their packages, bundles and bags onto the couch and coffee table. There in the middle of the front room was a six-foot-tall Christmas tree, balanced delicately on a wooden stand.

"I know each year we have a little tree inside the house,

because our big tree is outside, so I thought this year we'd just decorate a bigger tree inside the house."

Mr. Pérez scanned his children's faces.

They looked at the tree. It was a pretty green. Its branches were nice and even, and it had that wonderful pine smell. But it wasn't their tree, their family tree.

"It's a real nice tree," began Tonia.

"Yeah, Dad, thanks," added Roberto.

"This isn't the surprise Santa promised," thought Marika. "I know it isn't."

"We'll decorate it tomorrow on Christmas Eve like we do every year," interjected Mamá. "Thanks, honey, for finding such a nice tree. Now, let's wash up for dinner, so we can begin wrapping all these presents."

Dinner was quiet that evening. Mrs. Pérez described the gifts she had found for the grandparents. The children listened and poked at the food on their plates.

"Come on, finish your dinner. You always have a good time helping me wrap the presents," Mamá insisted.

After the dishes were cleared, the children all got into their traditional Christmas-wrapping roles. Tonia was the expert bow-maker. Her slender fingers twisted and darted, transforming flat strips of ribbon into beautiful curving loops that sat atop the presents like clusters of red and green butterflies. Roberto was the packager. He transformed the flattened gift boxes into square and rectangular containers. His keen sense of space knew exactly the right size for each item. He could always tell the exact length he needed to cut the shiny foil or candy-cane-printed wrapping paper. Mamá and Papá twisted the paper expertly around all the sides and corners of the gift boxes, but it was Marika who was always there as needed to attach the pieces of scotch tape that kept everything in place.

Mamá put on tapes of Christmas carols to help get everyone in a holiday mood. Everyone listened as they worked, but somehow no one sang along as they had other years.

By nine-thirty, towers of bright and shiny wrapped presents surrounded the Pérez family.

"Great job!" said Mamá, picking up the last scraps of wrapping paper.

"Yes, I'm impressed by how well you all did. Maybe I'll hire you out next year," added Papá with a wink toward Mamá.

Mamá moved toward each child and gave them a hug and kiss on the head. "Hurry on to bed now. Tomorrow's a big day. We still have a tree to decorate."

The children stole a quick look at the tree in the corner of the room, then said good night and headed down the hall toward their rooms.

"It is a nice tree, I guess," said Tonia.

Roberto just shrugged.

The next morning, the girls stirred in their beds as sounds of "O Christmas Tree" filtered into their room. They incorporated the sounds into their Christmas dreams until Roberto burst into their room.

"Tonia, Marika, get up, get up. Some people are here singing outside our door."

As the girls sat up, they saw their parents moving down the hall in their robes, their mother saying, "Who ever heard of Christmas caroling in the morning? Who do you think it could be?"

"There's only one way to find out," Papá replied, moving a little faster down the hall.

The girls leapt out of bed, and the three children ran to catch up with their parents.

As they entered the front room, the singing became louder.

Papá stepped ahead and opened the door. There assembled in a semi-circle in their front yard were about fifteen of their friends and neighbors, singing in loud smiling voices.

In the middle of the group in a large planter box was a beautiful eight-foot-tall pine tree, with long, full limbs reaching out in perfect symmetrical arcs.

Mrs. Sánchez stepped forward, the bell on her Santa hat jingling as she walked.

"We know it isn't the same as your own tree, and it's not quite as big yet, but if we plant it now we can all watch it grow together."

Mr. Pérez bit down hard to hold back the feelings that welled up in his chest and throat. He hesitated a minute, trying to find words that could express all the feelings of joy and gratitude he felt at that moment. He began, "What can I say to such generous friends?"

Before he could finish, Marika ran forward into the middle of the group.

"I know," she cried. "I know what to say. Thank you for delivering the tree Santa promised me."

Soft laughter rose from the group. Then the friends and neighbors pressed forward, sharing hugs and shaking hands. The women dabbed their eyes and some of the men rolled the huge planter box to a place near the old tree's stump. Together they began to break the earth with the picks and shovels they had brought along. Before long, the new tree stood securely in place, its graceful green branches reaching out towards the crowd.

Marika ran into the house, scooped up her red foil ball and returned quietly to the tree. Mamá nudged Papá to look at

Marika. He walked over and in one easy movement had her sitting high on his shoulders.

Marika reached up and with swift and careful fingers hooked the ball onto the highest branch.

The crowd clapped and cheered spontaneously. Marika smiled at the brilliant sunlight dancing on her foil ball and the warm and happy glow that it lit within her.

A Cold Night

Américo Paredes

The quintessential man of the border, anthropologist and folklorist Américo Paredes (1915–1999) developed a theory of culture clash to explain Mexican American identity. Long before his years as one of the most respected academics in the United States, winner of the Frankel Prize from the National Endowment for the Humanities (1989), Paredes was a prolific poet and fiction writer in Spanish and English. Like Hinojosa and Rivera in stories penned much later, Paredes concentrates on the bleakness of Christmas for the poor, within a framework of religiosity. Here the family's beliefs in God and the Virgin of Guadalupe are symbols as seemingly impotent and silent as Santa Claus.

Further Reading: Américo Paredes, *The Hammon and the Beans and Other Stories* (Houston: Arte Público Press, 1994); Américo Paredes, *Folklore and Culture on the Texas-Mexican Border*, ed. Richard Bauman (Austin: University of Texas Center for Mexican American Studies, 1993).

A Cold Night

The boy was playing on the floor, close to the tub full of glowing charcoal. Because the lip of the tub was hot, he sat tilted sideways, a buttock against the lower part, the rest of him leaning away, propped on one hand. With his other hand he played. He was a quiet, skinny little boy; his arms and legs looked like the limbs of those mechanical Mickey Mouses sold in the ten-cent stores: black, straight and very thin.

On the other side of the tub his father sat in a backless

kitchen chair, hunched elbows-on-knees over the coals, smoking a cornhusk cigarette. Occasionally he spat. The coals sizzled and steamed for a moment and then glowed red again. The room would be quiet after that, except for the subdued noise of dishes which the boy's mother was putting away. And now and then her hollow cough.

The boy was playing with an oblong piece of wood, whittled roughly at both ends to make it taper. The tapering made it look like a short, fat cigar. Or a boat, or a racing car or an airplane. That was the beauty of this piece of wood, it could be so many things. It was the boy's favorite toy and his only one, and because of that it was dirty and discolored from long handling. Its rough edges, where the boy had worked it clumsily, were beginning to smooth away.

Outside it was cold, one of the coldest nights of the year. The wind shook the little two-room house. There was a broken windowpane, into which an old pillow had been stuffed. Sometimes the wind would force its way inside. When it did, it caused a chill eddy in the room, especially along the floor, where the boy played, his sharp little nose close to the piece of wood, his big eyes soft with dreams.

Three days before the weather had been mild, and the boy had been playing outdoors. That was a long time ago. He had been squatting in the alley behind the church then, teasing a big red ant that was in a hurry to get home. He had been waiting for the church bells to talk to one another in the soft, warm twilight. That was when he saw death. But that was long ago. He tried not to think about it, not to let the thought interfere with his dreams about the oblong piece of wood.

Now the wind blew against the house in a mighty gust, and the pillow in the windowpane could not withstand it. The pillow pulled away slowly from the broken glass and slid to the floor. The boy shivered and looked at his father. His father did not move. He sat on the backless chair, his half-burned cigarette in one hand, his other hand stroking his swallow-wing mustache, his shoulders hunched. His matted hair was pressed down along his forehead where his hat had been. The boy looked at him, a half-smile on his thin, pointed face. Some day, he thought, some day I will have a beautiful mustache like that. His father did not notice him. He was dreaming too.

His mother left the dishes and crossed the room in heavy, clumping steps. She picked up the pillow and jammed it back in place in the windowpane, pushing so hard that the broken glass cracked a little more. His father looked up and met her eyes.

"I was getting up," he said. "I was going to do it."

"Tomorrow," she said. "Tomorrow you were going to do it."

"I'm tired too," he said. "And my back hurts pretty bad. You don't know what it's like, pulling stumps out of the ground from dawn to dusk."

"I guess I don't," she said.

The man turned back to the fire, his feelings hurt. He dragged on his cigarette and slowly let the smoke out through his nostrils. The boy stared at the smoke, fascinated.

His father said, "Why don't you go to bed? Or play with something else. All you do is slide that piece of wood back and forth."

"He doesn't have anything else to play with," his mother said. "He could have, if you had let him go downtown last week to see Santa Claus."

"Come along," she told the boy. "It is time for you to go to bed."

"It's cold in bed," the boy said.

His mother smiled thinly. "It will be warmer in bed. After a while."

The boy knew it would be warmer in bed. But the bed was

in the other room, and it was dark. He was afraid of the dark, but he was even more afraid to say so. Perhaps if he did not mention it at all, she would not make him say the prayer this time. So he left his toy and went with her, and after he had creaked into bed, he burrowed about in the cold bedclothes to warm them as quickly as possible.

His mother said, "Haven't you forgotten something?"

He stopped burrowing, and pushing away the covers he knelt on the bed. "Not the one about the Virgin Mary!" he said. "Please!"

His mother smiled her thin, distant smile. Her brown face seemed to float above the flame of the candle she was holding. It reminded him of the face of the Virgin of Guadalupe in the church. Except that his mother's smile frightened him. "It's a very important prayer. The Virgin Mary will look after you all your life."

"I don't want *her* to look after me!"

"Say the words with me." His mother's voice was firm. He straightened his back, shifted his knees and repeated the words after her. The Padrenuestro first and then the Avemaría, down to the last terrible words. "Now and at the hour of our death. Amen."

His mother blessed him, kissed him and said, "Now go to sleep." And she went back into the other room, taking the stump of a candle with her.

But he couldn't sleep. He was thinking about God. Through the chinks in the wall he could see the light in the other room, and he wished he were there, watching his father smoke and playing on the floor with his piece of wood. He did not like it at all, lying in the dark with nobody but God. It made him think of things he didn't want to think about. But he couldn't stop thinking them, because they were God's business. That's what his mother had called it, God's business. "One must leave

God's business to God," she had said when he told her that evening three days ago. But now he was alone with God, and he had to think of all those things.

He had seen death, that was why. He had come home, still shaking, and he had told his father, "I just saw death."

His father was sitting on the doorstep, smoking. He had been surprised into a quick upward glance. After that one glance his father had settled back to his smoking. "Hush," he said. "Don't talk wild talk."

His father was a dreamer, he did not believe in death. But his mother, who spit blood into a dirty rag, was not a dreamer. When she heard what the boy had said, her eyes glittered with a feverish interest, a hint of recognition. She called him inside, questioned him.

He had been in the alley, squatting, his back against the brick wall at the rear of the church. Just beside him was a door, and in front of him were two garbage cans belonging to the church. He was squatting there, teasing the red ant and waiting for the bells to ring before he went on home through the alley.

A man had come down the alley, hatless, the end of his tie over his shoulder as he hurried along. He stopped to light a cigarette and looked about but did not see the boy. After puffing on his cigarette, he started off, then stopped. There was another man standing at the mouth of the alley. The man with the cigarette swung about and started walking back the way he had come. Then he stopped. Still another man was at the other end of the alley.

The man with the cigarette just stood there. The other two men quietly came up to him. No one said a word. The two men took something out of their back pockets and beat the other man over the head. There was no sound except for the whack-whack of the blows and the men's heavy breathing. The beaten man put his hands on top of his head. The others tore the hands away, and the whack-whacking sound went on. Again the man put his hands on his head, again they pulled his hands away. Then they began to push at him after each blow. The man staggered this way and that but he didn't fall. Finally one of the two men took out a knife and stabbed him in the side. Now the man fell.

The other one kept looking at the fallen man until the one with the knife said, "Come on, let's go. He's dead."

The one who was looking muttered something. The other one said, "God damn! Haven't you ever seen death before?" Then they went away.

The boy came out from behind the garbage cans. He had never seen death before, so he went and looked at the man on the ground. Lying in his bed in the dark, alone with God, the boy wished he had not looked. But he had looked, a long, long look, and then he had run home and told his mother. She had listened eagerly. When he finished he exclaimed, "Why did they do it, Mama?"

"God knows," his mother said. "It's God's business."

"It was awful!" he said. "I wish I hadn't seen it."

His mother had looked at him calmly. "Awful?" she said. "There's nothing awful about death. All of us have to die some-time. Some day you'll be like that man in the alley."

"Oh no!" he cried, "I don't want to die! I'm not going to be like that!"

His mother gave him a hungry smile. "Of course you'll die. When God wishes, not one moment later or sooner. You don't know how or where or when." She paused to cough. "It's time you learned how to pray, no matter what your father says."

That night he had prayed with her, terrified by the thought that at any moment he could become a corpse like the man in the alley. She had taken a grim satisfaction in his terror. "There's nothing to be afraid of," she had said. "Just love God."

But lying there in the dark that cold night, he could not love God no matter how much he tried. Fear choked him, he wanted to get up and scream. But he remained quite still. He wondered how God could be so cruel to be like He was, and he said to himself, "Oh, I hate Him! I hate Him!"

It came out before he could stop himself. He felt he was sinking, and he started to pray, fervently and with trembling lips. Cupping his amulet of the Virgin of Guadalupe in his hand, he kissed it over and over. It was a tin likeness of La Guadalupana, which hung around his neck on a string. This image of her, though just a lump of tin, was a constant reminder of the Virgin that stood in church to the left of the altar. He liked her much more than he did the Virgin Mary. She was the most beautiful thing in the church, she and the bells.

It would have been very dull in church, except for La Guadalupana. She was dressed in red and green robes. The moon and the stars were at her feet, and there was a blue canopy above her, decorated with glass pendants shaped like huge drops. The inside of her robe was painted gold, and there was a frame of gold all around her. Below her there was a table with a white lace cloth, and on it there were little glass cups filled with short, fat candles in many colors, flickering and throwing all sorts of shadows on the wall, making the colors of the Virgin's robe sparkle, and the glass drops on the canopy too. It was a beautiful sight.

But best of all was her face. It was a nice, familiar Indian face, brown and smiling. It was beautiful, that smile, all-embracing, all-forgiving. When he was in church, the boy always fixed his eyes on the Virgin's smile, and he prayed to her instead of to the Christ that writhed bloodily on his cross at the right side of the altar. This was before he had seen the men in the alley. Since then his mother had sent him to church once, and he had not been able to look toward the right of the altar without shuddering.

So now, lying in the dark, in the cold of the night, while the wind pried at the window and at the cracks in the wall, he stroked his image of La Guadalupana and tried to see her not as she was in his tiny medallion but as she was in church, brilliant and colorful, smiling down on him. He had done this before, on other nights when he lay alone in the dark, and it helped him go to sleep. He tried to do it now, but tonight he could not see her. Instead, the writhing figure on the cross kept swimming into his vision, with its bloody head and wounded side. Except that the face was like that of the man in the alley.

He was alone with God and God's business. And it made him very much afraid. He began to weep, silently, and with the tears there came rebellion, exasperation with himself and everything else, and he said to himself over and over, "Goddam! Goddam!"

The words became monotonous, meaningless, and he tried to give them new force. "Goddam everything!" he said. "Goddam everything! Goddam God!"

His mouth twitched violently. He put up his hands as if to avert a blow. But nothing happened.

He waited. He did not even think of praying, he knew he was beyond any such help.

Above the foot of the bed, close to the roof, there was a little window not much larger than a picture frame, and beyond it was a square of sky. It was a clear, bright piece of sky, and in it were several stars. The stars were white and shiny, and they seemed to wink at him. There was no sound outside except for the swirling wind. It seemed to be calling his name. "Ramón. Ramón. Ramón."

In the other room his father hacked and spit into the coals, and after the coals had hissed, there was no sound except the wind calling his name, "Ramón. Ramón. Ramón." It didn't sound angry, it didn't seem to care at all.

Whatever there was inside of him that had crouched and shivered suddenly stood up, courageous and erect. He took a deep breath and said deliberately, "God damn God!"

A wild spasm seized him, shook him violently, then passed away, leaving him weak but victorious. No thunderbolt. In the sky the stars still shone. He tried again, adding the names of Christ, of Saint Peter and Saint Paul. After that he added the Holy Ghost. He was delighted with the supreme meanness of it all. He lay there, saying the words over and over to himself until he got tired. He closed his eyes, for he was very sleepy, and soon he was floating about on the edge of sleep, thinking. His father had been right, after all.

His head was dipping and rising in airy blackness. What was he . . . trying. . . . He blinked into half-wakefulness again. What was he trying to . . . oh, yes. He was trying to call the Virgin of Guadal. . . . But no! He sat up in bed. That wasn't it! That wasn't . . .

He sat there with his mouth open, catching his breath. Cupping the image of La Guadalupana in his hand, he raised it to his lips. But before his lips touched the piece of tin, he closed his fist about it in a quick, almost violent movement. He pressed his clenched fist against his chest and sank down on the pillow, staring at the dark. The wind sighed and swirled about the house. "Ramón. Ramón. Ramón," it said.

It was a lonesome sound, the lonesomest sound he had ever heard.

The Night before Christmas

Tomás Rivera

Tomás Rivera's poetic novel of life among migrant farm workers, . . .
y no se lo tragó la tierra / And the Earth Did Not Devour Him,
was the first great work of fiction of the Chicano literary movement
and remains a classic to this day. A former migrant worker himself,
Rivera (1935–1984) struggled through a piecemeal education all the
way to Ph.D. and became a university professor and administrator.
In his literary life, however, he continued to identify with the working
class and the downtrodden—and he was a pioneer in opening up uni-
versity education to the disadvantaged. Rivera's grim view of Christ-
mas surely derives from his and his people's experience of always viewing
the glitter, affluence, and commercialism of American Christmases from
the outside, from the vantage point of the poor and marginalized.

Further reading: Tomás Rivera, . . . y no se lo tragó la tierra / And the Earth Did Not
Devour Him (Houston: Arte Público Press, 1987); *Tomás Rivera: The Complete Works*,
ed. Julián Olivares (Houston: Arte Público Press, 1995); Julián Olivares, ed.,
International Studies in Honor of Tomás Rivera (Houston: Arte Público Press, 1986).

The Night before Christmas

Christmas Eve was approaching and the barrage of commercials,
music and Christmas cheer over the radio and the blare of an-
nouncements over the loudspeakers on top of the stationwagon
advertising movies at the Teatro Ideal resounded and seemed
to draw it closer. It was three days before Christmas when Doña
María decided to buy something for her children. This was the
first time she would buy them toys. Every year she intended

to do it but she always ended up facing up to the fact that, no, they couldn't afford it. She knew that her husband would be bringing each of the children candies and nuts anyway, and so she would rationalize that they didn't need to get them anything else. Nevertheless, every Christmas the children asked for toys. She always appeased them with the same promise. She would tell them to wait until the sixth of January, the day of the Magi, and by the time that day arrived the children had already forgotten all about it. But now she was noticing that each year the children seemed less and less taken with Don Chon's visit on Christmas Eve when he came bearing a sack of oranges and nuts.

"But why doesn't Santa Claus bring us anything?"

"What do you mean? What about the oranges and nuts he brings you?"

"No, that's Don Chon."

"No, I'm talking about what you always find under the sewing machine."

"What, Dad's the one who brings that, don't think we don't know that. Aren't we good like the other kids?"

"Of course, you're good children. Why don't you wait until the day of the Reyes Magos. That's when toys and gifts really arrive. In Mexico, it's not Santa Claus who brings gifts, but the Three Wisemen. And they don't come until the sixth of January. That's the real date."

"Yeah, but they always forget. They've never brought us anything, not on Christmas Eve, not on the day of the Three Kings."

"Well, maybe this time they will."

"Yeah, well, I sure hope so."

That was why she made up her mind to buy them something. But they didn't have the money to spend on toys. Her husband worked almost eighteen hours a day, washing dishes and cooking at a restaurant. He didn't have time to go downtown and buy toys. Besides, they had to save money every week to pay for the trip up north. Now they even charged for children, too, even if they rode standing up the whole way to Iowa. So it cost them a lot to make the trip. In any case, that night when her husband arrived, tired from work, she talked to him about getting something for the children.

"Look, viejo, the children want something for Christmas."

"What about the oranges and nuts I bring them."

"Well, they want toys. They're not content anymore with just fruits and nuts. They're a little older now and more aware of things."

"They don't need anything."

"Now, you can't tell me you didn't have toys when you were a kid."

"I used to *make* my own toys, out of clay . . . little horses and little soldiers . . ."

"Yes, but it's different here. They see so many things . . . come on, let's go get them something . . . I'll go to Kress myself."

"You?"

"Yes, me."

"Aren't you afraid to go downtown? You remember that time in Wilmar, out in Minnesota, how you got lost downtown. Are you sure you're not afraid?"

"Yes, yes, I remember, but I'll just have to get my courage up. I've thought about it all day long and I've set my mind to it. I'm sure I won't get lost here. Look, I go out to the street. From here you can see the ice house. It's only four blocks away, so Doña Regina tells me. When I get to the ice house I turn to the right and go two blocks and there's downtown. Kress is right there. Then, I come out of Kress, walk back towards the ice house and turn back on this street, and here I am."

"I guess it really won't be difficult. Yeah. Fine. I'll leave you some money on top of the table when I go to work in the morning. But be careful, vieja, there's a lot of people downtown these days."

The fact was that Doña María very rarely left the house. The only time she did was when she visited her father and her sister who lived on the next block. And she only went to church whenever someone died and, occasionally, when there was a wedding. But she went with her husband, so she never took notice of where she was going. And her husband always brought her everything. He was the one who bought the groceries and clothing. In reality she was unfamiliar with downtown even though it was only six blocks away. The cemetery was on the other side of downtown and the church was also in that direction. The only time that they passed through downtown was whenever they were on their way to San Antonio or whenever they were returning from up north. And this would usually be during the wee hours of the morning or at night. But that day she was determined and she started making preparations.

The next day she got up early as usual, and after seeing her husband and children off, she took the money from the table and began getting ready to go downtown. This didn't take her long.

"My God, I don't know why I'm so fearful. Why, downtown is only six blocks from here. I just go straight and then after I cross the tracks turn right. Then go two blocks and there's Kress. On the way back, I walk two blocks back and then I turn to the left and keep walking until I'm home again.

God willing, there won't be any dogs on the way. And I just pray that the train doesn't come while I'm crossing the tracks and catches me right in the middle . . . I just hope there's no dogs . . . I hope there's no train coming down the tracks."

She walked the distance from the house to the railroad tracks rapidly. She walked down the middle of the street all the way. She was afraid to walk on the sidewalk. She feared she might get bitten by a dog or that someone might grab her. In actuality there was only one dog along the entire stretch and most of the people didn't even notice her walking toward downtown. She nevertheless kept walking down the middle of the street and, luckily, not a single car passed by, otherwise she would not have known what to do. Upon arriving at the crossing she was suddenly struck by intense fear. She could hear the sound of moving trains and their whistles blowing and this was unnerving her. She was too scared to cross. Each time she mustered enough courage to cross she heard the whistle of the train and, frightened, she retreated and ended up at the same place. Finally, overcoming her fear, she shut her eyes and crossed the tracks. Once she got past the tracks, her fear began to subside. She got to the corner and turned to the right.

The sidewalks were crowded with people and her ears started to fill up with a ringing sound, the kind that, once it started, it wouldn't stop. She didn't recognize any of the people around her. She wanted to turn back but she was caught in the flow of the crowd which shoved her onward toward downtown and the sound kept ringing louder and louder in her ears. She became frightened and more and more she was finding herself unable to remember why she was there amidst the crowd of people. She stopped in an alley way between two stores to regain her composure a bit. She stood there for a while watching the passing crowd.

"My God, what is happening to me? I'm starting to feel the same way I did in Wilmar. I hope I don't get worse. Let me see . . . the ice house is in that direction—no it's that way. No, my God, what's happening to me? Let me see . . . I came from over there to here. So it's in that direction. I should have just stayed home. Uh, can you tell me where Kress is, please? . . . Thank you."

She walked to where they had pointed and entered the store. The noise and pushing of the crowd were worse inside. Her anxiety soared. All she wanted was to leave the store but she couldn't find the doors anywhere, only stacks and stacks of merchandise and people crowded against one another. She even started hearing voices coming from the merchandise. For a while she stood, gazing blankly at what was in front of her. She couldn't even remember the names of the things. Some people stared at her for a few seconds, others just pushed her aside. She remained in this state for a while, then she started walking again. She finally made out some toys and put them in her bag. Then she saw a wallet and also put that in her bag. Suddenly she no longer heard the noise of the crowd. She only saw the people moving about—their legs, their arms, their mouths, their eyes. She finally asked where the door, the exit was. They told her and she started in that direction. She pressed through the crowd, pushing her way until she pushed open the door and exited.

She had been standing on the sidewalk for only a few seconds, trying to figure out where she was, when she felt someone grab her roughly by the arm. She was grabbed so tightly that she gave out a cry.

"Here she is . . . these damn people, always stealing something, stealing. I've been watching you all along. Let's have that bag."

"But . . ."

Then she heard nothing for a long time. All she saw was the pavement moving swiftly toward her face and a small pebble that bounced into her eye and was hurting a lot. She felt someone pulling her arms and when they turned her, face up, all she saw were faces far away. Then she saw a security guard with a gun in his holster and she was terrified. In that instant she thought about her children and her eyes filled with tears. She started crying. Then she lost consciousness of what was happening around her, only feeling herself drifting in a sea of people, their arms brushing against her like waves.

"It's a good thing my compadre happened to be there. He's the one who ran to the restaurant to tell me. How do you feel?"

"I think I must be insane, viejo."

"That's why I asked you if you weren't afraid you might get sick like in Wilmar."

"What will become of my children with a mother who's insane? A crazy woman who can't even talk, can't even go downtown."

"Anyway, I went and got the notary public. He's the one who went with me to the jail. He explained everything to the official. That you got dizzy and that you get nervous attacks whenever you're in a crowd of people."

"And if they send me to the insane asylum? I don't want to leave my children. Please, viejo, don't let them take me, don't let them. I shouldn't have gone downtown."

"Just stay here inside the house and don't leave the yard. There's no need for it anyway. I'll bring you everything you need. Look, don't cry anymore, don't cry. No, go ahead and cry, it'll make you feel better. I'm gonna talk to the kids and tell them to stop bothering you about Santa Claus. I'm gonna tell them there's no Santa Claus, that way they won't trouble you with that anymore."

"No, viejo, don't be mean. Tell them that if he doesn't bring them anything on Christmas Eve, it's because the Reyes Magos will be bringing them something."

"But . . . well, all right, whatever you say. I suppose it's always best to have hope."

———

The children, who were hiding behind the door, heard everything, but they didn't quite understand it all. They awaited the day of the Reyes Magos as they did every year. When that day came and went with no arrival of gifts, they didn't ask for explanations.

The Gulf Oil Can Santa Claus

Rolando Hinojosa

Born into a Mexican and Anglo-American family in a small Rio Grande Valley town, Rolando Hinojosa (1929–) has experienced the tug and pull of two cultures his entire life. The most prolific and respected of Mexican-American novelists, Hinojosa has written works in both Spanish and English with the facility of a bilingual merchant on the border and the artistry of Ambrose Bierce and Carlos Fuentes, with whom he is often compared. "The Gulf Oil Can Santa Claus" is one of the few memoirs penned by Hinojosa and clearly exhibits his minimalist talent for reducing complex social movements and human emotions into humble, concrete images and symbols. Santa Claus, the central cultural symbol of the American Christmas, here becomes the symbol of the growing American identity of Mexicans in the United States during the historical period when this process was most salient: World War II and the Korean War.

Further Reading: Rolando Hinojosa, *Ask a Policeman* (Houston: Arte Público Press, 1998); José Saldívar, *The Rolando Hinojosa Reader: Essays Historical and Critical* (Houston: Arte Público Press, 1984).

The Gulf Oil Can Santa Claus

By the time the Japanese imperial forces were deep into the mopping-up operations in the Bataan Peninsula, preparations for the siege and fall of Corregidor were also underway. One of the defenders was Clemente García, a twenty-three-year old youngster from Mercedes, Texas, down in the Valley.

He was born not in Mercedes, but in Northern Mexico; his

mother, two brothers, and a sister had crossed the Rio Grande at Río Rico, Tamaulipas, Mexico, and settled in Mercedes some two or three years after the death of don Clemente senior who had died during one of the Spanish influenza epidemics that swept Mexico and most of the world, at the end of World War I and well into the Twenties.

Don Clemente had been a veteran of the Mexican Revolution; upon his death, as an enlisted careerist, his widow began to receive a smallish pension from the Mexican government.

Mrs. García's decision to cross the Rio Grande was an economic one and thus no different from the hundreds of thousands of European and other immigrants who settled in the United States. The choice of Mercedes was no accident, however: it was, and remains, an overwhelming Texas Mexican town. Its history and demography reflect that fact, and if not all of the newly arrived Mexican nationals remained there, they did make it a type of half-way house for transients who later spread out all over Texas, the Midwestern United States, and beyond.

These Garcías, then, were merely the newest crop of Garcías to blossom there; to my recollection, there were at least twenty García families in Mercedes. I say "separate" to indicate that these twenty were neither first nor second cousins germane; these were all the main families, and thus the number of affiliated García families could have numbered fifty units or more. García, however, was not the commonest name, it was merely one of the most popular. As popular, say, as Saldívar or Paredes which are as common as cotton bolls in the month of July.

So, these Garcías settled in Mercedes. Aurora, an only daughter, did needlepoint and constructed some remarkably intricate crepe paper designs to be used as cemetery decorations. Two of the youngsters, Arturo and Medardo, were apprenticed off to neighborhood *panaderías*—bakeries; Arturo to the *El Fénix* and

Medardo to *El Porvenir*. Clemente, clearly the brightest according to the family, was enrolled at the all-Texas Mexican neighborhood school: North Ward Elementary.

He logged in the mandatory six years there, and, at sixteen years of age, had learned to read and write enough English to hire on as a sackboy for a local grocery store. Later on, he became the deliveryman as well as the driver.

On his twenty-first birthday, he came to our home and knocked on the east porch door. I was the only one home at the time and invited him in. He thanked me but said that he was in the middle of a delivery; he had stopped, he said, to ask my father's advice on some matter, but that he'd call again.

He was there the same evening after supper. He was typical of many Northern Mexicans, as many of us are, with greenish eyes peering out of fair skin now darkened by a fierce sun.

Our people came to the Valley, as had his, with the Escandón expedition and colonists in 1749; our family happened to live on the northern bank of the Río when it became part of the American Union; his ancestors had lived on the southern bank and thus with the proclamation of the Treaty of Guadalupe Hidalgo, they became Mexican, nationals, and we, American citizens.

Later, with the Rio Grande acting as a jurisdictional barrier, the northern and southern bank cultures changed somewhat but not to any marked degree: relatives remained relatives, and *conocidos*—friends-distant-kin-and-acquaintances—were as firm as ever. It was not, then, unusual but rather customary for northern and southern borderers to marry one another. During those times of weddings and other celebrations, the legal crossings of the international bridges were dispensed with; not by the immigration authorities, of course, but certainly by the families and guests involved and then for as long as the wedding parties lasted. The same was true for *pedidas*—betrothals, or baptisms, wakes, and funerals.

Since Clemente had no father, he called on mine for advice; this was in the late Nineteen Thirties and there were still some strong remnants of the old patriarchal system established in 1750. "It's a serious matter, don Manuel," he said to my father.

This was the obligatory phrase and it would encompass almost anything, anything from a request for my father, as a sponsor, to ask for a girl's hand to my father selecting a commission for that same purpose. It could also mean putting in a good word—*dar una recomendación*—on his behalf for whatever was needed; in short, it could be anything, but certainly something of importance to the petitioner.

The Great Depression was still hanging on in the Valley and elsewhere, and steady jobs were hard to come by. For Valleyites jobs were harder still given the Valley-wide agrarian economy which afforded little opportunity. In Clemente's case it was something different: during one of his deliveries in the Anglo Texan side of town, he had met a man named Claude Rodgers. According to Clemente, Mr. Rodgers was going to own and operate a Gulf Oil gas station in the Texas Mexican part of town. And, Mr. Rodgers had asked Clemente if he wanted to work there, full time. Clemente had not known what to say to this, but Mr. Rodgers solved that when he said, "Think it over. Let me know in a week or so."

My father listened to Clemente, nodded, and then pointed to a chair. Clemente sat down, and one of my sisters brought him a tall glass of limeade. I was about to leave them, but my father said I could stay, and I did so.

The upshot was that he took the job; the gas station was directly across the street from our house, and I would see him on a daily basis on my way to and from North Ward Elementary.

In November of 1940, a week before Thanksgiving, as I was crossing North Texas Avenue on my way home, I heard a series of shrill whistles: it was Clemente. "Acá," he said. "Over here." He grinned and yelled out: "Ándale. Come on, hurry it up." He was standing under the car wash which doubled as the car repair section of the garage. It was supported by four solid metal posts, and the sixteen-to-twenty-foot high roof was on a slant.

"What's up?" I asked.

"Look."

"At what? The oil cans?"

"Yeah; I've been saving them."

"Can you sell 'em, like milk bottles?"

He laughed then, and said, "No. I'm going to weld them; all of them. I'm going to weld them and make us a Santa Claus for Christmas."

"Really? Out-a cans?"

"Yeah, you just wait."

"Can I help?"

"You better; it's my Christmas present for you."

"For me?"

"Sure! We'll begin by rinsing and drying them out. What's your dad going to give you?"

"A pair of khaki pants. And a leather belt, from Matamoros."

"And this'll be your third present; everybody's entitled to three, you know."

Thanksgiving came and went, and every afternoon after running errands and doing the daily chores, I'd run over to Rodgers Gulf, rinse some more cans and watch Clemente weld them for the Santa Claus.

"We're going to put it up there, on top of the roof; I'll get me some good, strong wire and nothing'll blow it down; not even the Gulf wind."

That Santa Claus had the biggest belly I'd ever seen; it was matchless in paunch, in roundness, and the black belt was forged out of a series of flattened out cans which gave an even bigger impression of the girth of that old man.

Clemente finished it a week before Christmas, and then in January, on *El Día de los Magos*, the Day of the Magi, or Epiphany as the Church Calendar calls it, he received a notice from the local Selective Service Board.

He took and passed his physical in San Antonio that March of 1941, and he was on his way to the Philippines by October of the same year. What letters he wrote to his mother were brought to my father to read.

Mrs. García, proud but fearful, worried about her two remaining sons. Arturo was found unfit for military service, but Medardo, when he came of age, was drafted and, coincidentally, found himself in the Luzon offensive of 1944; after that campaign, he was sent to Okinawa where he managed to survive the end of the War.

The Santa Claus stayed on top of the car wash for some ten years after World War II. Korea came and went and some of us found ourselves in that "nasty little war" as some correspondent once called it. The Santa finally came down—rusted away, most probably—but due, in greater part, to urban renewal.

In the way of the world of the living, I forgot about it, and I had almost forgotten Clemente García, 'La Norteñita,' as we called him. It was an affectionate name, and a feminine one too. But, he was called that, in the singular, in honor of his favorite song, "Las Norteñitas," "Those Oh-so-sweet Northern Girls."

I had forgotten my Christmas gift from him, as I said, and then, one day, I went down to Mercedes on some now forgotten family business.

Urban renewal had also taken care of the house in which I

was born; in its place stood an empty but paved parking lot. Across the street, the old Rodgers Gulf Station had been replaced by a tire store; it was owned by a man named Leopoldo Martínez, a relatively newcomer to Mercedes. (As such he was called a "fuereño," a foreigner, the name usually given to those not born there.)

As I crossed the street to see Martínez, I thought I saw the Gulf Oil Can Santa Claus. I walked on, and I was sure I had seen it again. Somewhere. But how?

I ran inside the store and then almost knocked down a clerk taking inventory.

"Oh, it's you, Doctor. How are you?"

I stopped and looked at him for some sign of recognition but found none.

"I'm sorry," I said. "Who's your father?"

"Leocadio Gavira, the truck driver; he knows you."

I nodded and apologized again. He couldn't help noticing my searching for something and asked, "Can I help you?"

I didn't know what to say, where to begin. Images of the Thirties, Forties, and Fifties flicked on and off and on again as in a slide show until I finally said, "No . . . thanks; I thought I had seen something . . . it's nothing."

He nodded, and as I turned to go, I saw it again; not its reflection this time, but the article itself: a full-blown Michelin Tire Man. The Gavira youngster looked at it, and said, "Oh, that. It's a new line. You know, when some of the older people come in and look at it, they shake their heads. You know why they do that?"

I nodded and started out the door again when he said, "Good to have seen you again, Doctor."

I smiled back and on an impulse asked, "Did you ever know or hear of the Widow García on Hidalgo and First?"

"Sure; she must be ninety, ninety-five, a hundred, maybe. She's still alive; lives with a daughter, I think."

And with her memories, too, I added silently.

"Thanks . . . what's your first name?"

"John, sir."

"John! Well, thanks, again."

"Yessir." And he went back to his inventory.

The Michelin Tire Man. It looked grotesque, somehow, but—and again somehow—it looked like my third Christmas present, the one I got the year before the War.

◀ II ▶

Puerto Rico and New York

The Magi Kings

Anonymous

Unlike the jolly frolicking of "Las Arandelas" and other songs of the
asalto, *"The Magi Kings" is a serious* aguinaldo *commemorating the*
sacred coming of Christ to save humanity. Both music and lyrics reveal
ancient roots in medieval Europe.

Further reading: López Cruz, Francisco, *El aguinaldo en Puerto Rico* (San Juan: Instituto de Cultura Puertorriqueña, 1972); Canino Salgado, Marcelino, *El cantar*
folklórico de Puerto Rico (Río Piedras: University of Puerto Rico Press, 1974).

The Magi Kings

The Kings who came to Bethlehem
Announcing the coming of the Messiah
We too sing to Jesus Christ today . . .

From far-off lands,
We have come to see you
The eastern star
Has served as our guide.

Oh, brilliant star,
That announces the dawn,
Don't ever keep from us
Your beneficent light. [bis]

Come all ye shepherds,
Come to adore him,
The King of the Heavens
Who has just been born. [bis]

Los Reyes Magos

Los reyes que llegaron a Belén
Anunciando la llegada del Mesías
A Jesús con alegría le cantamos hoy también . . .

De tierras lejanas
Venimos a verte
Nos sirve de guía
La estrella de Oriente [bis]

Oh, brillante estrella
Que anuncias la aurora
No me falte nunca
Tu luz bienhechora [bis]

Venid, pastorcillos,
Venid a adorar
Al Rey de los Cielos
Que ha nacido ya [bis]

Glory on the highest
To the Son of God,
Glory on the highest
And Love on Earth. [bis]

Gloria en las alturas
Al Hijo de Dios
Gloria en las alturas
Y en la tierra amor [bis]

If You Give Me Meat Pies

Anonymous

Another in the cycle of Christmas songs that is traditional in the asalto *(see the Introduction), "If You Give Me Meat Pies" asks for the recompense of meat pies and rice pudding for singing at the patron's door.*

Further reading: Cancionero navideño (New York: Migration Division, Commonwealth of Puerto Rico, s.d.); Miriam Transue, ed. and trans., *Aguinaldos de Puerto Rico / Christmas Songs of Puerto Rico* (New York: Migration Division, Commonwealth of Puerto Rico, 1960); Marcelino Canino Salgado, *El cantar folklórico de Puerto Rico* (Río Piedras: University of Puerto Rico Press, 1974).

If You Give Me Meat Pies

If you give me meat pies,
Give them nice and hot,
Because cold meat pies
Leave us all bloated.

If you give rice pudding,
Don't give me a spoon,
'Cause my mother told me
To bring her some.

Si Me Dan Pasteles

Si me dan pasteles,
Denme los calientes,
Que pasteles fríos
Empachan a la gente.

Si me dan arroz,
No me den cuchara,
Que mamá me dijo
Que se lo llevara.

The Arandelas

Anonymous

"Las Arandelas" is one of the series of songs from oral tradition that are standards in the repertoire of the asalto *during the Christmas* parrandas *in Puerto Rico (see the Introduction). In the song, the singers ask to be let into a house to partake of the Christmas foods. The meaning of* arandela *in the chorus and the title is, for the most part, lost and forgotten, just used for rhyme and rhythm rather than meaning.*

Further reading: Cancionero navideño (New York: Migration Division, Common-wealth of Puerto Rico, s.d.); Miriam Transue, ed. and trans., *Aguinaldos de Puerto Rico / Christmas Songs of Puerto Rico* (New York: Migration Division, Common-wealth of Puerto Rico, 1960).

The Arandelas

Open up the door,
Open up the door,
'Cause I'm in the street
And everyone will see
That you're rebuffing me.
And everyone will see
That you're rebuffing me.

Sing the *arandelas*,
Sing the *arandelas*,
Sing the *arandelas*,
To my heart.

Las Arandelas

Abreme la puerta,
Abreme la puerta,
Que estoy en la calle
Y dirá la gente
Que éste es un desaire
Y dirá la gente
Que éste es un desaire.

A las arandelas
A las arandelas
A las arandelas
De mi corazón.

What is that I see?
What is that I see?
Something covered up
Oh, could it be
A roast suckling pig?
Oh, could it be
A roast suckling pig?

[*Chorus*]

When we assault your house,
When we assault your house,
We all come singing
All very excited,
All very happy,
All very excited,
All very happy.

[*Chorus*]

Allá dentro veo,
Allá dentro veo
Un bulto tapao,
No sé si será
Un lechón asao.
No sé si será
Un lechón asao.

[*Coro*]

A darte un asalto,
A darte un asalto,
Venimos cantando
Todos bien alegres
Con mucho entusiasmo,
Todos bien alegres
Con mucho entusiasmo.

[*Coro*]

Down from the Mountains

Anonymous

The following Puerto Rican Christmas song celebrates the singing, revelry, and parrandas *that are part of the Christmas tradition of* jíbaros *or highlanders descending to the cities to sing carols and participate in the* asaltos *(described in the Introduction). Especially important are the traditional foods, such as* lechón *or roast suckling pig, mentioned in the lyrics.*

Further reading: *Cancionero navideño* (New York: Migration Division, Commonwealth of Puerto Rico, s.d.); Miriam Transue, ed. and trans., *Aguinaldos de Puerto Rico / Christmas Songs of Puerto Rico* (New York: Migration Division, Commonwealth of Puerto Rico, 1960).

Down from the Mountains

We're down from the mountains
To invite you to eat
Suckling pig on the spit
And rum *coquito* to drink.

Ay, Doña María,
Ay, Compadre José,
Open up the door,
I want to see you both.

We're down from the mountains
To invite you to eat
Suckling pig on the spit
And rum *coquito* to drink.

De las Montañas Venimos

De las montañas venimos
A invitarte a comer
Un lechoncito en su vara
Y buen coquito a beber.

Ay, Doña María,
Ay, Compay José,
Abrame la puerta,
Que los quiero ver.

De las montañas venimos
A invitarte a comer
Un lechoncito en su vara
Y buen coquito a beber.

Open up, compadre,
It's already three a.m.
And I haven't had
Even a taste of coffee.

Ay, Doña María,
Ay, Compadre José,
Open up the door,
I want to see you both.

Don't bring me nothing
That I don't want,
At Christmas time,
Just give me *lechón*.

Ay, Doña María,
Ay, Compadre José,
Open up the door,
I want to see you both.

Abrame, compay,
Que ya son las tres
Y yo no he probao
Buche de café.

Ay, Doña María,
Ay, Compay José,
Abrame la puerta,
Que los quiero ver.

No me traigan ná
Que no quiera yo,
En las Navidades
Tráiganme un lechón.

Ay, Doña María,
Ay, Compay José,
Abrame la puerta,
Que los quiero ver.

Santa Clo* to La Cuchilla

Abelardo Díaz Alfaro

After graduating with a degree in social work and serving as a social worker in Puerto Rico, Díaz Alfaro (1917–) developed a career as a writer for radio broadcast and print. Perhaps because of his broadcasting experience, his stories are orally effective, capturing colloquial speech and the nuances of dialogue. The following tale that he weaves runs in direct opposition to the ideology exemplified in the Americanizing tales of such writers as Juan B. Huyke, also included in this collection. Díaz Alfaro, with tongue in cheek and razor-sharp satire ridicules the folly of imposing English as the official language of education in Puerto Rico and displacing Puerto Rican customs with those of the United States.

Further reading: Abelardo Díaz Alfaro, *Terrazo* (San Juan: Institute of Puerto Rican Culture, 1967).

Santa Clo* to La Cuchilla†

Peyo Mercé's school was the one which had a red flag out in front waving from a bamboo pole. The school was made up of two large halls made by a long room divider. In one of those two halls a new instructor was teaching: Mister Johnny Rosas.

The area supervisor thought it prudent to appoint to the barrio of La Cuchilla† an additional teacher, one who would

*The pronunciation of "Santa Claus" in Puerto Rican Spanish.

†The name of the town, La Cuchilla, means guillotine, among other types of very sharp blades. Guillotine is the ironic meaning intended by the author.

show Peyo new pedagogical methods and bring the light of progress to the dark barrio.

The supervisor called into his office this recently graduated young and fortunate teacher, who had even traveled to the United States. He said only this: "Listen, Johnny, I'm going to send you to La Cuchilla so that you can put into practice the latest methods you've learned. That Peyo doesn't know anything about methodology; he's about forty years behind the times. Try to get him to change his ways and, above all, teach the kids English, lots of English."

One day, Peyo Mercé spied a weary old horse struggling up the hill to the school with the new teacher on his back. Peyo didn't feel any resentment. He even sympathized somewhat with the young man, saying to himself, "Life will start wrinkling his brow, like a plow cutting furrows into the earth."

And Peyo ordered some *jibaritos** to remove the harness from the horse and take him to pasture.

Peyo knew that life would be hard on the young man. Life is hard in the hill country. The food is humble: rice and beans, garlic sauce, *avapenes*, tiny freshwater fish, salt-dry codfish, soup and with a lot of water to make it stretch. Impassible roads, almost always filled with giant potholes. For bathing, there's the waterfall and for drinking, rain water. Peyo Mercé had to draw up his lesson plans by the shimmering light of a kerosene lantern or a wooden torch.

Johnny Rosas became bored at nightfall. The hilltops wood slowly turn black and ghostly. Here and there tiny yellow lights would blink on and off in the monotonous shadows of the landscape. The tree frogs were the pulsing heartbeat of each night. A rooster would suspend its slow and tremulous crowing

*Country people, hillbillies. Here, the diminutive form, *-itos*, is used endearingly.

in the air. Far off in the distance a dog would stretch out its painful bark as the stars began to bloom above.

And Peyo Mercé would head off to play cards or dominoes down at Tano's general store.

One day, Johnny Rosas told Peyo, "This barrio is very backward. We have to renovate it. New things are needed urgently. We need to replace what's antiquated, traditional. Remember the words of Mr. Escalera: 'Down with tradition.' We need to teach a lot of English and copy the customs of the Americans."

And Peyo, without getting upset much, uttered these words: "That's right, English is good and it's needed. But, by gosh, we don't even know how to pronounce Spanish well enough! And a hungry child is a slow learner. The fox once said to the snails, 'You first have to learn to walk before you can run.'"

And Johnny didn't understand what Peyo was saying.

The tobacco plantation was becoming more animated as the Christmas holidays approached. Peyo had already seen some of his students making *tiple* and *cuatro* guitars from cedar and *yagruma* wood. The holidays always brought back memories of good times in the past. Celebrations of the coming of the Magi, wonderful dances. Back then tobacco leaf sold well. And the best cuts of pork were sent to neighbors as a symbol of the ties of god-parenting. It seemed that he could still hear that old Christmas song:

> *This the house that has*
> *A door made of steel*
> *The person who lives here*
> *Is kind and genteel.*

Yes, a gentleman who was languishing away like a dying moon over the swamps.

Johnny Rosas awoke Peyo from his reverie with these words:

"This year Santa Claus will make his debut in La Cuchilla. That celebration of the coming of the Magi is out of date. It's hardly seen at all in San Juan these days. It's part of the past. I'll invite Mr. Rogelio Escalera to the party; that'll please him a lot."

Peyo scratched his head and responded dispassionately, "You're just like Juana and her chickens. But me, I'm just a *jíbaro* who has never left this place, and I hold the Three Magi deep in my soul. It's that we *jíbaros* know how to smell things out . . . they can be as pungent as dried cod fish."

And Johnny started making preparations for the "Gala Premiere" of Santa Claus in La Cuchilla. Johnny showed his students a magazine illustration of Santa Claus in a sled pulled by reindeer. And Peyo, who happened to be standing in the doorway that divided both school rooms, imagined a different scene: an old, decrepit *jíbaro* mounted on a mare being pulled by goats.

And Mr. Rosas asked the little *jíbaro* school children, "Who is this?"

And Benito, as sharp and quick as he could be, answered, "Misteh, that's the old year, all red."

And Johnny Rosas marveled at the ignorance of those children and at the same time got angry at Peyo Mercé's carelessness.

Christmas Eve arrived and all of the barrio parents were invited to the school.

In his class, Peyo organized a typical *fiesta*, which turned out wonderfully. Some of the *jíbaro* children sang Christmas songs accompanied by *tiple* and *cuatro* guitars. And to top it off, the Three Wise Men made their entrance while the old folk singer Simón improvised verses on the theme of "They come and go, but us, no." Peyo dished out rice pudding and candies, and the children exchanged little trick gifts.

Then Peyo asked the children to go into Mr. Johnny Rosas' classroom, because he had a surprise for them, and he had even invited Mr. Rogelio Escalera.

Right in the middle of the room there was an artificial Christmas tree. Red streamers were hung from bookshelf to bookshelf. Hanging on the walls were little wreaths made of green leaves with a red fruit in the middle. Snow-covered letters spelled out "Merry Christmas." Everything was covered with icicles.

The parents and family members were speechless as they took in all that they had never seen before. Mr. Rogelio Escalera looked very pleased, indeed.

Some of the children stepped up to the teacher's platform and arranged themselves in an acrostic that spelled out Santa Claus. One retold the tale of Noel and a chorus of children sang "Jingle Bells," while ringing some bells. All the parents could do was look at each other in amazement. Mister Rosas disappeared for a moment, and the supervisor, Rogelio Escalera, congratulated the children and parents of the barrio for such a beautiful party and for having such an involved and progressive teacher like Mister Rosas.

And then, Mister Escalera asked for complete silence from the assembly, because he was about to introduce a strange and mysterious personage. A chorus immediately broke into song:

Here comes Santa Claus . . .
He walks so slow.
Tic, tac, tic, tac.

And suddenly there appeared in the doorway the red and white person of Santa Claus carrying an enormous sack on his back, and saying in a thunderous voice, "Here is Santa, Merry Christmas to you all!"

A cry of terror shook the entire classroom. Some of the

campesinos jumped out the window, the smallest children began to cry and grab onto the skirts of their godmothers, who were quickly scattering. Everyone was looking for an escape route. And Mister Rosas was running after them, to explain that it was he who was dressed up so strangely, but his yelling just increased the panic.

One old lady crossed herself and said, "He's been conjured up! It's the devil himself and speaking in American!"

The supervisor was making useless attempts at detaining the crowd, openly shouting, "Don't run, don't be silly little Puerto Ricans. Santa Claus is human, a good man."

From afar the shouts of people scattering could be heard. And Mister Escalera, on seeing that Peyo Mercé had remained cool and indifferent, dumped all of his resentment on him, accusing him at the top of his voice, "You, Peyo Mercé, are to blame for the savage behavior of this barrio, right in the middle of the twentieth century."

And Peyo, without reacting, answered, "Mister Escalera, I'm not to blame if that little saint is not part of Puerto Rican hagiography."

A Story about Santa Claus

Juan B. Huyke

"The creating in our youth a spirit of loyalty and a true love for the American flag and for all American institutions, in order to induce Puerto Ricans to feel, think and act as true Americans" was Juan B. Huyke's goal as Commissioner of Education under the American military government of Puerto Rico. As a curriculum developer, textbook writer, and author of children's literature, Huyke (1880–?) carried on his Americanization project. It is within this framework that Huyke's adaptation of the Santa Claus myth can be understood.

Further reading: Juan B. Huyke, *Cuentos de Puerto Rico* (Chicago: Rand McNally and Company, 1926); José Solís, *Public School Reform in Puerto Rico: Sustaining Colonial Models of Development* (Westport, Conn.: Greenwood Press, 1994).

A Story about Santa Claus

"A story? But my soul is not up for stories, my children. Let me sleep, let me forget."

"But we want to hear one, and play."

"Come on, a story."

"Come on, a Christmas story. A pretty story like those you tell. Just imagine that Sarín will be listening to you too."

My children have named my beloved departed child, who also would ask her father to tell a story.

That's life! The memory of my recently departed child still in my heart. And in front of me, asking for a happy tale from my sad lips, stand my happy children who as yet do not know how to suffer. A Christmas story, no less!

Once again these words are pushing to escape from my soul: "But I'm not up to telling a story right now." My will impedes it.

Nevertheless, seeing that my children are calling for a story from my old font of happiness, one starts to come out: "Gather around me, kids. Get close to me, all of you. Don't anybody talk, because I'm going to tell you a story about that old man Santa Claus. I bet you don't know why children who behave badly also get gifts from Santa Claus on Christmas?"

They look at each with curiosity written all over their faces and settle in to listen as closely as students in old time schools.

"You'll see: When I was a child, that didn't happen at all; only well behaved children were rewarded on that glorious day by the kind old man with the white beard and the red suit. But something happened on Christmas day and things haven't been the same since then.

"Santa Claus would come to earth in his great big coach, happy to bring more toys than ever for Christmas. He would walk around in space, all covered in his grand red suit trimmed in white fur and he'd relish in the thought of his little friends, the children of earth, that planet he could see off in the distance looking like a giant shiny ball.

"The only thing old Santa worried about was having to be the cause of sorrow for some children during his Christmas visits, because, as you know, there are well behaved children and then there are the badly behaved ones. Those who lie, those who don't obey their parents, those who don't want to go to school . . . they are children who really don't deserve Santa's gifts.

"Just because this was fair that didn't mean that it didn't bother the good old friend of children. To come into a home and fill up the bags of good kids with toys and to leave nothing for the children who had seriously misbehaved! It was truly disagreeable to him.

"It so happened that on the Christmas I'm talking about, more than any other time Santa Claus was noticing all of those children's souls that were rising up to heaven as he was floating down to earth. They looked like little points of light ascending in the dark sky, ascending until they were out of sight. There were big ones and tiny ones. He knew that they were souls from all different times in history who were crossing through space on their final voyage to God's mansion. All of a sudden Santa's coach hit something hard. He stuck his venerable head out the side window and saw a little light begging for help. The little soul just had to speak to Santa before rising up to join the celestial hordes.

"Santa hesitated for a moment. He just could not lose any more time; he just had so many hours in which to do his work. But determination was always weakened by children, so he gave in and asked, 'What can I do for you?'

"A three- or four-year-old boy as beautiful as the angels took on visible form. A happy smile was playing on his little face because he was on his way to join God.

" 'Do you remember me?' the child asked.

"Santa hesitated again. How can I possibly remember all the children who live on earth? But, he still made an effort, and then, happily, perhaps because he would soon have that child in heaven, he exclaimed, 'Rubén!'

"Rubén was the smallest child in a home on earth that Santa Claus would visit with joy. It was one of those crowded little homes in which it seemed that an invisible hand united all the souls.

"That scamp Rubén, who was spoiled by everyone, was the king of the household. His slightest wishes were always met by his parents. His brothers and sisters loved him very much, without ever feeling jealousy or envy. Rubén was the indisputable ruler of that happy home, in which preparations were being made to celebrate the best ever children's festival: Christmas.

"All the children had been good. That is, all except for Luis and Daniel, two unruly little boys who always had to be reminded of Santa's upcoming visit in order to behave well.

" 'Santa Claus is not going to bring you a thing,' their father would warn.

" 'Santa Claus is going to punish you,' their mother would warn.

Evidently, these warnings had their effect. But after a few minutes, Luis and Daniel would forget them and return to their mischief without any regard for their parents' authority.

"Santa Claus had already punished them the previous year. All of the children had received valuable presents except for Luis and Daniel, who only received a few trifling gifts from Santa.

"But the boys did not change their habits because of the previous year's punishment. Santa's effort was wasted on them.

"When their parents were discussing how hard this year's punishment should be, they could not agree upon what to recommend this year. Their mother thought Santa Claus should be just as severe as last year.

"Their father thought that Santa Claus's kindness would not allow him to keep on punishing them. 'It's our responsibility to punish them, not Santa's,' he said.

" 'But Santa will help us,' their mother answered.

"Then the father assured her, 'They're still at a mischievous age. They grow out of it.'

" 'Not if it's left up to you,' the mother said. "You let them get away with everything."

" 'You'll see. Don't worry,' he said patiently as he left so that he would not have to continue this delicate discussion.

"Santa Claus invited Rubén to step into the coach, at which the little boy hopped in next to Santa.

" 'What happened at your house?' Santa asked him.

"This is what Rubén related: 'I got sick yesterday. I didn't really understand what was going on. It felt like a strong hand was squeezing my throat. I complained to my parents, and they sent for the doctor, but nothing; that hand kept squeezing me without mercy. There was a horrible moment. My brothers and sisters were all around me, crying, when they were suddenly sent from my bedroom. They weren't allowed to stay. And my mother and father were crying also. I, too, wanted to cry, but I just couldn't; that cruel hand just kept tightening around my throat. I remember noticing Luis and Daniel at the instant that they were leaving my room. The poor things were crying. Seeing them crying like that, I thought to myself that they were not so bad, after all.'

"Santa Claus was moved by Rubén's story, but the boy just kept telling his tale: 'Finally, I no longer was concerned with Earth. All of my pain suddenly left me and I started ascending, ascending as if angels were taking me up in a soft cradle. In the midst of my joy, I was taken over by some sad thoughts. I thought of my brothers, who would not be receiving toys from you this year, according to my parents. But they're good, because they were crying for *me*. When I saw your coach floating in space, I decided to stop you in order to make a request of you.'

"Santa Claus, who had been listening carefully, immediately interrupted him. 'How can I possibly take them presents if your parents believe their behavior has been bad?'

"The little soul blurted out, 'No, my parents don't understand these things well enough. I assure you that Luis and Daniel are good.'

"Then, thinking like a heavenly angel, Rubén added this phrase that made a good impression on Santa: 'All children are good. Evil is a thing of adults who do not understand children.'

"Santa lowered his head onto his chest. Later, resting his head on the palm of his hand, he spent a long while thinking. He thought that what the little child had said was the truth. 'Why punish the children when there is goodness in all of them? The most mischievous child on earth is worthy of my mercy and my forgiveness.'

"Then, addressing the child in a booming voice, he said, 'Go on up, content, to your new celestial mansion. From now on, I'll bring gifts to all of the children. You have convinced me. In all of them there is goodness.'

"The little glowing light continued on its journey to heaven, and Santa Claus went on down to Earth to inspire forgiveness in the souls of his helpers, the parents.

"When Santa arrived at Luis and Daniel's home, he saw the Christmas tree on the living room piano that the parents had prepared before their little son had died. The children were playing on the balcony. The parents were in their bedroom, crying.

" 'Come, dear, we have to make an effort for them. It's not fair that they should suffer. Deep down, they're good kids,' Santa heard the father saying.

"A few moments later, all of the children were immersed in their happiness and had forgotten about everything else, even their parents' suffering.

"Santa Claus, the spirit of Santa Claus, had triumphed."

The Day We Went to See the Snow

Alfredo Villanueva-Collado

A professor of English at Hostos Community College in New York, Villanueva-Collado (1944–) was born in Puerto Rico, raised in Venezuela, and received his Ph.D. from the State University of New York in Binghamton. Despite being an English teacher, Villanueva prefers to write creatively in Spanish and sees it as part of the effort to preserve Hispanic culture. He hopes that his writings offer an alternative history to that proffered by the American Dream. The present story is revisionist in its challenge not only to the idea that Christmas is part of the culture of the snowy North, but that Puerto Ricans are deprived by not sharing northerners' experiences.

Further reading: Julián Olivares, ed., *Cuentos hispanos de los Estados Unidos* (Houston: Arte Público Press, 1993).

The Day We Went to See the Snow

That day it dawned all of a sudden, with the sun grabbing the venetian blinds as if it wanted to melt them. I heard my mother in the kitchen already preparing breakfast, my father in the bathroom flushing the toilet, and Roberto rummaging around in cabinets in the room next to mine. I suddenly remembered what day it was and my heart began to beat faster. I rushed to wash up and get dressed. I put on a cream-colored sweater, some corduroy pants and thick socks. On seeing me in such attire, Mami began to laugh.

My father, in his slow, heavy pace, let out a grunt and said, "The traffic jam is gonna be a b——," he said to no one in particular. "It's already nine o'clock, and it'll take us two hours to get to San Juan.

"With so many people, I don't doubt it," Mami added. "We'd better get a move on."

We were already in the car, when Papi got a sudden urge to go to the bathroom, so we lost another twenty minutes. Roberto and I were sitting in the back seat, each by a window. Mami had already warned us what would happen if we didn't keep still. As she said it, she flourished her long fingernails, immaculately manicured and painted a deep red; on more than one occasion they had spiked us into tears as her means of gaining immediate control over us. Papi came back and we hit the road.

Getting out of Bayamón was easy, but once we got to Santurce, the traffic jammed to the high heavens. We moved just four feet every half hour and, with the intense heat and not even a breeze, the car interior was as sticky as a steam bath. Roberto started shooting at Indians, because on that day he happened to be wearing his cowboy outfit, complete with a wide-brimmed hat, gun belt and pistol. "Pow!" and an Indian would hit the dust, and "pow!" down went another Indian, until Mami noticed the horrified looks coming from other rolling steam baths, and she quickly turned and grabbed Roberto's arm and told him to drop the toys, because it was not polite to point at people, much less with a gun, that what would they think, that she hadn't left home to be embarrassed in public, and if he didn't straighten up, we were going to return home immediately. Right, Casimiro?

She let Roberto go and turned to the other side to see what I was doing. But my game was much more peaceful. My obsession was counting cars of certain makes, specifically Studebakers, which, you should realize, wasn't very easy in that monster traffic jam. At least I could try without attracting too much attention from the front seat. There was a Ford, and in front of that a Chrysler; there were tons of Chevrolets and here and there a Cadillac, but I didn't even see one Studebaker. So I started lifting myself up to see out the back window when, pow, a heavy hand knocked me back down into the back seat as I was warned that we would all die in an accident because Papi would not be able to see the cars in back with me blocking the view, that I and nobody but I would be responsible, and that it would be better that right then and there we turned back for home in order to avoid a tragedy.

Finally we arrived at the Condado bridges; a sea breeze alleviated the itching I was feeling all over my body. I was going to take my sweater off, but Mami, who had eyes in the back of her head, told me that she'd see me in the hospital with pneumonia, I was so drenched in sweat, in addition to the swatting she'd give me, because decent people did not disrobe in public. Roberto was in a worse way: he was itching in an inappropriate place and was trying to scratch himself without anyone noticing. The result was that after one quick tug, he found himself in the front seat, leaving a sweat stain on the red plastic seat cover by the side window; he was warned forthwith that the health of his soul was in danger for sticking his hands in certain places. The radio was announcing the coming gift to the people from the first lady, which only incited Papi's furor more.

"Damn all these people and damn that old lady, getting it into her head to bring that garbage here so that every idiot in San Juan can feel like an Eskimo for a day."

"Look, Casimiro, you're the one who promised it to the kids, and you're the one who's dying of curiosity. Isn't that why we're stuck in this traffic? Wouldn't it be better to leave the car here and to go on foot to the park? Oh, you're such a lazy butt; well, here we are, anyway."

As if he had conjured it up, a parking space appeared, and a rabid Papi inserted the car with one swoop of the steering wheel.

"Are you sure it's legal to park here?" Mami asked, always fearful of breaking the law.

"Go to Hell," Papi answered, closing the door to any possible debate.

We got out and Papi and Mami led the way, he in his *guayabera* shirt and Mami with a shawl on her shoulders, just in case, as she would say. Roberto and I walked hand in hand, he hopping up and down and trying to shake loose from his sweaty cowboy pants, which had begun torturing him, while I was battling with the sweater, which felt like it was crawling with ants. It was almost noon.

Once in the park, we made our way through the multitudes all headed in the same direction, enduring the screams, either of excitement or anguish, of millions of children dressed in Levies, corduroy, gloves and even red wool caps with colored balls on top. And there, in the middle of everything, was the snow: white, or almost white, shining but already very watery. I leaped forward and took off running to the snow, getting mud all over my pants on the way, because the melted water was being mixed with the dirt of people's shoes from all over the island. I touched the snow. It was no big deal; it occurred to me that, if I wanted to, I could make it in the refrigerator freezer back home, or play with the shaved ice from snow-cones. All this trouble for this? But obviously, my critical attitude was not shared by others. People were going crazy with the snow. They would circle around the snow pile with their eyes bulging out, while kids went splashing through the mud hole or posed for snapshots taken by their parents. To one side, the people's benefactor, who had made this miracle and my disenchantment possible, was smiling as she turned her silvery head from side to side and cooled herself with a lace fan.

Evidently, the refreshing spectacle had not improved Papi's mood, because I saw him with a purple face at Mami's side, holding on to Roberto, who was screaming inconsolably with his pants fallen down to his knees. I started to hurry up and, coming up to where they were standing, I slipped and fell, about five inches from my Mami's fingernails, who only picked me up, looked over my ruined sweater and remarked, "Just wait till we get home." On top of everything, when we finally found the car where Papi had left it, it had a ticket stuck to the windshield. Papi picked it up, put it into his pocket and, exasperated, said to Mami, "Well, sweetheart, one more bright idea from you and I'll join the statehood party!"

Christmas Was a Time of Plenty

Nicholasa Mohr

Nicholasa Mohr (1935–) is the creator of numerous stories for children, adults, and young adults based on growing up in New York City during the 1940s and 1950s. She has populated her tales with a richly diverse array of characters who reveal the heartbreak, humor, and contradictions of Puerto Rican biculturalism in the big city. In "Christmas Was a Time of Plenty," Mohr reminisces about the ability of poor families to scrape by one way or another, especially at Christmas time.

Further Reading: Nicholasa Mohr, *In Nueva York* (Houston: Arte Público Press, 1988); Nicholasa Mohr, with Antonio Martorell, *The Song of El Coquí and Other Tales of Puerto Rico* (New York: Viking, 1995).

Christmas Was a Time of Plenty

Compared to the rest of the year, Christmas was a time of plenty when I was a child. That was saying a great deal for me and my six older brothers. We were the children of Puerto Rican migrants, living in New York City at the height of the Great Depression. Where and how my parents and the older folks were to get money for Christmas each and every year depended on "un milagro," "God's mercy," or "just plain luck."

At the beginning of World War II, and just before my older brothers left for the Armed Forces, we were all still home. I was quite young, but I can still remember the electricity that permeated the air at Christmas time. My parents together with aunts and uncles would purchase a large sow from the local butcher. They would carefully spice and fix that sow in the traditional Puerto Rican manner. Then, it was sent to an "out of town" bakery . . . a place far from where we lived on 105th Street and Madison Avenue, called Queens. The reason was that no one had an oven large enough to roast the sow. It was delivered to us hot and ready to serve on Christmas Eve, which was when we had our celebration. Traditional dishes like arroz con gandules (seasoned rice with tiny, dry, green peas and pork), pasteles (delicate meat pies, made from root plants and plantains), and rice pudding were also served. I thought that the building itself would surely elevate to heaven just from the sheer goodness and delight of all of those flavors floating and steaming around in the atmosphere.

We all got ready to party by piling the living room furniture into the small bedrooms, making room for wooden kegs of beer and creating a dance floor. We also cleared an easy path to and from the kitchen.

That entire night and into the early hours of the morning, friends and neighbors would come into our home, eat and visit. Some brought their guitars and their accordions; others recited poetry. Speeches were made to the effect that we should all unite and help win this terrible war that was threatening all of mankind. Prayers were offered asking God to be on our side against the enemy and protect our young men, who would have to leave home. In between the speeches, prayers and entertainment, our record player sounded out all the latest Latin hits, including patriotic war songs. "PON PON CAYO EL JAPON . . . PIN PIN CAYO BERLIN" was a favorite.

The younger children like myself fell asleep sooner than the others. We were bedded down in one of the overcrowded bedrooms. Exhausted and happy, we slept soundly, oblivious to the noise and excitement in the other rooms. We were too busy dreaming of the special brand-new toys that might be waiting for us under the brightly lit, tinsel-trimmed, Christmas tree. I hoped this year the adults would be more generous with the gifts I wanted, instead of the practical sweater or the woolen knee socks needed for school.

The next day and for about a week we ate Christmas food without worrying about asking for seconds. Then one day it was over. The Christmas tree was undressed and thrown out, its fate, to be burned in the street. Later we all watched the warm blaze illuminate the cold winter night. Once more we were reminded of the lean times, the daily monotony of school and getting to bed early.

Soon my four oldest brothers went into the service to fight in the second World War. We at home were issued ration books for meat, milk, clothing and other items.

There were good times in between the hard years that followed; some of us moved far away; others died. Most of us just grew up.

Many years went by before we could all manage to get together once more at Christmas time. When we did, everyone could still recall almost vividly those magical Christmases back then . . . in our urban village set in the heart of New York City.

La Nochebuena: The Best of Nights

Jose Yglesias

Jose Yglesias (1919–1995) was one of the first contemporary writers to bring the culture of Hispanics, as part of the American mosaic, to a broad English-speaking public. Over the decades, Yglesias chronicled the bicultural life of Cuban and Spanish Americans through a series of finely wrought novels, short stories, and reportage. Many of his most beloved novels are evocations of growing up in a community founded and dominated by cigar-factory workers in Ybor City (now part of Tampa), Florida. As an early and, perhaps, the best interpreter of an American Hispanic community of the early twentieth century, Yglesias always had an eye for quaint customs and an ear for nuanced and poetic speech.

La Nochebuena: The Best of Nights

Nochebuena. I have never been able to find out how Christmas Eve came to be named this by Spaniards, but in Ybor City, the Latin section of Tampa, it was truly a good night. Indeed, it was the best of nights. Why this was so is difficult to explain. After all, there were other occasions that should have been more exciting for me and my cousins and the other kids on the block—children's day at the State Fair, outings to the beach in summer, the times the Ringling Bros. Circus came to town, the training games of the Cincinnati Reds. Our happiness was not due either to the expectation of gifts left by our bedside while we slept that night; there was no Christmas tree and hardly any toys in the 20s and 30s, not for the children of

{190}

workers. The gifts we did receive were mostly clothes, and we had a pretty good idea of what those would be. Why then was *Nochebuena* so special that it has left me with the finest of gifts—the belief that like most Latinos I was given a touchstone for true gaiety and good feeling?

Let me describe it. For us it was a secular holiday. True, some Latinos went to the Catholic Church for midnight mass, *la misa del gallo*, but these were mostly the few who attended the parochial school and it was another way of not letting go of the day, for *Nochebuena* was the one night when we were allowed to stay up as long as we could. The younger kids were carried off to bed when they turned up into little heaps of sleep, and the older ones were guided there in their stumbling daze. I don't remember ever wanting to cross the backyard that joined my aunt's house, where we all gathered, to our own, but I never walked the few yards home, while my Cuban grandfather firmly grasped my elbow, with any energy left to spare or any room in my bloated belly for another mouthful of *turrón*. I once said to him, "I stole a third glass of wine when no one was looking," and he replied, "Aha!" in a tone I heard myself use years later with my son when I pretended to have been taken in by some maneuver of his.

When I think back about *Nochebuena* in Ybor City, I can see that although it was not a religious occasion it was certainly a reverent one. Our altar was the dinner table. All the preparations and expectations and excitement of the day led to that marvelous feast. We sat down to it at least four or five hours later than our usual 6:30 dinner, reverting in this way, by a kind of racial memory, to the right time for a proper Castilian *cena*. The very timing creates suspense: in any Spanish city, even today, you can observe the happy buzz of anticipation that invades the people out for the *paseo*. Whether they are dashing out on last-minute errands or meeting friends at cafes or simply strolling down the main street, they are all really preparing for the *cena*.

But whereas the Spaniards in the cities are somewhat blasé about their *paseos* and *cenas*, we in Ybor City never could be about *Nochebuena*. Ours was a cigarmaking community that kept U.S. working hours, and although on ordinary days the men went after dinner to the canteens at the Cuban, Spanish, Asturian, and Italian clubs to play dominoes and chat and have a second cup of *café solo* with perhaps a *trago* of cognac, everyone was back home and ready for bed at eleven o'clock. On *Nochebuena* this was reversed: about six o'clock, when they were assured that there were no more errands to do—the pork well on its way to being perfectly done, the house stocked with wine and liquor, the long Cuban loaves brought home from the last freshly baked batch at the bakery—the men of the family went off in little groups to make the rounds of the cafes and the homes of friends. We boys would see our fathers and uncles leave and we longed for the day when we too could go off to be treated (making the women a little anxious that we might return too drunk to appreciate the dinner) and come back four hours later flushed and happy, sneaking dimes and quarters to the kids.

Not that the men were uninterested in the preparation of the dinner. In Ybor City families, they took no part in shopping for food or in preparing meals on ordinary days, except, of course, to make the *café solo* when dinner was done: handling the *colador* was a man's job. But *Nochebuena* was another matter. A week earlier began the discussions of where to buy the big fresh hams that, crisp on the outside, juicy inside, are the great baked wonder of the meal. Sometimes it was the men who cooked it too. I was startled out of bed one Christmas Eve morning by agonized squeals coming from the backyard and ran to help whoever was in trouble. Mother yelled from the kitchen, "Don't go there!" Too late. The men of the family were struggling with a pig, and I was just in time to see Cousin Viola's husband, who had been reared in the Cuban countryside, plunge the knife. I was rooted to the back steps by curiosity, and I did not turn away despite the blood and my mother's calls, because it would have been unmanly.

The pig had to be degutted, scrubbed with boiling water, and its hair plucked, while others dug a pit for the charcoal fire. It took much work and discussion to do all this and set the dressed pig on a spit. Also, many swigs from the gallon of wine. Cousin Pancho had prepared a huge pot of the *mojo*, made with sour orange juice, garlic, and paprika, and during the long hours ahead there were always two men there to turn the pig and baste it with *mojo*. After the novelty of this had worn off for them, I was allowed to dip the new paint brush into the delicious-smelling pot and coat the now unscarifying pig. My mother and aunts no longer live in those three houses on Ybor Street with a common backyard. Some have died and all have scattered to better homes, but to this day Cousin Pancho, now in his mid-seventies, prepares the *mojo* on the 23rd and takes it round in half-gallon jars to three or four of our family's homes. He insists on personally puncturing the legs of pork to show the women, who are certainly no novices, just how to soak *mojo* into these interstices.

That *Nochebuena* they cooked an entire pig because we were sharing it with neighbors. Otherwise, two hams (eighteen pounds each) cooked at two stoves will do. We were never less than two dozen at dinner. Some families took their pork to the bakery to be done. On our block there were always variations of this sort from family to family, but what made *Nochebuena* a true rite was that the menu never changed. There were (and are) no surprises in that—only confirmed delights. The menu was black beans, white rice (each grain firm and separate), sweet potatoes, yuca, salads, chicken baked in lemon and garlic sauce (in families with closer ties to Spain than Cuba, this might be substituted by whole red snappers in *escabeche*) and the pork. The hams were not brought to the table whole. They were sliced in the kitchen, the brown crisp skin put to one side, and the slices and drippings placed in long pans and given a last turn in the oven just before being served with the crackling skin as garnish. On the table was red wine and *sangria*.

This menu rolls off the tongue so easily that I forget how complicated is the preparation of the least dish. Take the black beans; they must be soaked overnight, fortified with garlic, onions, green peppers sauteed in fine olive oil, along with oregano, wine, and hot pepper, and simmered for hours. These ingredients are added at careful intervals so that the sauce will coagulate while the beans remain whole and firm. No mean trick. No less than getting the white rice perfect and hot to the table. One *Nochebuena* the rice was ruined because at the last moment, when the men were already late from their rounds of the clubs, two empty homes behind our alley burst into flames. So suddenly, so thoroughly, that we all knew without being told that the fires had been set. It was 1932, the Depression was well under way, and the insurance would come in handy. What a memorable *Nochebuena* that was for us kids— what a disaster for the cooks!

Of course, no one owned a dining table that could seat 24, and kitchen tables were brought from the other houses, placed in a row, and made to seem one by overlapping tablecloths. Our excitement was already at a high pitch by the time we sat down at it, but the very novelty of so long a table made for further happiness. Also, the tolerance and good humor that prevailed. We children did not cease to be children, and our mothers and aunts yelled at us when we threatened to get out of hand, especially when the table was cleared and the *turrones* and guava paste and cream cheese and flans and *brazos gitanos*, brought out for dessert; but the admonishments carried no threats: everything the adults said, and especially the laughter of the men, contained a license for our youthful mischief, so long as it was harmless. After all, it was *Nochebuena*.

There was enough of everything for everyone. On this one night we were the privileged of the earth. Or so that groaning board made us feel. Only the adults knew what sacrifices it may have taken to provide this plenitude, but I believe that even they when they sat at the table felt they had achieved the good life. Not just for themselves, nor for what in the non-Latino world is called the immediate family, but for the whole of the family—the least cousin or in-law—and the neighbors on the block and that island of Latinos called Ybor City. If an *americano* had wandered down our street, we should have gathered him unto us with a whole heart.

There is not much left of my home town. It is scattered and broken up, and its old *ambiente* seems to me almost entirely gone. I am bitterly sad about it, but three years ago my wife and I were down there for Christmas and our two grown sons, who are New Yorkers, joined us there. Mother got up at six on the morning of Christmas Eve to start the pork cooking, and we three fellows got out of the way by driving to the beaches 40 minutes away and spending the day with the tourists from up north. It was after six when we started back, so interested in our talk that we had no sense of what day it was. As our car approached Nebraska Avenue, the outer rim of old Ybor City, the car was invaded by a new odor. "What's that?" one of them asked, and I immediately recognized it—pork baking in that pungent *mojo*. Heavenly pollution, may no wind ever waft it away.

Those with Less Shared More

Piri Thomas

Author of perhaps the best known memoirs of growing up within the Hispanic culture of poverty in New York, Piri Thomas (1928–) has cultivated in his writings a poetic love-hate relationship with American culture and its most famous Metropolis. His weaving together of the elements of Puerto Rican and Anglo Christmas practices, with Catholic and Protestant rituals in this reminiscence of a World War II era holiday is an affirmation of Hispanics' ability to unify diverse and conflicting tendencies in their own complex experiences.

Further reading: Piri Thomas, *Down These Mean Streets*, (New York: Vintage, 1991); Piri Thomas, *Stories from El Barrio* (New York: Knopf, 1992); Piri Thomas, *Seven Long Times* (Houston: Arte Público Press, 1995).

Those with Less Shared More

Las Navidades de mi niñez eran más que Kris Kringle, alias Santa Claus, alias Mami y Papi, o quién sea. Para mi las Navidades eran la alegria de ester con la familia—pobres de bolsillo, pero ricos de corazón.

Las calles del barrio se llenaban de alegría. Villancicos salían de las vitrolas y radios, de las esquinas y las iglesias y las casas—cantados en muchas lenguas, pues nuestro barrio no era sólo puerto-rriqueño. En Nochebuena nos olvidábamos de que éramos pobres. La mesa rebosaba con la cena tradicional; todo sabía tan delicioso que nadie pensaba en el costo.

Sí, recuerdo las Navidades y los Días de Reyes de antaño, pero más que nada recuerdo las sonrisas de cariño que nos regalábamos unos a otros.

Christmas to me, from childhood on, has been a kaleidoscope of things. Christmas was, as I remember it, Momma's version of Seventh Day Adventist Christ and having to deal with hopped-up prices. Poppa was always the kind of pops that strained his brains digging up ways on the WPA to make the extra pesos needed at Christmas times.

It wasn't that moms and pops didn't know how to save. But in order to save, there had to be some moneys left after pop's emaciated paychecks got through taking care of rent, food, clothing, etc. Mostly there were but few pennies, quarters, dimes, nickels left. The big glass jar set in its closet shrine would celebrate a rare holiday when a crumpled, count-worn dollar bill sulkily floated down through its slot and came to rest on coppers and silvers. Unfortunately, the bottle would never fill and most times would become very empty, because of emergencies like no leche, no pan, no carfare, no breakfast, no lunch, no dinner. Middle-class kids and on up the class ladder weren't the only ones with appetites. Poor *barrio* children were often accused of having hollow legs and two stomachs, like camels.

Anyway, economics was the main reason many of us got to Christmas time broke, and that, pardon the rhyme, was no joke. To force Christmas cheer and joy for the kids was to accept that Christmas was going to meet you broke and leave you even broker.

But "what the hell" was the jolly wartime cry in 1942. Enjoy while you can. You're a long time dead. So deck the halls with boughs of holly, falalalala and *p'alante* for the credit line—that is, if you can apply. Somehow, someway, the money was found. It seemed that those who had more shared less, and those who had less shared more.

Moms and pops were always that way and, diggit, they weren't alone. *Muchos* were of the same *corazón*. And to many of us of all colors and all creeds, Christmas was more than shopping sprees to *La Marqueta* or Kresge's Five and Dime or, for the elite among us, to Macy's, Bloomingdale's or even Klein's, which was the store for the poor who had a millionaire's taste for champagne with a Pepsi Cola pocket.

As a Puerto Rican, I saw how other ethnic groups in all class levels celebrated Christmas. As a child, I was always pleased that they had only one Christmas on December 25th and that we Puerto Ricans had another on January 6th, *El Día de los Tres Reyes*. Both days were for sharing and exchanging gifts. We celebrated not only the birth of Christ but also the three kings who followed the bright star to Bethlehem and found Jesus born in a stable, worshipped him and offered him fine gifts. In my home, Christmas presents were given out on Christmas morning, the idea being, of course, that Santa Claus had done his thing down a nonexistent chimney and out a nonexistent fireplace. So as not to hurt our parents' feelings, we went along with labored letters in English to a cold North Pole, asking an overweight Santa Claus for a list of never-to-come toys, while suspecting him of overindulging in 150 proof Ron Rico because his nose was too tomato red.

But anyway, Christmas to me was more than Kris Kringle, alias Santa Claus, alias my moms and pops, or whoever gave. To me Christmas was the joy of being with my family, poor in pocket and rich in a whole lot of love and understanding. It is true that the cruelties of forced poverty got in the way, but that was purely physical. Spiritually, it wouldn't relate.

The *barrio*'s streets would be alive with Christmas carols sung from juke boxes and radios and street corners and churches, especially in the homes, all in *muchas lenguas*, of course. For our *barrio* was not just made up of Puerto Ricans. It was mixed with almost all the nationalities represented on the branches of ghetto Christmas trees.

In my home in those never-to-be-forgotten days, the preparation of Christmas food was underway, giving promises of
delight. Food that was seen not too many times a year was in
the making, and the dishes had exotic names that often brought
blank stares from those unable to understand that the food
tasted even better as *lechón asado*, prepared with spices and
roasted slowly until crunchy beyond compare. This melted in
your mouth to your heart's content, and you forgot its cost.
Arroz con gandules, pasteles (wrapped in banana leaves or boiling
paper, which gently held the blending plátanos, potato,
yuca and spiced meats), *arroz con dulce* (teasing the tongue with
coconut, cinnamon and raisins), flan, and on and on. And of
course, Christmas cheer from *ron* and milk, eggs and spice
which is called *"coquito,"* a creamy delight that goes down
smoothly, but, if you're not careful, can blow your mind.

Christmas to me as a child was this and more. For it brought
many large families together. Guitars would appear, and songs
of Puerto Rico would be sung, with most people leaving the
room if anyone was uncouth enough to play *I'm Dreaming of a
White Christmas*. Considering the constant lack of heat in apartments in winter time, you could hardly expect the singing of
"White Christmas" to be a big hit.

Religion played big on Christmas—all religions. Momma
was Seventh Day Adventist; aunts and uncles were Pentecostal;
poppa was a death-bed Catholic who would only see a priest
long after he was dead. The church we went to on 116th Street
and Madison Avenue was on the second floor, above a bank. In
churches all over, plays were being enacted, *La Santa Cena, La
Crucifixción, La Natividad. Caramba!!* I even played Tiny Tim
in *A Christmas Carol*, by Charles Dickens. Tiny Tim, who was
crippled, walked fine compared to me. For I hammed it
so much, it took what seemed hours for me to dramatically
drag my "crippled" body six inches across the stage into

the arms of my stage father as played by Reverend Samuels.

The dancing was beautiful in our Christmas lives as well as on Three Kings' Day. As a matter of fact, songs and dances were every day, for it is a matter of our culture—*a nuestra manera*. Slow romantic boleros, fast mambos, smooth island *danzas* full of love and grace. And Three Kings' Day brought *asalto* time. People came singing at your door with music and instruments galore. They would be invited in, served food and drink. Then the whole family would join them, and all went singing and dancing on to the next house—and on and on far into the night and early morning light.

The hardships of reality were set aside in the warmth of the Christmas illusions. But who cared? Reality returned soon enough. We knew when Christmas was over. It was over as soon as they came to collect the rent, the light bill, the gas bill, the furniture bill, the Household Finance, the *bodega* bills and all the rest of the little hells . . . But what the heck! Later!

I remember Christmas and *Día de los Reyes* in the *barrios* of long ago, and, of all, I remember best the smiles of love we gave to each other. To me they were better than all the rest. They weren't wasted smiles.

❧ III ❧

Hispanic Immigrant Christmas

Christmas Eve

Aurelio Luis Gallardo

*A poet, novelist, and playwright who came to San Francisco from
Mexico as a political refugee, Aurelio Luis Gallardo (1831–1869)
published his last book in the port city a year before he died in Napa,
far from his birthplace in Guadalajara. His "Christmas Eve" nostalgically evokes all the color, hubbub, and pageantry of the holiday
celebration in the big city of Guadalajara and contrasts them with
the simple religious fervor of Christmas in a small town. His romantic
re-creation gives us the best representation, by far, of what Christmas
was like in mid-century Mexico. Gallardo, in typical immigrant fashion, feared for the loss of tradition far from his native land; in the
introduction to this last book,* Leyendas y romances, *he states that
he wrote and published it as a legacy for his children. He also wrote
so that those in exile could remember their beloved homeland: "If those
who are living in the bitterness of exile, dispersed along these foreign
shores, cry remembering the homeland they lost, as they turn through
these pages, perhaps they'll encounter here a brief diversion and will
see reflected something of that homeland that is so beloved to them."*

Further reading: Aurelio Luis Gallardo, *Leyendas y romances. Ensayos poéticos.* (San
Francisco, 1868).

Christmas Eve

I

Drizzle, what a drizzle this be:
What a night! It's Christmas Eve,

La Noche Buena

I

Llovizna está que llovizna:
¡Qué noche! y es Noche Buena,

Not a blue piece of sky to be seen,
Not even the crown of stars above.
Frost is covering the fields,
The north wind blowing, almost snowing,
And the little white drops of water
Are tiny pearl-like granules.
A night of many memories,
And happy reminiscence,
Of that august anniversary
Of that greatest Redemption.
In the largest of cities
When midnight is nigh,
From the cathedrals so holy
How large the bells sound!
The multitude comes crowding,
Into the vast temple penetrating,
Beating on the tall metal sheets
Of the enormous bronzed doors.
At twelve o'clock midnight,
With the orchestra sounding strong,
In the light of one hundred torches,
High mass is now celebrated
Amid the incense and the singing,
The deep purple and the grandeur,
The pomp and circumstance
of all the churchly rituals.
Perfume, everywhere, and majesty,
Light, splendor, brilliance, riches,
Beautiful altar pieces manifesting
The piety of regal jewels.
What a procession now crossing
Below the ample dome,
The musicians in the chapel,

Ni un pedazo azul de cielo,
Ni una corona de estrellas.
Cubre á los campos la escarcha,
Sopla el cierzo, casi nieva,
Y las blancas gotas de agua
Parecen granos de perlas.
Noche de grandes recuerdos,
De gratas reminicencias,
Del augusto aniversario
De la Redencion excelsa.
En ciudades populosas
Cuando las doce se acercan,
De las santas catedrales
¡Cuál los esquilones suenan!
La multitud agolpándose
Al vasto templo penetra,
Batiendo las altas hojas
De enormes broncíneas puertas.
A las doce de la noche,
Y al estruendo de la orquesta,
Y al fulgor de cien antorchas,
La misa magna celebran,
Entre el incienso y los cantos,
La púrpura y la grandeza,
Y la soberana pompa
De los ritos de la Iglesia.
Doquier magestad, perfumes,
Luz, fausto, brillo, riqueza,
Lindos altares que cuaja
La piedad de alhajas régias.
¡Qué procesión la que cruza
Bajo la bóveda extensa,
Los músicos de Capilla,

The children's chorus singing!
The young acolytes singing,
The chaplains praying,
And wearing their winter capes,
The priests come in tow
Of the bishop's pallium,
He who sports the richest robes
As he blesses all the faithful
Who kneel awaiting him.
Flooding into the holy temple
Is a throng of diverse classes;
The refinement, the luxury
Of the leading ladies seen
And the genteel young men
Bedecked in their elegant attire.
The crowds of common folk,
Dirty, ragged or arrogant,
Resplendent in their tatters
But clothed and covered, no less.
They mill around, they jostle
This varied congregation,
Nursing babies sobbing,
Women jostling each other.
Young men busy greeting
Beautiful female acquaintances,
Perhaps those who are in love
Chortling in urgent whispers.
Behold this vast ocean
Whose incessant tide
Rises and falls in grand waves
Like the sea during a storm.
It is that everyone tonight
On this happy Christmas Eve,

Los infantes que corean!
Los cantores, los acólitos,
Los capellanes que rezan
Y con sus capas pluviales
Los canónigos, y miéntras
Bajo de pálio el obispo,
Que un trage soberbio ostenta,
Vá bendiciendo á los fieles
Que arrodillados lo esperan.
Inunda el templo un gentío
De condiciones diversas;
El refinamiento, el lujo
En las principales hembras,
Lo propio que en los mancebos
Que elegantes trages llevan.
La muchedumbre del pueblo
Súcia, andrajosa ó soberbia,
De arambeles relumbrantes
Mas ridículos cubierta.
Vaga, se aturde, se choca
Tan variada concurrencia,
Lloran los niños de pecho,
Las mugeres se codean.
Los mozalvetes saludan
A sus conocidas bellas,
Quizá los enamorados
En voz baja cuchichean.
Es aquello un oceano
Que en su incesante marea
Sube y baja en grandes olas
Como la mar en tormenta.
Y es que todos esa noche
De la feliz Noche Buena,

Is here at midnight mass
As if attending a grand party.

II

Let us emerge from the church now
To the large plaza out in front,
To the beautiful portals
Arching over an immense crowd.
With hundreds of stands selling candy
And statuettes made of wax,
And out in the plaza itself
All sorts of pastry on well set tables.
Little cutout figures and shapes
Made of flowers and of paper
Fashioned by the holy sisters
And saturated with fragrance.
There are wonderful toys
Made of wood and porcelain,
Fragrant jars from Tonalán
Of the tastiest preserves and jams,
Pastries, pumpkin candy, jellies,
Turnovers, baked and candied fruit,
Delicious bars of almond marzipan,
Sweet sugary meringues,
A spread of savory fruits,
Giant nuts from Castile,
And an abundance of tasty creams.
Standing out is the gracefulness
Of the French women vending,
And the pretty trifles they sell
On their stands and in their stores.
To be seen are boxes and drawers

Ván á la misa de gallo
Como se asiste á una fiesta.

II

Trasportémonos ahora
A la gran plaza de fuera,
A los vistosos portales
Llenos de una turba inmensa.
Con sus mil puestos de dulces
Y sus muñecos de cera,
Y de antes y confites
Las bien adornadas mesas.
Figuritas recortadas
De cartón y flores hechas
Por las madres del Beaterio,
Y saturadas de esencia.
Hay primorosos juguetes
De porcelana y madera,
Los olorosos jarritos
De Tonalán, las conservas,
Mas gustosas, confituras,
Calabazates, jaleas,
Empanadas, fruta de horno,
Ricos turrones de almendra,
Almibarados merengues,
Sabrosa fruta cubierta,
Grandes nueces de Castilla
Y harto deliciosas cremas.
Distinguiéndose en la gracia
Las vendedoras francesas,
Por las lindas chucherías
De sus puestos y sus tiendas.
Se hallan en nuestros cajones

Of rag dolls, rattles, figurines,
Little houses made of straw,
Drums and stringed instruments,
Made of rubber, glass and clay
All competing against each other.
Here is seen the ingenuity
Of all that man can contrive.
Who knows, perhaps art
Is also present here,
Maybe in a rare painting
Or a magnificent statue.

III

What confusion in the plaza!
What shouting, what hubbub!
Passersby, vendors, all at once
Creating such a clamor.
"Tiny pastries and turnovers,"
Yells a hoarse old voice,
"Come on in to dine, *señores*,
On this night of Christmas Eve."
Tables set with clean cloths,
The flowers and the lettuce
That adorn the *enchiladas*,
The chicken and the sandwiches.
Resin candles of *ocote* pine
Illuminating immense piles
Of peanuts, citrus fruits
And *jícamas* from the mountains.
Bundles of ripe sugar cane,
And all the overflowing
Whitewashed and patched baskets
Of suckers and hard candy.

Rorros, matracas, muñecas,
Las casitas de popote,
Los tímpanos, las vihuelas,
El barro, el cristal, la goma
En desigual competencia.
Revelando por la industria
Cuanto los hombres inventan.
¡Quién sabe! también el arte
Allí á veces representa
Ya en una rara pintura,
O en una estátua soberbia.

III

¡Qué baraunda en la plaza!
¡Qué gritería, qué gresca!
Paseantes, vendedores,
Todos á la vez vocean.
"Pastelitos y empanadas"
Grita una voz ronca y seca,
"Pasen á cenar, señores,
Que esta noche es Noche Buena."
Mesas con limpios manteles,
Con flores, lechugas frescas,
Que adornan las enchiladas,
El pollo y tortas compuestas.
Las luminarias de ocote
Frente á las pilas inmensas
De cacahuates, naranjas
Y gícamas de la sierra.
Haces de maduras cañas,
Y canastas bien repletas
De ojos de buey y mamones,
De encaladas y soletas.

Boxes and boxes of sugar twists,
Milk and cinnamon confections,
And honey-dipped caramels,
And wheels of almond-covered pastry.
In the atrium of the Sanctuary
Above the marble steps,
Standing o'er their braziers
Are the makers of *buñuelos*.
Out on the plaza itself
Under improvised canopies
Festooned with green garlands,
Are dispensed the fruit ades.
What confusion! What hubbub!
What crying and wrangling!
From a lost child here,
From a thief who is escaping,
From a harpy there complaining,
From some idiot swearing up and down,
And over there a belligerent barbarian.
The rogues say, " 'Tis good
To seek out the love
Of some elite little filly,
Not a total waste of time;
And these are good too:
Those petticoats at mid calf,
The embroidery on that blouse,
The roundness of those sequins.
That shawl a lark-gray color,
And those luxuriant flannels,
And those fulsome breasts,
Those pearly colored shoes
Worn by the maidens

Las cajas de charamuscas,
Dulces de leche y canela,
Y enmielados caramelos,
Y rosquetitos de almendra.
En el átrio del Sagrario
Sobre las gradas de piedra,
Frente de sus bracerillos
Se ven á las buñoleras.
En los cuadros de la plaza
Bajo improvisadas tiendas
Que ramos verdes festonan,
Se expenden las aguas frescas.
¡Qué confusión! ¡qué algazara!
¡Qué de lloros y reyertas!
De algún niño que se pierde,
O de un perro que apalean;
De un ratero que se escapa,
De una harpía que reniega,
De algún zángano que jura,
De un lépero que pelea.
"Bien hallan, dicen los tunos
Que el tiempo no mal emplean.
Cortejando enamorados
A alguna gentil mozuela;
Bien hallan esas enaguas
Rabonas, á media pierna,
Y la bordada camisa,
Y el ruedo de lantejuelas.
Ese rebozo calandrio,
Y esas lujosas franelas,
Y esas henchiladas puntas,
Zapatos color de perla
Con que se lucen las chinas

On Christmas Eve."
What an embarrassing assortment
Of thieves stealing ponchos and pants,
Rolled up shirt cuffs,
And well-ironed shirt bibs!
Look how they carry their loot
Through the milling crowd,
A cigarette dangling from the mouth
And a bold, insolent stare!
Wrapping their arms 'round waists
Of women of the night,
Who wear a dagger
Even on such sacred days.
Provocative little tarts
Of funereal spirit, willing
For a walk or a dance in the plaza,
Ready for a harangue or a squabble,
With their lightning fast smiles,
And their shimmering eyes,
And feet so diminutive
They resemble those of dolls,
So crazy about men,
So charming when they're happy,
With more glorious batting of eyelashes
Than that of one of those Andaluz girls
Who leave behind them as they pass
The fragrance of cinnamon,
And their hearts are veritable
Oyster beds producing pearls.
What young women and what young men!
What love affairs and what a din!
Causing envy among the dandies
And scandal among the old ladies!

Durante la Noche Buena."
¡Qué desgarro el de los pillos
De jorongo y calzoneras,
De puños encarrujados
Y bien planchadas pecheras!
¡Cuál llevan entre la banda
Mal envueltas las monedas,
El cigarrillo en la boca
Y en los ojos la insolencia!
Enlazando la cintura
De esas muchachas de cuenta
Que usan daga hasta en aquellos
Días Santos de Cuaresma.
Mozuelas provocadoras,
De aire lúbrico y resueltas
Para el paseo y el baile,
La jarana y la pendencia.
De risa como el relámpago,
De ojos que lanzan centellas,
Y de piés tan diminutos
Que parecen de muñeca.
Descocadas con los hombres,
Con mas sal cuando se alegran,
Con mas desparpajo y gloria
Que una andaluza de aquellas
Que ván dejando en la calle
El olor de la canela,
Y que son sus corazones
Como criaderos de perlas.
¡Qué mozas y qué galanes!
¡Qué amores y qué protestas!
¡Envidia de los *catrines*
Y escándalo de las viejas!

What *chinas poblanas* from Jalisco,
Ardor, youth, vivaciousness
In the beauty of their *jarabe* dance.
And indoors, even more beauty!
Oh, Guadalajara Plaza,
How animated you show yourself
In your commerce and hubbub
Every Christmas Eve.
Stir up that movement,
What turbulence, what a dust cloud!
Oh, how cold it is tonight!
And how bright shine the stars!

IV

Just for the sake of contrast
Which is to be found in towns,
How tender is the night
When the baby Jesus is recalled!
Through the fields and valleys
Covered by a dark cloud,
From the only church bell
That is owned by an antique church
A holy prayer is heard
As if it were announcing
To mountain lasses and shepherds
The glorious Good News.
You can hear the shepherds' flutes
And the resounding notes of drums
As they descend in bands
From surrounding mountains and hills
These humble country folk
Who in those rural spaces
Are the owners of their farms

¡Qué chinas las de Jalisco,
Fuego, juventud, viveza;
En el jarabe lo lindo.
En la casa lo de veras!
Plaza de Guadalajara,
Qué animación manifiestas
En tu comercio y bullicio
Durante la Noche Buena.
Aturde ese movimiento,
¡Qué vaivén y qué humareda!
¡Cómo hace frío esta noche!
¡Cuánto lucen las estrellas!

IV

En tanto, como un contraste
Bien diverso, en las aldeas,
¡Con qué ternura esa noche
Al Dios niño se recuerda!
Por los prados y los valles
Cubiertos de oscura niebla,
De la única campana
Que existe en la antigua Iglesia,
Se oye la santa plegaria
Cual si anunciase preexcelsa
A serranos y pastores
La dichosa Buena Nueva.
Ya las flautas pastoriles
Y los tímpanos resuenan,
Y descienden en cuadrillas
De los montes y las sierras
Los humildes campesinos
Que, en las comarcas aquellas,
Poseen sus alquerias

And the fertile fields around.
Up there the herd of goats
Has been left behind in a grotto
To be guarded by a mastiff
Like a zealous sentinel.
Commemorating that night
When the celestial spheres witnessed
Reclining in a humble manger
He Who sustains the very heavens;
And an angel was announcing
The honoring of all the promises
That were, in the holy books,
Predicted by the prophets,
For the simple shepherds,
Pure of faith and clean of soul,
Those who in the holy prophecies
Have maintained their beliefs;
And choruses of angels were singing,
And all the heavenly powers:
"Glory be to God in the heavens
And peace on Earth to men."
And three powerful kings
From the farthest of lands
Came to worship Him
Guided by a star.
Commemorating that night
As a Christian festival,
Pretty shepherdesses arrived,
Their golden tresses so silken,
A pretty flower plucked by a stream
Casually planted in their hair.
Their little straw hats,
Their aprons of silk

O productivas dehesas.
Allá el ganado cabrío
En gruta silvestre queda
Con el mastín que lo guarda
Cual celoso centinela.
Conmemorando esa noche
En que vieron las esferas
Reclinado en un pesebre
Al que á los cielos sustenta;
Cuando un ángel anunciara
Se cumplían las promesas
Que, en volúmenes sagrados,
Predigeron los profetas,
A los sencillos pastores
De fé pura y alma recta
Que en las santas profesías
Tenían firme creencia;
Y cantaban coros de ángeles,
Y potestades excelsas:
"Gloria á Dios en las alturas
Y paz al hombre en la tierra."
Y llegaban á adorarlo
De las mas remotas tierras
Tres poderosos monarcas,
Guíados por una estrella.
Conmemorando esa noche
Y en son de cristiana fiesta,
Vienen bellas pastorcitas
De sedosas rubias trenzas,
Con la flor de algun arroyo
Luciendo al descuido en ellas.
Sus sombreritos de paja,
Sus delantales de seda

Trimmed with little ribbons,
And garlands and pearls.
Here come the brave young men
With their crooks held to the right,
And a little kid, the whitest
Of the herd, honey from the hive,
Bouquets of thyme
And a pitcher of fresh milk,
All to give as gifts,
As simple offerings.
Here comes a gallant horde
Of smiling, beautiful children,
Who fill us with joy
And delight us with song.
Here come the trembling aged
With their snow-white hair,
Their canes in their hands
And piety in their souls.
They all arrive in town
Amid the dancing of shepherds,
Relating all these tales,
So soulful and simple,
That virtue sanctifies
And tradition teaches us.
Entering into this revelry
That gladdens the surrounding fields
Is a shepherd disguised
As a religious hermit.
What festive little songs!
What pleasant praises are heard
As the invasion of shepherds
Crosses through the Church!
There's no glitter and gold there,

Cuajados de listoncitos
Y de guirnaldas y perlas.
Vienen mancebos gallardos
Con su cayado en la diestra,
Y algún cabrito, el más blanco
Del redil, miel de colmena,
Ramilletes de tomillos
Y un tarro de leche fresca.
Para presentar sus dádivas
Como sencillas ofrendas.
Viene de preciosos niños
Turba galana y risueña,
Que alboroza con su risa,
Y con sus cantos deleita.
Vienen ancianos temblosos
De nevada cabellera,
Con báculos en las manos,
De piedad sus almas llenas.
Y entre danzas pastoriles
Al pueblo inmediato llegan,
Diciendo esas narraciones
Tan sencillas y patéticas,
Que la virtud santifica
Y la tradición enseña.
A esas comparsas preside,
Que aquellos campos alegran,
Un pastor que se disfraza
De piadoso anacoreta.
¡Qué festivas cancioncitas!
¡Qué alabanzas placenteras
Cuando invaden los pastores
El crucero de la Iglesia!
Allí no hay fausto, ni brillo.

Only purity and humility.
With a thousand sylvan branches
And strands of clinging ivy
They gently decorate
The antique Gothic nave.
The old mechanical organ
Replaces the orchestra there,
Though happy little ballads
Are resounding throughout.
Instead of expensive incenses
They spread the rare essences
Of flowers from the mountains
And branches from the woods.
Perhaps an ancient priest,
The patriarch of their village,
An august and noble pontifice,
Will sing this holy mass
And a chorus of virtuous maidens
Will join in with the organist.
And God the Child on the altar
In a humble manger will be seen,
Amid the straw and hay
The King of heaven and earth!
He smiles upon his young mother,
An eternal sun of beauty,
Amid his aura full of glory,
Shining on His golden air.
His eyes that have lighted
All the sparkling planets
That twinkle so brightly
On that throne on which is seated
His Father who art in heaven;
And his brow—Where does its expression

Sino humildad y limpieza.
Con mil nemorosas ramas
Y guías de enredaderas
La gótica antigua nave
Gentilmente la aderezan.
Un órgano melancólico
Sustituye allí á la orquesta,
Aunque alegres romancicos
Por todas partes resuenan.
En vez de inciensos preciados.
Esparcen raras esencias
Las flores de las montañas.
Los ramages de las selvas.
Quizá algún párroco anciano,
Patriarca de aquella aldea.
Noble pontífice augusto.
Canta la misa, y corean
Los cantos del organista
Las más virtuosas doncellas.
Sobre el altar, el Dios niño
En un pesebre se ostenta;
¡Entre la paja y el heno
El, Rey de cielos y tierra!
Sonríe á su jóven madre,
Eterno sol de belleza,
Y luce un íris de gloria
En el oro de sus crenchas.
Sus ojos que han encendido
Los chispeantes planetas
Que tachonan luminosos
Aquel trono en que se asienta
Su Padre que está en los cielos;
Y su frente—¿á do me lleva

Take me, pure, ineffable,
The most tender gratitude?
That God Child is the image
Of nothing less than He who came
To save the human species
By fulfilling his holy promise.
In the meantime, in that haughty Rome,
Midst an arrogant court
A grand monarch enters ostentatiously
With Cesarean majesty;
Jesus was born not on the steps
To the throne of inherited royalty,
But in a humble archway,
He was born in Bethlehem, in Judea.

La espresión pura, inefable,
De la gratitud más tierna?
Ese Dios niño es imágen
No más de Aquel que viniera
A salvar la especie humana
Cumpliendo santa promesa.
Que en tanto, en la altiva Roma,
Entre una corte soberbia,
Ostentaba un gran monarca
La magestad cesaréa;
Nació Jesús, no en las gradas
Del sólio, de estirpe régia.
Allá en un portal humilde,
Nació en Betlhem de Judea.

A Sad Christmas Eve

Salvador Calderón

Little is known about Salvador Calderón's life in the United States, whether he was in voluntary or forced exile in New York, but much of his nonfiction writing, published in Central America, dealt with historical and contemporary political themes. Born in El Salvador, Calderón (1869–1941) has become a national literary figure there only in the last twenty years, with the reprinting of his various books. "A Sad Christmas Eve" is a story from a book written for his daughter while he lived in New York.

Further reading: Salvador Calderón, *Stories for Carmencita* (Brooklyn, N.Y.: Brooklyn Daily Eagle, 1914).

A Sad Christmas Eve

Well, then, the Holy Child was born in Bethlehem. He was as sweet as dawn, as luminous as the stars and as peaceful as the Aurora . . .

Every year, this is the way I begin my story about the coming of Baby Jesus, and my little ones, hanging onto my knees, restless and astonished, insistently ask me to tell the details of this tender and delicate poem.

. . . There was a resplendent celestial light coming from a grotto, and a child was happily smiling; in the snow-white and rosy complexion of his enchanting visage the shepherds perceived an unknown glory which made their simple hearts beat as they kneeled in adoration. And the cold gusts of December rocked the limbs of trees outside, creating a soft harmony like that of heavenly harps . . .

And that's the way I have had to follow the narrative thread, inspired by the tender rapture enveloping my tiny ones.

But how sad things are in life! At another time, my imagination would unleash my reverie and I would continue weaving the story of Baby Jesus, recounting to my children all of the incidents of that prodigious miracle. The shepherds paraded by with their gifts, and the richness of language provided the means to satisfy the sweet curiosity that would arise in them.

Back then, close to us, presiding over the group, was their mother, radiating her soul's overwhelming peacefulness, shining her soft and caressing virtue throughout our home. Just fixing my gaze upon her, my thoughts would take flight and the telling of the story would go on and on, unending, until our children were immersed in a peaceful sleep.

How we would await their awakening, when their shouts of joy would announce that the Holy Child had brought them toys! We would not sleep in our feverish excitement, awaiting the moment when they would open their eyes to the morning light.

Oh how can my wounded heart compare the present to the memories of the past!

Filled with feelings of loneliness, depressed by the memories of the happiness that filled my life, I keep vigil over the beds of my little children!

Perhaps I am not alone! Her soul in the fullness of its immortality, shining in the light of the heavens, guided by Baby Jesus, will return quietly, quietly, to our abode to give us a saintly kiss of blessing and solace.

Loves Me, Loves Me Not

Anilú Bernardo

In her books for young adults, Anilú Bernardo (1949–) often writes of the types of experiences she faced as a young immigrant from Cuba. Growing up between cultures, negotiating the proper response and attitude for each situation, relating to new friends of a different language and background, hanging onto the old ways while experimenting with the new — her characters have to find their way through a maze of customs and meaning in their coming of age. In this excerpt from Loves Me, Loves Me Not, *Bernardo's young heroine experiences her first Christmas dinner in an Anglo-American home. Shy and slightly ashamed about the modest means of her background and customs, she is on pins and needles the whole time.*

Further reading: Anilú Bernardo, *Loves Me, Loves Me Not* (Houston: Arte Público Press, 1999).

Loves Me, Loves Me Not (excerpt)

Chapter 8

I didn't hear from Susie for a few days, and I didn't bother to call her. I was still stinging from her attitude towards me at Justin's house. I decided to call her the day after Christmas to give her my present. I was sure she'd be curious about my day at Zach's.

Mami and I went to Misa de Gallo, the midnight mass on Christmas Eve named after the roosters whose morning crowing began as the mass let out. In spite of our late bedtime, I managed to get up before seven on Christmas morning so that we could enjoy time together before she left for work. Mami scrambled eggs with chorizo, my favorite Spanish sausage, and I warmed up the milk for cocoa. We opened presents and had our traditional breakfast in the living room by the elaborate Nacimiento, with its tiny ceramic statues of the Holy Family, the three wise men, shepherds and countless animals witnessing Jesus' birth. Every year we added special ceramic pieces to it. Mami and I set up the figures on a miniature landscape of boxes covered with sheets of crumpled brown and olive green paper. Over the years, the Nacimiento had expanded so that now it rambled over a grouping of side and coffee tables and cascaded down to floor level. It was the centerpiece of the season's decorations.

As I had hoped, Abuela sent me the running shoes I wanted. She also inserted a ten-dollar bill into each shoe to spend on anything I pleased when I wore the shoes. I ran to the phone to thank her, forgetting how early it would be in Chicago because of the difference in time zones. Abuela said she didn't mind the early hour. She said that for me, she'd wake up anytime.

Our celebration was short, but this year I was so excited about having Christmas dinner with Zach that I didn't complain about Mami's work schedule.

After she left, I showered and worked on my hair until every strand was smooth and perfectly in place. I selected a cotton sweater from the presents Mami had given me. It was royal blue, a shade that brought out the pink in my cheeks, and also went well with my new black pants. I wore silver earrings, one a stick figure of a girl, the other a boy, and a matching bracelet that alternated boys and girls holding hands. Among all my presents, these had been my favorite.

I was ready ahead of time, but I didn't want to hang around

on the front porch and appear anxious. So, I stepped out for a jasmine and returned to the living room to wait. Mrs. Maxwell would have Zach pick me up as soon as he arrived at her house. I let the plucked petals of the jasmine tumble onto my pants. I didn't care about the mess. The last petal said he loved me, and that was all I cared about. As I brought it to my lips to kiss it for luck, Zach tapped the Blazer's horn three times.

I ran to the door, slipping on the wood floor in my new chunky-heeled moccasins. "I'll be right out," I shouted through the crack of the door.

Zach was coming up the steps of the porch, while the Blazer idled in the driveway.

"Merry Christmas!" I said.

"Yeah. Merry Christmas!" He stepped into the house behind me.

"I just have to grab a few things," I told him, tossing my black purse over my shoulder and rushing into the kitchen.

"Would you believe Grams made me come in to get you? She said it was rude to blow the horn."

"Everybody does it. I'm used to it," I was trying to sound casual but I was mortified. Mami had baked ripe plantains for me to take to Mrs. Sherwood. She said it wasn't necessary to buy my hosts presents, especially since I had never met Zach's parents. But a gift of food was the right thing and could be enjoyed by the whole family, Mami had said. The dish went well with ham, turkey or pork and they were bound to have one of those as the main course. I dreaded to see their reaction to a Cuban dish at an American Christmas party.

"Geez! This is the biggest manger scene I've ever seen!" I heard him exclaim.

"The Nativity?" I carried the warm casserole wrapped in clean dish towels into the living room.

"The darn thing takes up a third of the room!" He scratched

the blond cowlick at the crown of his head. "It must take you hours to put it together!"

"We love setting it up. The landscape turns out a different way every year." The ceramic angel blowing the trumpet over the stable had slipped on his side. I made a mental note to straighten it when I got back. "Every time we unwrap a figure, it's like making a discovery."

"Is this a Cuban thing? Making such a big production of this?"

"I never thought of it," I answered, examining the scene in a new light, as if seeing it through someone else's eyes. "I guess it's a Cuban tradition. Every Cuban family I know sets one up."

"Do they put this much work into it?"

"Sure. After all, the birth of Jesus is what Christmas is all about."

"Where's your tree?"

"Over there." I thrust my chin in the direction of the family room.

He eyed the tree with surprise. I was sure he thought it was strange that the tree had a secondary role in our home.

"Can you bring that present on the couch? It's for your grandma. And grab my keys and lock the door, please."

Seeing that I was balancing the dish with caution, Zach opened the front passenger door for me.

"Merry Christmas, Maggie," Mrs. Maxwell piped up from the back seat. "You look beautiful in that shade of blue."

"Thank you." I was annoyed at the rush of warmth that flushed over my face. I didn't dare look in Zach's direction. "What are you doing in the back seat? You should be sitting up front."

"No, no. The front seat is for the young people. Besides, I've got to hold on to all these presents I'm bringing."

Mrs. Maxwell was surrounded by packages in colorful wrappings and ribbons. Her forest green suit showed off her creamy skin and her halo of white curls. Over her heart, she had pinned a lacquered brooch in the shape of a red poinsettia.

"Well, Grams, here's one more," Zach said, as he slid into his seat and handed her my present. "It's from Maggie to you."

For a moment, Mrs. Maxwell looked confused. My ears and face warmed up with added embarrassment. Zach left the package in his grandmother's hands and started the engine.

"Zachary! Where's your courtesy?" Mrs. Maxwell gasped. "If it's Maggie's present, then it's not your place to hand it to me!"

Zach stole a smirking glance at me. "Oops!" he said.

"Don't mind him, Maggie. When we open presents, I'll know this one is from you." Mrs. Maxwell sighed deeply and, though I didn't turn around to look at her, I could picture her wagging her head of white curls. "If it wasn't so hard to get in and out of this truck, I'd move to the front seat to keep you in line, young man."

Zach chuckled. "Oh, Grams . . ."

The Sherwood home was a two-story stucco structure with impressive Spanish arches and dark wooden shutters. On the moist and shady sections of its red barrel tile roof, moss and ferns had taken hold. Though built in the early part of the century when the elegant city of Coral Gables was carved out of the rocky hammocks, the house seemed to have been transported from a medieval Spanish village. I'd always wondered how Americans found the architecture of my ancestors so appealing while often disliking the ways of their descendants.

Enormous live oaks flanked the corners of the house, cooling the front yard with their protective shade. Where the sun-loving St. Augustine grass was sparse, English ivy rambled over the ground and wound around the gnarled trunks. Masses of pink, purple and white impatiens lined the stone path and edged the foot of the foundation plantings. A pair of twig deer, wearing plaid bows at their necks, decorated the lawn for the season. Though resembling a Southern woodland, the wild nature of the landscape had been carefully studied and planned by someone.

A girl, whose age I pinned at thirteen and whom I guessed to be Jennifer from Mrs. Maxwell's descriptions, came out the door. Her straight blond hair bounced on her shoulders as she hurried to the driveway. A younger, tow-headed boy rushed past her yelling, "They're here! Grams is here!"

"Brian! Come give Grandma a hug!" Mrs. Maxwell said, standing by the car door. The boy reached up and smacked her on the cheek.

"Merry Christmas, Grandma," said Jennifer.

"Merry Christmas, sweetie," Mrs. Maxwell said, planting a kiss on her cheek. "I want you to meet Maggie." She put her arm around my shoulder. "This is my granddaughter Jennifer. I think you girls will get along just fine."

"Hi, I'm Brian." The boy had slipped into the back seat and was holding an armful of presents.

"Oh, yes. This is the youngest member of the family." Mrs. Maxwell grinned, a warning pointer wagging at his perky face. "Take those presents in the house, but don't open any until I'm with you."

As I watched Brian heading back to the house, I saw that Mr. and Mrs. Sherwood were now coming down the path. Mr. Sherwood's dark blond hairline was sprinkled with gray, though his tall frame had the athletic strength of a younger man. Mrs. Sherwood had ageless beauty: her figure slim, her hair a natural blond, her manner gracious. I could see where Zach had gotten his good looks. After exchanging hugs with Mrs. Maxwell, Mrs. Sherwood turned to me.

"I'm glad you came, Maggie."

I was somewhat flustered because I couldn't offer a handshake. The warm casserole was still in my hands. "Thank you. My mother made me bring . . . Oh! What I mean is, she made a Cuban dish for your Christmas dinner."

"How wonderful!" Mrs. Sherwood's eyes didn't crinkle like her mother's when she smiled.

"You remembered," Mrs. Maxwell exclaimed. She turned to her daughter and son-in-law. "I asked Maggie for more Cuban food. What she brought me at Thanksgiving was so delicious."

"What is it?" Jennifer asked.

I braced myself for the looks on their faces. "Baked sweet plantains."

"I've had that at a fancy Cuban restaurant. I think you'll love it," Mr. Sherwood said to his family as I breathed a sigh of relief. "Zach, take the dish and put it in the kitchen."

"I'm bringing in the presents," Brian shouted as he zoomed past us with another armful.

As Mrs. Maxwell, her daughter and I started down the stone path to the house, Mr. Sherwood and Jennifer took out the rest of the presents in the truck and shut the door.

"Your house is beautiful!" I said.

"Thank you. We're proud of it," Mrs. Sherwood answered.

"It dates back to the 1920s. It's as old as me." Mrs. Maxwell winked a clear blue eye at me.

"Come on, Mom," Mrs. Sherwood said.

"I guess you love gardening as much as we do," I said to the younger woman. "It must be a lot of work keeping your plants so healthy and beautiful."

Mrs. Maxwell's laugh was fresh. "Oh, dear, no! She doesn't set foot in the yard. The landscapers do all the work."

Mrs. Sherwood gave her mother a gracious smile, but I detected a touch of irritation behind it. "Be fair, Mom."

"She's right," Mrs. Maxwell said to me. "She has little time left after all her civic meetings and fund raisers and looking after the house and the kids."

"And you!" Mrs. Sherwood added.

"Just teasing, darling. You're a wonderful daughter. Between you and Maggie, I'm very well cared for."

"There's still the matter of getting your house cleaned, Mom. You're in no condition to be doing it yourself. You know that's what I expected from the arrangement." Her voice trailed off into a whisper, as though the comment was meant only for her mother's ears.

My mouth went dry. It seemed Mrs. Sherwood had only wanted me as a maid for her mother.

"Now dear, Christmas is not the time to nag." Mrs. Maxwell put an arm around my shoulder and drew me to her. "Besides, I've brought a guest that I'd like you to make welcome in your home."

Mrs. Sherwood stepped aside for her mother and me to enter the foyer. The home was impeccably decorated in fashionable plaids and flowered prints, in sunny yellows, peach and green. Though the furniture was new, its style was in keeping with the age of the house, if not its Spanish lines. The sound of Christmas carols grew more distinct as we passed the formal living room. I moved along with the group to the family room, which opened to a large modern kitchen and on the opposite side had a wall of windows to the swimming pool and patio. The tallest Christmas tree I'd ever seen inside a house stood at the end of the room, and its base was now surrounded by the packages Brian had brought in from the truck. I scanned the room for a Nativity, but there was none.

"Let's open the presents you brought, Grams!" Brian pleaded.

Mrs. Sherwood slipped into the kitchen. "Not until we've had dinner."

"But I can't wait that long to see what Grams got for me," Brian moaned.

"You'd think you didn't get any presents this morning," said Mr. Sherwood.

"What's the big deal? Why should feather-brain have to wait until he eats?" Zach snapped.

Mrs. Sherwood gave him a warning glance. "Zach, be nice."

"We're not just eating, Zach," his father said. "We're having Christmas dinner. That's a big deal."

Jennifer brought glasses of iced soda for me and her grandmother. She changed the CD from choir hymns to lively carols, then sat on the couch next to me.

"Just one present, Grams?" Brian held up a box and gave his grandmother a look worthy of Tiny Tim.

"Let the boy open his presents," Mrs. Maxwell said, handing me a cracker that she'd lathered with salmon spread. She whispered, "Eat, dear. Don't be shy."

Mrs. Sherwood put a dish of freshly baked finger food on the counter that separated the kitchen from the family room and, without a word, Jennifer transferred it to the coffee table. The flaky pastries were topped with colorful dollops of green (which I guessed to be spinach), red (probably chopped tomatoes), and a cheese and sausage mixture. Though the aroma of baked cheese and onions was teasing my appetite, I waited for Mrs. Maxwell to place one of each on a little glass plate for me. I smiled gratefully, taking it and a cocktail napkin from her hands.

From the kitchen side of the counter, Mrs. Sherwood gave her youngest child a nod of approval. "Okay. You can open all your presents before dinner."

"Yes!" Brian screeched, tearing the paper from the box he'd picked.

"Take it easy, son. Don't tear up what's inside too," Mr. Sherwood advised him.

"It's the latest set of Inter-galactic Reptomorphs," Brian shouted, jumping up and down. "I needed these to complete my collection! Thank you, Grams."

"Let me see that, you kangamorph!" Zach snatched the box from the boy.

"Give it back!"

It seemed Zach had a knack for chafing his little brother with funny names and teasing. I wasn't sure I liked that. He had the advantage of age and size over Brian. For some reason, I realized I'd never heard Justin call others names. Then again, he didn't have the aggravation of little brothers and sisters.

Zach took out a couple of the plastic reptilian-looking creatures and pretended to speak for them. "Argh! We'll eat the kangamorph when it gets dark. Wroof! We'll come to life when the quasi-human is alone in his room."

In spite of his anger, Brian laughed. Jennifer and I joined in.

"Don't worry, Brian," Mrs. Maxwell assured the boy. "Plastic figures can't come to life. I don't want you to be scared later."

"I know that, Grams. Zach can't scare me."

"Yeah, right. Wait 'til Mom and Dad go out one night and leave me in charge. I'll turn into a spiny specter."

A picture of Justin and me stepping into the dark water raced through my mind. Instead of adding to my fears that night, Justin had reassured me. I wondered if Zach would have done the same.

"You're *already* one, Zach," Mr. Sherwood told him.

"He's just showing off, Dad," Brian said. "He's being cute for Maggie."

Jennifer broke out in giggles and once more, I felt the heat travel to my cheeks.

"Maggie's just a friend, bronto-breath." Zach handed back the box to Brian and searched under the tree for presents. "Here's one for Miss Pretty Prissy," he said, handing a box to his sister, who rewarded him with an ugly grimace as she took it from his hands. "One for Grams; one for Maggie . . ."

"For me?" I asked shyly. I was troubled about not having gifts for the Sherwood family. I hoped Mami was right about bringing food instead.

"Jennifer helped me find the right gift for you." Mrs. Sherwood added milk to the mashed potatoes in the mixer. "I hope you like it."

After emptying out bundles of colored tissue paper from the large decorated gift bag, I brought out a black denim jacket and a matching skirt. "They're beautiful! Thank you."

Mrs. Maxwell's eyes widened with delight when she saw the present I gave her. "This is a gorgeous throw." She spread open the cotton blanket and admired the pattern of boxes with potted plants in the center of each.

"The colors are rich, Mom," Mrs. Sherwood said, glancing at it from the other side of the counter. "It's perfect for your lap, when you sit in the Florida room to read the morning paper."

"I have a present for you too," Mrs. Maxwell told me. "Zach, would you hand me the small box for Maggie?"

The little package was covered in black and gold metallic wrap, with a tiny gold ribbon and bow. "It's too pretty to open."

Zach laughed. "Oh, no! Another one of those silly girls like my sister, who hates to tear nice paper."

Jennifer leered at him. "Pretend he doesn't exist. He's a spiny specter."

I opened the package carefully, setting aside the precious gold ribbon. The little box snapped open when I pressed a button in the front. Inside the red velvet lined box were pearl earrings with a small ruby on each. "Oh, Mrs. Maxwell, you shouldn't have. This is too nice."

"Nonsense. This is what I want to give you."

"Ooh!" Jennifer leaned closer to peek in the box. "I like them. Look, Mom."

Mrs. Sherwood glanced over the counter at the contents of the box. "Very nice," she said distractedly. "Maggie, do the plantains need to be warmed up? Dinner's almost ready."

"I guess they can go in the microwave for a couple of minutes." I got up and made my way into the kitchen, unsure whether I should be helping with the meal. At home, I usually gave Mami a hand.

"Time for my performance." Getting up from his chair, Mr. Sherwood rubbed his hands together. I thought perhaps he played a musical instrument and it was their tradition for him to play it now. But he joined us in the kitchen, tested the sharpness of the knife and began to carve the turkey.

Jennifer and I helped Mrs. Sherwood take the serving dishes into the dining room. The vegetables were served in bowls that matched the flowered china. Condiments and bread had been placed in various silver servers. I was aware that my casserole wasn't fancy enough for such a dressy table. The dark wood pedestal table was set with sparkling crystal and china, and topped with a centerpiece of gold sprayed pears, apples and nuts and gold ribbons laced in the spaces between the fruit. "Jingle Bells," a song I associated with the cold winters of the north more than with a spiritual Christmas, played in the background.

As I hung back waiting to be assigned a seat, Mrs. Maxwell placed her hand on the backrest of one of the dark carved chairs. "Sit here, Maggie. Right between me and Jennifer."

I noticed that Zach had taken the seat across from me and the skin of my neck prickled as our eyes met.

"Can you pass the smashed potatoes?" he asked me.

"They're mashed, Zach, not smashed!" Jennifer glared at her older brother.

"They look smashed to me." Zach grinned.

Jennifer rolled her eyes to the heavens.

I lifted the dish, which had been placed in front of me, and stretched my arm across the table. The serving dishes traveled around the table as each person took a helping. I scooped up small amounts, not wanting to let them think I was fainting with hunger, though the steamy aroma of onions, green beans and turkey was making my mouth water. At home, I would have heaped my plate with food this good.

Mr. Sherwood raised his glass of white wine. "Here's to health, to a happy family and to our guest."

We raised our stem glasses, though the children's were filled with Sprite instead of wine.

"And to lots of money!" Brian piped in.

"That's a pretty materialistic wish at Christmas, Brian." Mrs. Sherwood set her blue eyes on her youngest child.

"What's that?"

"Greedy. You bronto-brain." Zach snickered. "But I'll have to admit that's a pretty cool wish."

"Zach!" His father gave him a stern look.

Our hands and glasses were still raised.

"Okay, okay," said Mr. Sherwood. "May all our Christmas wishes come to pass."

The room was filled with the clinking of crystal. Then, each person took a sip of his drink. I set down my glass, laced my hands together on my lap and dipped my head. But, instead of a prayer of thanks before the meal, I heard the familiar plink-ing of silverware as the others sliced the food on their china plates. At home, we always said a prayer before a holiday meal. I peeked through lowered lashes. Everyone at the table had started eating. Hoping no one had noticed my bowed head, I quickly thanked God for all the good things in my life. I didn't make the sign of the cross; I felt too self-conscious. I simply picked up my fork and caught up with the activity at the table.

The first morsel in my mouth was white meat. It was tender, with just the right amount of moisture. I kept my eyes on my plate, too shy to look up across the table at Zach while I chewed.

"Were you able to spend time with your mother this morning?" Mrs. Maxwell asked.

I gave her a series of nods, as my mouth was full at the moment.

She smiled. "I'm glad. I was afraid she'd have to work so early."

"How come she has to work on Christmas?" Brian asked.

"Because she works in a hospital and hospitals have to keep running, even on Christmas," Mrs. Sherwood answered.

"Is she a doctor?" Jennifer asked.

As I was ready to answer, Mrs. Sherwood shook her head and a subtle smile appeared on her lips. "She changes beds and cleans up. Right, Maggie?"

As if zapped by lightning, my body stiffened. My mom wasn't an orderly! She'd worked hard for her nursing degree.

Mrs. Maxwell came to the rescue. "Mrs. Castillo is a nurse. And Maggie's father was a doctor, mind you."

Mrs. Sherwood raised an eyebrow.

"He's not a doctor anymore? Was he kicked out of the hospital or something?" Zach asked.

It was Mrs. Maxwell's turn to blush, though I was sure it was from anger at her grandson's tactless ways rather than embarrassment. "Maggie's father died, Zachary."

Zach pressed his lips together. "I'm sorry. I didn't know."

I accepted his apology with a nod.

"What was his specialty?" Mr. Sherwood asked, interest warming his blue eyes.

"He was going to be a pediatrician, but his illness took hold when he was interning."

"That's a foot doctor, right?" Zach offered.

Mr. Sherwood inhaled. "A foot doctor is a podiatrist. A pediatrician works with children."

"I was just kidding." Zach grinned. But he didn't fool me. I figured he'd claimed to be kidding to save face.

"Maggie's mom works in the pediatrics wing of the hospital. She takes care of patients just as Maggie takes care of me," his grandmother said.

"Are you a nurse?" Jennifer asked me, wide eyed.

"I'm gonna be one," I said.

Mrs. Maxwell patted my hand. "As far as I'm concerned, she already is one."

"That's impressive, Maggie," Mr. Sherwood told me, but instead of glancing in my direction, he glared at Zach. "I don't know too many kids your age who know what they want in life."

"Frosty the Snowman" blared from the family room. Mrs. Sherwood broke the uncomfortable silence that followed. "I'm grateful your mother took the time to cook this dish for us. Tell her the plantains are delicious," Mrs. Sherwood said.

"What country is this dish from?" Brian asked.

"Cuba," Mrs. Sherwood offered. "Maggie is Cuban."

I smiled shyly. Though I'd been taught it wasn't polite to correct adults, I couldn't help it this time. "I'm not Cuban. I'm American. I've never been to Cuba. I was born in Miami."

"Well, her parents were born on the island," Mrs. Sherwood told Brian. "That makes her Cuban-American, I suppose."

"The plantains aren't cooked the way I'm used to having

them," Mr. Sherwood interrupted, his purposeful tone indicating the previous subject was closed. "I don't think I've had them in a sauce before," said Mr. Sherwood.

I was glad that the plantains had been very ripe, because they'd cooked to sweet perfection. The sauce had thickened to darkest brown from the red wine, brown sugar and cinnamon in it. "That's because restaurants usually fry them," I explained. "When they're baked with red wine and sugar we call the dish 'Temptation.' "

"They are tempting," Mrs. Maxwell said.

"I thought I detected the wine in it." Mr. Sherwood smiled.

"Wine?" Brian perked up. "I'm gonna have some more and see if I get drunk."

"You can't get drunk from gravy, you gobbler!" Zach teased.

"How would you know?" Brian retorted, lifting the lid from the casserole. "You haven't even tried it."

I ventured a glance at Zach's plate. There were neither plantains nor a tell-tale puddle of sauce.

"You never like to try exotic stuff," Jennifer said. "You could be missing out on something good."

"I'm just watching to see if any of you passes out." Zach's lips curled into a mocking grin. "If the food is safe, then I'll try it."

I stared down at my plate.

Brian rested the glass lid on the table and began to select another small piece.

"Brian, don't put the lid on the linen tablecloth. Red wine stains don't come out!" When Mrs. Sherwood lifted the lid, its square edges were outlined in dark sauce on the white tablecloth.

I was sorry to see that the food I brought had been the cause of a problem. "I'll take the tablecloth home. I'm sure my mom knows how to get rid of the stain."

"That won't be necessary, Maggie," Mrs. Sherwood said, turning to set the lid on the buffet behind her. "But thank you anyway."

"I want some more to see if something happens to me." Jennifer laughed. She dripped a spoonful of the sauce on the plantains on her plate.

"Okay," said Zach. "I'll try the stuff. Shovel a little on my plate, Maggie."

By now, the casserole had made its way to me. Zach shoved his plate in at me over the fruit centerpiece. I spooned a portion of plantain, then tried to steady his plate with my other hand, but to my horror, the sauce dribbled from the spoon onto the white tablecloth.

"Zachary!" I heard Mrs. Sherwood exclaim.

But everyone could see that it wasn't his fault. "I'm so sorry," I said.

"It's all right, dear," Mrs. Maxwell said, patting the spots with tissues she'd dug out of her pocket.

"This wouldn't have happened if you kids hadn't been playing games with the food." Mrs. Sherwood dampened a few paper napkins with iced water from her glass and passed them down to her mother. "The alcohol is cooked out of the wine, anyway."

"Hey, you're always telling me to try new foods," Zach snapped at his mother. "Now I get blamed for going for it. I can't win."

"You could have asked her to pass the serving dish," said Mrs. Sherwood.

Brian craned his neck to check the damage, as his grandmother continued to rub the spots. "They won't come out. They're spreading."

"Don't start acting so innocent," Jennifer told her little brother. "You ruined it first."

"That's enough!" Mr. Sherwood stared at his children. "If the tablecloth is ruined, we'll buy another one. What's the big problem?"

"Another Irish linen tablecloth?" Mrs. Sherwood raised her eyebrows at her husband who sat at the head of the table. "Do you know how expensive linen can be?"

I wanted to slide under the table.

Mrs. Maxwell tucked her chin and gave her daughter a meaningful look. "Well, that's the price we pay for raising children. Anyone can have an accident. Right, dear?"

Mrs. Sherwood nodded, but I could detect displeasure through her veil of politeness. "Yes, it was an accident. I didn't mean to make you feel uncomfortable, Maggie."

I was sure my face glowed deep crimson. "I'd like to take it home and see what my mom can do about the stains."

Mrs. Sherwood shook her head but her eyes didn't meet mine as she said, "That's all right. I'll try cleaning it myself."

"Why don't you let Maggie take it home? I'm sure Mrs. Castillo has battled this kind of stain before. Anyway, it will make Maggie feel better," Mrs. Maxwell told her daughter.

Mrs. Sherwood gave in. "Oh, I suppose she can."

Jennifer took me to her room after dinner to show me the clothes she had gotten for Christmas. I was relieved to be away from the adults, as my mood had changed from happy anticipation to deep embarrassment. I think Jennifer was aware of my feelings, because after going over every one of her gifts, she asked me to help her put together outfits for school. That took up the better part of the afternoon. I was grateful.

I was too flustered to be around Zach. For some reason, I didn't mind passing up on a chance to be with him. For days I had dreamed of the special talks Zach and I would have today. I had nursed hope that he'd overcome whatever was holding him back from asking me out. In my mind, I had pictured his room in the same condition as his Bronco, basketballs and books on the floor and his smelly jersey thrown in a corner, and I'd accepted his messy habit as a charming quality. But I hadn't even peeked in his room. And I wasn't sure I wanted to anymore. As for his asking me out, I was beginning to wonder if it was meant to happen after all. But one thing I knew: It wasn't going to happen this Christmas day.

When Zach knocked on the door to tell us Mrs. Maxwell thought it was time to go, I was glad. I thanked Mr. and Mrs. Sherwood for inviting me. Zach gave me a hand carrying to his truck my presents, the casserole and the stained tablecloth, which Mrs. Maxwell had folded and placed in a shopping bag. Jennifer and Brian helped Mrs. Maxwell with her packages. The family stood in the front yard waving as Zach backed the Bronco to take us home.

"I hope you know what you're doing with Mom's tablecloth," he said with a snort as he drove.

Anger roiled in my head.

"It'll be fine," Mrs. Maxwell assured him.

"I'd hate to be around Mom if it doesn't clean up."

"It's only a tablecloth, Zachary. It can be replaced." Mrs. Maxwell reached up from the back seat and patted my shoulder. I wondered if she could feel it sizzle from the angry heat boiling in me. "You and Brian had a part in the spills, Zachary. Don't make it sound as though Maggie was responsible for the stains. She's not. What happened was an accident."

In spite of what she said, I couldn't help thinking that if I hadn't brought the plantains, there wouldn't have been any stains.

"Yeah, Grams!" Zach answered her. "But I'm the one who'll have to put up with Mom's bitching."

"Zachary! Watch your tongue with me, young man!"

The Good Night

Roberto G. Fernández

By all accounts, Roberto G. Fernández (1951–) is the poet laureate of Cuban-American satire. Himself an immigrant at an early age, he has dedicated his novels to the tongue-in-cheek analysis of the Cuban immigrant psyche as it is represented in the magic-realist culture of Miami. In his typical style of exaggerated contrast of life in Havana and Miami, Fernández has created in "The Good Night" a caricature of a Cuban-American Christmas.

Further reading: Roberto G. Fernández, *Raining Backwards* (Houston: Arte Público Press, 1997).

The Good Night

It was the Good Night, and Mima was boiling cassava and cutting radishes to garnish the Christmas Eve Pig. She had cut her fingers six times. The cuts looked accidentally inflicted, but they weren't. Mima was hoping for a wound deep enough to be hospitalized so she could avoid preparing the meal. Unfortunately, her wounds were mere nicks.

She looked through the kitchen window into her yard. It was bright out, and the mangos were ripe on the tree. She turned the ceiling fan on to stir up the air. She was hot, even though she wasn't wearing underwear. She had promised God many years before that if her son Keith got his visa waiver to come to the U.S., she would never wear panties again. Keith got the visa, though at times she wished he hadn't. Keith and his father always argued. She tried to remember the last time they had said a friendly word to each other and couldn't come up with a date. A gust of wind blew through the screen, waking her from a daze just in time to see a mango shower inundate the back porch.

"*Coño*. And now I'll have to spend the rest of the week making marmalade!"

Mima hated making marmalade. This fact would surprise even her husband. Making marmalade is one of those things that every one thinks Mima enjoys. This is because she always sings when she cooks. She sings only to console herself. When she is very depressed she even composes her own songs.

"Every year the same old people, the same old shit."

She sang the lyrics to the tune of "You and the Clouds," originally by Celia Cruz and now one of The Merengues super hits.

About forty participants were expected for the special gathering, all relatives and close friends. As usual, Mima kept everyone in suspense again this year, threatening until the Wednesday before the holiday to cancel. She only confirmed that she would host the party after her husband Jacinto menaced her with a promise to rent a boat, sail to One Hundred Fires and join the urban guerrillas. To prove he meant business he began wearing camouflage fatigues and marching around the house.

The telephone rang.

"Hello."

"Listen to me. It's Manolo, your cousin. I want to know how many bottles of wine we should bring."

The same old question, Mima thought. Why do people have to ask the same old question year after year? She was tempted to say a bad word, but she answered with the same response she always gave him.

"Same number as last year. Ten bottles, since each bottle

yields four glasses and most people have two glasses and the children only have soft drinks."

"Thanks, little sky, but be careful with the sodas. Make sure the metallic seal is intact. Remember the twenty kids that were poisoned last year, and don't get any diet drinks because they cause cancer."

"Okay."

Manolo hung up and went straight to Pepe's Grocery-Bar to buy the cheapest wine he could find, but first he flirted with Annabel, cashier by morning and vedette at night. He told her what nice breasts she had and tried to slip a five dollar bill into her cleavage. Annabel wouldn't let him get near her breasts, but she needed the money, so she flirted back, playing the coquette.

Manolo bought exactly ten bottles of a rare North Florida vintage at 99¢ each. He went home to proceed with his annual ritual. He steamed each bottle, then carefully peeled off the labels. After drying and polishing every inch of the bottles, he pasted on the famous brand labels he had been collecting from friends throughout the year. He practiced praising the bouquet of this year's selection.

Mima went out to the back yard and tried to place the pig on the grill over the pit. "How the hell do they expect me to place this thing on this grill? There isn't a big enough space here for a chicken! I should be frying plantains instead of wasting my time on this. Pepe needs 75 bags by Monday and I'm here playing Nitza Villapol, the recipe lady." She punched the dead animal and cursed her husband, wondering if she'd have to continue playing the hostess if he were dead.

A few blocks from her house, Manolo was still pasting labels on wine bottles while Barbarita, his wife, was complaining.

"I am not going to the Good Night at Mima's! I don't know why you expect me to have dinner with a woman who makes of her husband a cuckold. It is not possible that Keith is Jacinto's son."

"Barbarita, stop the nonsense."

"Manolo Gonzales, you know very well that Keith is Che Guevara's son. Mima was having an affair with him, and that is precisely why she didn't want to leave One Hundred Fires and we were stuck with Keith for a year. Of course, you, like a fool, were happy to take him in and let him ruin our family life."

"Whether you like it or not we are related. Family is family. We are going! Period! Why do you have to fight over this every year?"

"Look at my hair! If you'd give me more money, I could afford to go to Samy's, but no, not you. It doesn't match with my outfit. Ouch!"

"What is it now?"

"I broke a nail," screamed Barbarita, kicking her dresser drawers.

Manolo ignored her and continued pasting wine labels. Isabelita, their oldest daughter rushed back to her parent's bedroom to calm her down.

"Mama, mama, calm down. You know you're prettier and younger-looking than Mima. She looks ten years older than she is. You look like a woman in her forties, the prime of life. You should be proud that you still make men turn their heads. Don't be so upset!"

Barbarita looked at her sixty-five-year-old face in the mirror and tried to see the young woman who had once stared back at her.

"You really think so?"

"I know so! It's true, mama. Now come on and go to Mima's

with us. You should go just to prove it to yourself. It'll make you feel a lot better."

Barbarita agreed to go along to reassure herself that her daughter spoke the truth.

———

The telephone rang. Mima answered the phone then hung up after a short, whispered conversation.

"Hello."

"Hello, it's Keith. I'm not going to be able to make it until later on tonight, Mom. Something has come up."

"Oh, Keith, please, don't be too late. You know how important it is to be with the family for the holidays. Where are you going to be? Don't make me suffer anymore. You know how I hate all the bad company you keep. You should stay away from all those South Americans. They'll only cause trouble for you."

"Don't worry about it, Mom. I've been taking care of myself for a long time now. I know what I'm doing."

"Okay, okay! If you want to keep living like this, then you're going to be the cause of your father's death. You know he's very worried about your life."

Keith answered with a loud "click."

"Mima! Who was that on the phone? Is someone cancelling out?"

"No, Jacinto. It was just Keith. He said he'll be a little late for dinner. He had to work late. Something came up."

Mima headed down the hall to the bathroom to ease her bladder, but the phone rang again.

"Hello."

"Hello. This is Clavo. I won't be able to make it tonight." Mima knew why, but she asked anyway to be polite.

"Why not?"

"If I come it will just make me sad. Happiness died the day she left me."

"Well, I think you should come. It will do you good to be out."

The resplendent Miami sun was sinking and it was starting to get dark. Mima stayed outside by herself to calm down before the guests arrived. She stood over the pit sobbing. She wasn't sad for the pig, but for Pucho, her parrot, who had died exactly one year before. She had loved Pucho. He was an amazing little bird who really seemed to understand her. He had always cheered her up with a song when she was feeling blue or thinking about her mother in One Hundred Fires. She wiped away the tears and went into the house to shower and dress before the tribe began to arrive.

———

The festivities were about to begin, and the pig, cramped as it was, tried to observe everything from its position on the grill. Barbarita was worried. The dinner was being held outside and she thought it was going to rain. She tried to convince the others to move inside.

"It's going to rain. We're going to get wet. It's going to rain. I saw the weather report on television. Marty said there was an eighty percent probability. Listen it's thundering already! Manolo, Manolo, I'm talking to you! Help me move the chairs inside."

"Please, Barbarita, don't you see I am busy rehearsing my speech? Why don't you go inside and help Mima?"

"You know I don't have anything in common with that woman. I've only had one man. I'll have to talk to her if I go inside. You don't want me to end up like her, having lovers and my own business, do you?"

"Then go sit quietly somewhere."

Barbarita sat by herself under the mango tree for five minutes, but her husband's glaring eyes made her feel self-conscious.

"Okay, okay! I'll go in and give her a hand. But I warned you what might be the consequences!"

Mima walked toward the kitchen door.

"Mima, can I help you with anything?"

"Why don't you cut the '*turrón*.'"

"Sure, where's the knife."

"In the left drawer. By the way, Manolito and Purita came by earlier. Tatiana is such a beautiful little girl. I know you are proud to have her for a granddaughter. They said they couldn't stay very long because they're having Christmas Eve with her parents. I hear they are making a bundle with the candy business."

"Yes, her parents work very hard."

"I think she drank a little bit too much. She belched twice."

"You must be mistaken. Purita is a very proper lady."

"Let me tell you, your son is really getting fat."

"Well, he's slightly overweight."

"You should tell him to join a YMCA."

"It's going to rain."

"Do you think so?"

"Marty the weatherman said so. There is an eighty percent chance."

"Don't worry. They are usually wrong. Just like the communists, don't believe anything they say. Hey, who is that on T.V.? Isn't he the guy that played 'El Puma?' It must be a rerun."

"I don't know. I don't watch soap operas. Don't you ever turn that television set off?"

"Not really. It is an American custom."

"When are your kids coming?"

"They should be coming anytime now," Mima answered a bit curtly.

Jacinto called the guests to sit down to dinner. There was chaos at the beginning since no one knew where to sit. Mima directed the traffic, ordering everyone to a seat and keeping one chair empty for Clavo. He would be served in absentia. There was a small table to the right for the kids. They were kicking and biting each other, fighting over an orphaned Cabbage Patch Doll. The adults began to quibble over which child would make a better parent to the homeless waif.

"Her name is Holly Ann and she's from Maine."

"No she isn't. Her name is Lolona from Tallahassee."

"It's like Susy says. Her name is Lolona."

"No way! That's Holly Ann and she is mine!"

"Shut up, you little brat!" Barbarita finished her admonition by slapping Janetica.

"Aaaahh! Mommie, Barbarita hit me!"

"Barbarita, don't you see they are just children arguing."

"I don't care. Susy is right. Her name is Lolona. She ought to know. She is the doll's mother."

"No, she isn't. Janetica is better fit to be a mother than Susy. At least Janetica has both of her parents at home."

"Okay, okay, okay, break it up!" Jacinto intervened.

"Jacinto, she slapped my daughter."

"Try to be more understanding," Jacinto whispered. "She is under a lot of stress. Her cousin, the poet, is dying in Cienfuegos and her daughter's divorce has really affected her. The fact that her granddaughter has to fly alone to her father's in Tallahassee doesn't help any."

Barbarita went back to her seat to talk to one of her friends.

"What was that all about?"

"Nothing, Mirta. That spoiled Janetica was trying to boss Susy around. I just don't go for it."

"Barbarita, calm yourself."

"And how are you feeling? You look a little pale."

"It's nothing, just a little nausea. You know the first three months are kind of hard. So what is new with Emelina?"

"Promise me you won't tell anyone."

"I promise. You know I am like a tomb."

"Well, you know she and Clavo got divorced a few years ago. Now she is trying to get the marriage annulled and have herself declared a *señorita*, after four children!"

"Did she really only marry him for money?"

"Surely. Her family had lots of hot air, but no cash. That's why they married her to my brother-in-law, Clavo."

"I hear she doesn't get along with her oldest daughter, Linda Lucia."

"She can't stand her. I think she reminds her of Clavo. Emelina's now trying to join the band."

"A band? I thought she was into classical music."

"She used to be. She has a new boyfriend. He is the lead singer of the Westchester Engines."

"I've never heard of them."

"You haven't missed anything."

Most of Connie's father's conversations that night centered around Connie's new American boyfriend, Bill.

"He doesn't have any manners. He isn't even wearing shoes. Can you imagine wearing sandals on Christmas Eve? But, I know how you feel. You know we went through hell when Isabelita married that Wilson guy up in Tallahassee," murmured Manolo to Jacinto.

"Why she has to bring an American to a family gathering is beyond me. You know they don't even respect their parents. And Connie's just like one of them. She brought him just to bother me."

"Let me pour you a drink, Jacinto. It will make you feel better."

Connie, overhearing her father, turned up her nose at him and turned her attention to Isabelita.

"Izzy! You're looking great! What're you up to lately?"

"Just working," answered Isabelita in her usual lethargic style.

"How's your ex? You know, I never liked him from the very beginning. Let me tell you something, he's going to end up all alone. He'll pay for everything he did to you. I'm glad I'm so happy with Bill. Isn't he a babe? My life is great! Oh, I almost forgot, I have a gift for your little girl. Why don't you bring Susy to watch me at the cheerleading tryouts? I'm pretty sure I'm going to be the squad captain."

"Oh Connie! I feel so sick! Can you take me to the bathroom?"

"Sure. But we have to come back right away. We have so much to talk about."

Isabelita went to the bathroom leaning on Connie's shoulder. "Ok, Izzy. Here we are."

"Thanks, Connie."

"I'll wait for you to finish. Which one are you going to do, number 1 or number 2?"

Isabel kept her business to herself, giving Connie no answer. Connie waited for a while, then feeling tired, she went back to the table. She took her seat and crunched on a piece of pork rind.

"Connie."

"Yes, Dad."

"Will you please go to your room and change into something decent."

"Dad, quit it. I'm a Senior!"

"To your room, I say!!"

"Mom, Dad's doing it again."

"Jacinto, leave her alone."

"Her skirt is too short."

"It's modern fashion."

"Ha, fashions!"

"Jacinto, leave her alone and try to find your false teeth so you can enjoy the pork."

"Don't tell me how to live!"

"I swear by my mother's health that this is going to be the last year! I am tired of looking after you and everybody else. I should do like Emelina and move alone to a place where nobody'll ever find me, like Kendall."

"Mom, take it easy. Bill is here. Don't embarrass me, please. You're getting tense because Keith isn't here yet."

"Listen to this," Manolo shouted, interrupting the family squabble. "Youth, divine treasure, you are leaving never to return, when I want to cry I can't and sometimes I cry without wanting."

"My husband is a genius. He should run for president," Barbarita said.

"Wait till you hear my tribute to Columbus."

Jesusito and Deborah arrived a little late. Jesusito made a *"mojo"* dip for the occasion.

"Mima, where do I set the mojo?"

"Set it near the pig, Jesusito."

"I brought also a few reconds: The Big Dances of Anthony M. Romeu, Fajardo and his Stars, Congas and Carnival from the Orient, and Jacinto's favorites, The Moor Woman from Syria by Little Barbaro X, and They Are from the Hills by the Moorkiller Trio."

"Give them to Manolo. He's the musical director."

"Is my Dad here?"

"No, he isn't here yet."

Keith finally arrived, but he rushed straight to the garage closet to snort his last line. He came out and sat on Mima's lap, promising never to do it again. Mima thought he was sorry about being late and told him it was okay.

"But you should start taking care of yourself better, Kicito. You always have a cold. It is not normal."

Keith's new habit had replaced his old favorite: masturbation. At one time, he could masturbate seven times a day. He had a lot of nervous tension from being alone and fending for himself for so many years. Once, he told his father how many times he could do it and it made him very proud. In fact, it was the only thing about Keith that had ever made him proud. Jacinto told all his friends about his son's old habit, but he doesn't tell any of them now.

"Hey everybody stand up, my son, Quinn, is blessing us."

"May the saints keep protecting this family and our dear friends through the perils and tribulations in this land of the brave, this home of the free. Though many times we have been forced to work with dirt, we have never become soiled. Praise to Saint Barbara. Amen."

"Amen."

"Let's dance, everybody. Let's make a circle for my favorite song: "They Are from the Hills!' "

Dinner was almost over and the adults were getting ready for the children's Christmas presentation directed by Mirta, Barbarita's closest friend. Everybody quieted down while the kids were changing into their costumes.

"I am Gaspar," said Susy. "I have brought frankincense, and I have come here to say that life is good. That God exists. That love is everything. I know it is so because of the heavenly star."

"Isn't she talented?" said Barbarita. "Already she has a scholarship for the University of Miami!"

Deborita was anxious for her turn and she was chewing her dress.

"C'mon," said her mother, "it's your turn."

"I am Melchior. I have brought fragrant myrrh. Yes, God exists. He is the light of the day. The whitest flower is rooted in, mud, and all delights are tinged with melan melan melancholy."

Johnny, Mima's godchild, stood up at Mirta's ringing of a bell and shouted: "I am Balthasar, but my mother told me to make sure that everybody knows here that there is nobody black in our family. I have brought gold. I assure you, God exists. He is great and strong. I know it is so because of the perfect star that shines so brightly in Death's, diadem."

Mirta came to the forefront and recited while pointing with her index finger to the wisemen: "Gaspar, Melchior, Balthasar: be still. Love has triumphed, and bids you to its feast. He, reborn, turns chaos into light, and on His brows He wears the Crown of Life."

Clavo walked into the house in a stupor, babbling about his past millions, and interrupting Mirta's last verse. He grabbed his granddaughter, Deborita, who was still beaming from her role as Melchior, even though she stuttered a bit at the end. He forced Deborita to dial her grandmother's number.

"Grandpa, leave me alone."

"C'mon. Let's go and call Grandma."

"I don't want to. Ouch!"

"Just dial the number, punkin."

"No one is answering."

"Dad, please leave the child alone," says Jesusito.

"She wants to talk to your mom."

Clavo sat down, taking his shirt off. He was sweating profusely. Jesusito and Deborah tried to ignore him. Deborah got up and whispered in his ear not to embarrass her. Jesusito knew that he would have to carry his father home, undress him and give him a cold shower.

Manolo stood up trying to draw attention to himself and away from Clavo. Hardly anyone paid him any attention.

"Silence, please. This poem is dedicated to each and every one of you that come each year to partake of this Christian festival of hope, as did the Great Admiral many years ago on the island of Hispaniola among the wreck of the Niña. Listen carefully: 'Unfortunate admiral! Your poor Cuba, your beautiful, hot blooded, virgin love, the pearl of your dreams, is now hysterical, her nerves convulsing and her forehead pale. . . . ' "

"Mom, where's my Cabbage Patch Doll?"

"Hush! Wait till Manolo finishes."

"Let the child finish first, for children are the hope of the world."

"She's finished."

". . . a most disastrous spirit, the red spirit, rules your land where once the people raised their arms together, now there is endless warfare between brothers. Thank you!"

It had begun to pour and Barbarita was under the table, refusing to come out, for she had no make-up left. Deborah offered her a veil. Clavo was desperately banging at the bathroom door. He was about to throw up but Isabelita was crying beneath the sink. Connie was hoping tonight was going to be the big night. Mima couldn't bear the fact that Pucho was no longer with her and cut herself with a carving knife while cutting a piece of pork for her husband. The wound wasn't deep, but she demanded that someone call an ambulance. Manolo fell to the ground reciting poems and drinking at the same time. And on a rain soaked, cluttered table lay the bodiless

head of a pig with curly lashes and wide open eyes that remembered all it saw.

————————

*I had to cut it in half, it was just too big; Bill, when are we getting
married? He can't chew, he lost his false set; if business picks up maybe
next year; To Columbus: Unfortunate admiral! Your poor island, your
beautiful, hot-blooded, virgin love, the pearl of your dreams, is now
hysterical, her nerves convulsing and her forehead pale; Pucho, Pucho
why did you leave me, Pucho? people say she's pregnant, at her age?
Manolo it's raining; My God, it's raining, Mom calm down! So you
are going to Colombia on a business trip; roll her in flour and go for
the wet spot ha, ha, ha; hope she isn't crying for him; a most disastrous
spirit rules your land; where once the tribesmen raised their clubs together, now there is endless warfare between brothers, the selfsame races
wound and destroy each other; where are his shoes? They don't wear
shoes; Mom, Barbarita slapped me; that's Mirta Vergara, can you
believe someone tried to rape her three times! Okay, kids it's time to
change for the show, cut me a bigger piece, honey; she wants to call
her grandma; Quinn say the blessing, call an ambulance I'm bleeding;
Mom, she made me do it, I promise you I'll never do it again.*

————————

"Hey, everybody. It's time to go to midnight mass."

Next Year in Cuba

Gustavo Pérez-Firmat

"Life on the hyphen" is the term Gustavo Pérez-Firmat (1949–) coined to characterize the psychology and culture of Cuban Americans, that is, those who feel as comfortable or equally uncomfortable in both the United States and Cuba. In the following excerpt from his memoir, Next Year in Cuba, *he illustrates the process of negotiating an identity amid the conflicting traditions of an American Christmas and a Cuban Christmas.*

Further reading: Gustavo Pérez-Firmat, *Next Year in Cuba* (New York: Anchor/Doubleday, 1996); Gustavo Pérez-Firmat, *Anything but Love* (Houston: Arte Público Press, 2000).

Next Year in Cuba (excerpt)

The Ghosts of Nochebuenas Past

Havana, 1957

El hombre manda y la mujer gobierna—man rules and woman governs. This Spanish proverb accurately describes the balance of power in our family when my siblings and I were growing up. Although our father was the titular head, our mother ran the household and made most of the day-to-day decisions. If Gustavo was king, Nena was the prime minister. Both in Cuba and in Miami, she was the one who answered our questions, the one who solved problems and averted catastrophes. Perhaps because she herself grew up in a storm-tossed household, she governed with a loving and steady hand, always making sure that, whatever else happened in our lives, we had peace and stability at home.

When I reflect on my mother's life, I always think about Nochebuena, the Cuban Christmas Eve, a celebration of family togetherness. In my mind, my mother has always been the spirit of Nochebuena. When I was a child in Cuba, Nochebuena (literally, "the Good Night") was the most important family gathering of the year. As far back as I can remember, relatives and close friends always gathered at my parents' house on the evening of December 24. Bisected by Midnight Mass, this night oscillated, sharply but predictably, between the sacred and the profane, between religious observance and secular mirth-making. Since in the nineteen fifties Catholics were still required to fast before receiving Holy Communion, the part that accompanied the religious observance was not supposed to begin until one or two o'clock in the morning after everyone got back from *la misa del gallo,* Midnight Mass, whose name goes back to the Roman custom of holding mass at dawn, when the *gallos* or cocks crowed. But cultural differences being what they are, the Cuban roosters began crowing long before the Roman cocks. By the time Midnight Mass rolled around, my aunts and uncles had been celebrating for hours. Some of the men, who typically were less devout than their wives, were already well into their Bacardi cups. When they accompanied their wives and children to Midnight Mass, many remained on the steps of the Church while the women and children went inside to pray. It was a curious sight: from inside the Church you could see the crowd of men, impeccably dressed in their long-sleeved *guayaberas* with bow ties, milling around outside and talking. The hubbub was such that sometimes Father Spirali, the Italian-born pastor of the San Agustín parish in Havana, had to interrupt the service to hush the men congregated outside. I looked out jealously from within the church and couldn't wait to be old enough to join them.

Cuban Nochebuena was essentially a feast for grownups. Since in Cuba most children got their holiday gifts on January 6, the feast of Epiphany, nothing that happened on Christmas Eve had to do directly with us. At our house my brothers, my baby sister and I went to bed before *la misa del gallo.* The last couple of years in Cuba, Pepe and I were allowed to attend Midnight Mass, but since our American-tinged household was visited both by Santa Claus and the Three Wise Men (Santa brought the better gifts), we were still packed off to bed sooner rather than later with the pretext that Santa wouldn't come until all of the children were asleep. But it was hard to get to sleep on Nochebuena, a good but not silent night. After the dinner of roast pig, *yuca con mojo* and *congrí* (black or red beans and rice cooked together), which usually wasn't served until two o'clock in the morning, the celebration went on for several more hours. Those years when my parents skipped Midnight Mass, they and their friends would troop off directly from our house to a 5 A.M. mass at the Sacred Heart Church. From there they would go to breakfast. When my brothers and I woke up Christmas morning, my father would be sleeping, but my mother stayed up so that she could be with us when we opened our gifts. For her, Christmas morning with the children was no less important than Nochebuena with the grownups (for Gustavo, who slept until one or two in the afternoon, Christmas was the bleary day that inevitably followed the long good night). As we tried out our new toys, Vargas and the maids went about straightening up the house, which had that desolate post-party look, with smudged glasses and dirty plates and crumpled napkins strewn everywhere.

At least for me, the best part of Christmas wasn't Nochebuena or Santa Claus but the preparations that preceded the festivities. Like other Cuban couples, my parents had an uneven division of festive labor: Nena prepared, and Gustavo partied. Her job was to set everything up; his job was to make the most of her arrangements, for the benefit of others as well as himself. If Gustavo was the life of the party, Nena was its soul. Her preparations for Nochebuena began weeks earlier with the arrival of boxes of Spanish nougat, marzipan, filberts, sparkling wines and other holiday staples, gifts from the people my father did business with. We'd buy the tallest Christmas tree available at a nearby American-style supermarket, and then spend several afternoons putting up the ornaments and setting up the Nativity scene. The false fireplace in the living room was just the right size for the large plaster figures of Baby Jesus, Mary, and Joseph, and made a marvelous manger. Under the tree we built a replica of Bethlehem, complete with river, bridge, shepherds and sheep. Off to one side, somewhat in the distance, The Three Wise Men approached on their camels, bearing gifts. In the foyer my mother placed mirrors and cotton swatches to simulate snow and a frozen lake, which she surrounded with little cottages with red roofs and lights inside. Between early December and the second week in January, this incongruous wintry landscape was the first thing one saw as one entered our Cuban house, where even the walls were painted a leafy green.

Compared to the bushy Carolina balsams that I later became accustomed to in the States, the puny imported pines that reached the Ekloh Supermarket looked like malnourished third-world imitations of the real thing. They shed needles like rain, and no amount of watering could cure their wan, skeletal look. But to us they were marvelous. Other kids in the neighborhood, whose parents didn't believe in Christmas trees, came to our house for awed stares. The point was not the tree, anyway, but the decorations, whose abundance more than made up for the gaping holes in the foliage. Because Americans think of Christmas trees as natural objects, often their idea of decoration is a red ribbon with a pine cone or some paper cut-outs that their kids bring home from school. For us Christmas trees were cultural artifacts that provided an opportunity to demonstrate once again the triumph of man over nature *(dominé!)*, and so we smothered them with decorations: lights, endless rosaries of shiny marble-sized balls, and box upon box of ornaments, including some odd ones like a blown-crystal *bohío* (thatched hut). Any residual holes we buried under a canopy of *lagrimas,* literally tears, but in fact tinsel. Tears blanketed our sagging tree like kudzu. The crowning touch was a large, brightly lit figure of the Archangel Gabriel, who presided over the living room with arms outstretched. It was usually Vargas who got up on a ladder and, tottering above Nena's watchful eye, skewered the angel into the tree. By the time we were through, several days after we had begun, our formerly spindly tree looked splendid—an anorexic wrapped in fine jewelry and furs, and with an angelic tiara to boot.

When we got to Miami in October in 1960, we stopped celebrating Nochebuena. It seemed pointless to observe this feast in exile, with our unsettled situation and the family scattered all over—some relatives still in Cuba and others in New York or Puerto Rico. That first Christmas in Miami we put up a tree, though a smaller and greener one, but the only Nativity we could afford was a cardboard stable with fold-out figures. Instead of Nochebuena dinner, we had Christmas lunch; instead of the traditional roasted pig, Nena baked a turkey. My parents kept hoping that we would be back to Cuba in time to celebrate Nochebuena the way we always had, but it didn't happen. Sitting around the table on Christmas day, we weren't so much gloomy as dazed. We had been living in this house only a few weeks, everything was topsy-turvy, it wasn't clear what we were supposed to think or say. There we were, just my parents and us four children around the table, suddenly transformed into an American nuclear family. Instead of the noisy bacchanals we had been used to, our Christmas celebration was brief and muted. Earlier that morning Santa had left gifts for those of us who still believed in him, but two weeks later the Three Wise Men didn't show up.

After a few years, our family reinstituted Nochebuena. By the late sixties everybody in our family had left Cuba, and if they didn't live in Miami, they were able to come down for Christmas. Since the family had been brought together again, it no longer felt inappropriate to celebrate in exile. Indeed, the opposite thing happened: distance from the homeland made us celebrate the occasion all the more vigorously, for Nochebuena became one of the ways of holding on to Cuba. Although the Nochebuena in exile were less splendid than the Cuban ones, the essentials remained the same. During these years Little Havana was full of Cuban markets that carried all of the typical foods. *Turrón* and *sidra* (Spanish champagne) were easy to obtain; and if a family didn't have the time or the equipment to roast a pig at home, an already cooked pig could be bought at the corner *bodega*, along with containers of *congrí* and *yuca*. Like the food, the faces in our family gathering hadn't changed much. Our Miami Nochebuenas from the nineteen seventies included many of the same relatives that had attended the gatherings in Cuba. Tío Mike always arrived early to set up what he called his "intellectual laboratory," where he concocted mysterious martinis by looking up the proportions in one of his pocket notebooks. While Mike experimented, his wife Mary minced around in her gold high heeled thongs with the furred straps. Tony, an uncle who had been a cabaret singer in Havana and was now a waiter in New York, crooned *boleros* accompanied by my sister on the guitar, while Gustavo danced randy rumbas with any willing (and sometimes unwilling) partner. Tío Pepe and Josefina came, as did Tío Pedro and his wife Amparo, and Joseíto and his wife Encarnita. Also present were assorted boy-friends and girlfriends and current and prospective in-laws— all Cuban—and the one American in the family at this time, my cousin Evelyn's husband Jeff, the one whose name Constantina never mastered. And, oh yes, Constantina. At some point during these evenings, with her eyes sparkling from a glass or two of *sidra*, Constantina did her famous *jota*, which was followed by the ritual *pasodoble* with my father.

In spite of the similarities to Cuba, though, these lively parties weren't really clones of the old Nochebuenas. Even if we went to Church, pigged-out on roast pork, and drank and danced, the holiday had begun to change. Without anyone being overly aware of it, the Cuban Nochebuena and the American Christmas had started to get acquainted, to negotiate a compromise. Not only was Christmas sneaking up on Nochebuena; Nochebuena was converging on Christmas. Like Constantina doing the *jota* next to the Christmas tree, Cuban customs began to marry American ways.

On the face of it, the marriage was not an easy one. As a *prospective* celebration of the birth of Christ, Nochebuena has a high-strung, restive feel. Many Cubans spend the night in perpetual motion, going from one house to the next, a custom that supposedly goes back to the Biblical story of Mary and Joseph wandering around Bethlehem looking for a place to spend the night. On the evening of December 24, Cubans divide into two camps: the squatters and the roamers. The squatters stay put, cook, stock plenty to drink and keep their doors open. The roamers make the rounds. Since we were always squatters, part of the fun of Nochebuena was having people show up at our doorstep at any hour of the night, have a couple of drinks, eat, dance, and then move on to their next house. Needless to say, it's safer to squat than to roam, but it's the roamers who give the evening that extra burst of *embullo*, that extra hit of festive fuel. By contrast, the spirit of Christmas is neither raucous nor nomadic. As befits a family holiday, Christmas is merry but not moveable, joyful but not extravagant. Whereas Nochebuena is a nocturnal feast, Christmas is a daytime celebration, a holiday in the full sense of the word. If Nochebuena is all motion and commotion, Christmas is peace. On Christmas families gather to exchange gifts and spend time together, not to hoot and howl. Children are a big part of Christmas, but during Nochebuena they are a little more than a nuisance. Our Nochebuena photographs show bunches of grownups living it up; our Christmas photographs show parents and children gathered around the tree. When Christmas encounters Nochebuena, American days run into Cuban nights.

In our house the marriage of day and night occurred when my siblings and my cousins and I grew up and then began to have children of our own. By the mid-seventies and for several years thereafter, we had achieved a rough balance between the "Cuban" and the "American" ends of the family. The older Cubans, mostly men like my father and my uncles, celebrated Nochebuena; Nena and her American-born grandchildren did the same for Christmas. As a member of the one-and-a-half generation, I swung back and forth between one and the other, sometimes playing Cuban son to my father and at other times playing American dad to my son. During these balanced years, the prospect of Christmas morning made Nochebuena a little more sedate, and Nochebuena made Christmas a little more lively. Since the adults had to be up at the crack of dawn to open presents with the kids, we couldn't—as Nena always reminded us—stay up all night and then go for breakfast to La Carreta or Versailles. Besides, the house was too small for the kids to be able to sleep while the adults carried on outside. Since by the 1970s the Church had slackened its rules on fast-ing, most years Nena served dinner before Midnight Mass. By two or three in the morning Nochebuena was over.

I loved these hybrid celebrations, half day and half night, for they seemed to combine the best of both worlds. The problem, though, is that biculturalism is a balancing act that topples with the passing of generations, and by the end of our third decade in exile, our Nochebuenas had changed again. Tío Pepe, Constantina, Abuela Martínez, Joseíto and Tío Mike passed away in the nineteen seventies and eighties. Other aunts and uncles were either too old to travel to Miami every December, or became too infirm to leave their houses. When his wife Amparo died, my uncle Pedro stopped celebrating holidays altogether. (Now he gets on a plane on the morning of December 24th and spends Christmas Eve at the blackjack tables in the Bahamas; a *noche buena* for him now is when he doesn't lose too much money.) Then also, those in my generation have our own lives and can't always make it down to Miami for Christmas. My sister, who lives in Chicago with her husband and three children, has started holding Nochebuenas of her own; so has my brother in Atlanta. Maggie and Armandito, my cousins and drinking partners, now live in Mexico City. My younger cousin Anita is gay and doesn't feel comfortable bringing her lover to the party, so she doesn't come. Once every few years some of us still coincide in Miami for Nochebuena, but it seems to happen less and less often.

Every Nochebuena for the last four or five years, Nena has been grumbling that this will be her last, that she's getting too old for all of the preparations, but come the following year she roasts another leg of pork, cooks another pot of *congrí*, and tries to get the family together. However Americanized she may say she is, she doesn't seem willing to give up this Cuban custom. Old Havanas are hard to break, but for Nena and Gustavo Nochebuena has become a mournful holiday, a reminder of how much things have changed in their lives.

For exile families the impact of change is not only personal but cultural, for the passing away of a generation spells the extinction of a culture. As a friend of mine puts it, Cubans are not assimilating, they're dying. The ones who are still alive, he and I among them, are the ones who weren't totally Cuban to begin with. With every first-generation exile who passes away, we in the younger generations lose words, turns of phrase, habits of thought, gestures that are distinctively Cuban. No one could pack more devilishness into a wink, for example, than my father's cousin Joseíto, and no one could exclaim *"Oye, niña!"* like my uncle Pepe. The personal loss is inevitable, but the cultural loss, a consequence of prolonged exile, is much harder to accept. Every culture evolves, and the culture of children is never identical to that of parents and grandparents, but extinction is not evolution. Nochebuena used to be a time to remember and celebrate things Cuban. The ritual toast, "Next year in Cuba," set the mood for the evening, a mood both nostalgic and hopeful, for the Nochebuenas of yesteryear were a warrant on the Nochebuenas of tomorrow. During those very good nights in the 1960s, 1970s and 1980s, everything harked back to Cuba—the celebrants, the food, the music, the customs. Every year we heard my father's favorite chanteuse, Olga Guillot, singing "White Christmas" with a Spanish lyric. Every year we danced to "La Mora," an old Cuban song whose questioning refrain was uncannily relevant, *"Cuándo volverá, La Nochebuena, cuando volverá?"* "When will they return, those old Nochebuenas, when will they return?" Soon, we all thought, very soon. At no other time of the year did Cuba seem so close, did *regreso* seem so imminent.

With the death of the old timers, Cuba is dying too. Our

Miami Nochebuenas have become more and more American. It has been years since anybody showed up at my parents' doorstep at two o'clock in the morning. If they did, they would find the lights out and the family in bed. As the celebration has become geared to the American grandchildren, Nochebuena has become Christmas Eve, more an anticipation of the next day than a festivity in itself. With the arrival into our family of non-Cuban spouses, even the *lingua franca* of the night has evolved toward English, a language that my mother handles comfortably but that my father doesn't like to speak.

Gustavo and Nena have adapted to these changes with a mixture of resignation and good cheer. Although he sorely misses the company of his contemporaries, Gustavo compensates as best he can by showing off his dancing skills to his American daughters-in-law. He flirts with them with almost as much *embullo* as he displays flirting with the waitresses at his favorite Cuban restaurants, and somehow he manages to come up with bilingual dirty jokes. At the same time, however, he drinks less than he used to and gets bored or tired quicker. Sometime in the evening his mood will modulate from merry to melancholy; then he settles into his chair and turns on the TV. For Nena, the most difficult part hasn't been the Americanization of Nochebuena—after all, she grew up in Norfolk celebrating Christmas, not Nochebuena—but the fragmentation of our family. Until the last few years, she had been fairly successful in keeping everyone together. Both in Cuba and in Miami, her house was our oasis, our hospital, the haven to which we repaired in times of trouble, the temple where we celebrated birthdays, baptisms, graduations, engagements. Even during difficult years, she bore this burden lightly. No occasion was too insignificant, no party too big, no demand on her time or energy too onerous. In these tasks my father was an onlooker; once he stocked the bar and bought the bag of ice, his job was over. Nena was the one who cooked, who cleaned, who set everything up, who extended invitations and organized logistics. She was the one who kept finding reasons and occasions to gather children and cousins and aunts and uncles and nephews and nieces. For thirty years, her project has been keeping the family whole. She spun the thread that kept us tightly knit. As she says, give me a roof over my head and enough beds for my children and I am happy. I think she loved the Christmassy Nochebuenas even better than the Cuban ones.

But this doesn't mean that exile has been easy on her. If my father experienced exile as loss of wealth and status, she has experienced it as the diminishment of the family. Nena complains about exile when something goes wrong with the family, when it frays at the edges or comes loose at the seams. She complains when she cannot be at her daughter's or daughter-in-law's side during childbirth, when one son gets divorced and another gets into trouble, or when her sister-in-law has to be eulogized in English by a priest who doesn't know her. At times like these, she intones her eternal question, "Why has exile been so hard on us? Things would have been so different in Cuba." She views exile not as economic deprivation but as an assault on her family. For her the Cuban Revolution has been less a political than a cultural cataclysm. Compared to the dispersal of thousands upon thousands of families, financial hardship and expatriation are nothing. Fidel's greatest crime, she likes to say, the one for which he will roast in Hell like a suckling pig, is the breakup of the Cuban family. For Nena, the human cost of the Revolution must be measured in Nochebuenas, for it is then that the fractures in our family show up with the clarity of an X-ray.

This is why her adaptation to exile followed a very different curve from my father's. For him losing the *almacén* was the decisive blow. For my mother, however, exile was manageable so long as the family stayed together. If my father fantasizes about returning to his business, my mother dreams of a time when the family was whole. In spite of the plethora of day-to-day problems, for years Nena was basically happy in Miami. Even as she complained about the hardships of life in exile, she balked at the idea of returning to Cuba immediately after the fall of Fidel. She always said that what she missed was not Cuba but Kohly, the neighborhood where our house was located, and that Kohly would never be the same. She once told me, "Remember what Scarlett O'Hara says—she doesn't say she wants to go back to Atlanta. She always says, 'I want to go back to Tara.' Kohly was Tara."

In Cuba my mother's life had been a roller coaster of Friday nights at the Tropicana, Saturdays on the yacht, Sundays at the race track or the baseball stadium. The money that made possible the big house and the servants subsidized a lifestyle that she sometimes found unbearable. When my parents quarreled in Cuba, it was usually about partying. Gustavo wanted to, Nena did not. Being the king of the house, Gustavo usually got his way. In Miami all this changed. With the money went the maids as well as the fast-track lifestyle. No longer able to spend his evenings gambling or dancing, my father became a homebody. If he went out at night with his cousin Joseíto, it was to ride around Little Havana and have a cup of espresso at the Casablanca restaurant on Calle Ocho. In Cuba, it hadn't been so easy to track him down.

In exile, my father and mother made common cause. Old wounds healed and long-standing friction subsided. When my father is out of earshot, Nena says that exile saved her marriage. But when my mother is out of earshot, Gustavo says that exile ruined his life. Both exaggerate, but neither one is lying. Enervated by his losses, in Miami Gustavo became a spectator in his own family. He worked and he watched. Although he

remained the principle breadwinner, Nena took care of everything else. Partly by default and partly by design, she became
the family's solid center. Juggling husband, children, parents
and relatives, she never let any one of us drop. In Cuba she had
never worked outside the home; in Miami she held a full-time
job as a school secretary and served as a cook, chauffeur, financial planner, daughter, wife, mother, and maid. "Who could
have told me," she says, "that I would have to spend the rest
of my life pulling hair out of the bathroom sink?"

With my father emotionally disengaged, Nena picked up the
slack. Because we asked her all of the questions, she got good
at leaving all of the answers. Many of her answers were wise,
and some were cockeyed. Soon after arriving in Miami she made
my father turn down a job offer in the Dominican Republic.
Why? Because she wasn't about to raise children anywhere
where they didn't have *papel de aluminio*, aluminum foil, which
for her is a symbol of the advances of American civilization.
(Don't ask me how she decided that there was no aluminum
foil in the Dominican Republic.) When my brothers and I were
adolescents, she counseled us against marrying black women.
Why? Not because she found anything wrong with interracial
marriages, but "because the United States is not ready for
mulattas."

In times of crisis, Nena always shone. In my family, as in so
many Cuban families, the women like my mother display a
strength and stability that their husbands seem to lack. I have
observed this pattern over and over in other exile families, each
anchored by strong, resourceful women. Nena never cracked, or
at least never let it show. Always on call, she seemed tireless.
The accidents, the illnesses, the poverty—she could deal with
them all. For years Nena nursed her mother at home, long past
the time when Abuela Martínez, who not only was blind but
suffered from Alzheimer's (which we called only *chochería*),

stopped remembering who or where she was. But putting her mother in a home was something that Nena couldn't do. According to her, this is what Americans did, while Cubans took care of their own. When Nena went off to work in the morning, an old lady who lived down the block sat with my grandmother. At noon Nena came home to fix my grandmother's special lunch, a tricky undertaking since Abuela Martínez had a tumor in her stomach the size of a grapefruit. After work Nena spent the rest of the afternoon picking up and distributing children. When she wasn't cooking or cleaning or patching blue jeans or taking down cuffs or fending off Constantina, she was looking after her mother, who—because of the Alzheimer's—was not only recalcitrant but cruel. I remember that often Nena had to dodge insults and wipe shit from the floor at the same time. Years went by without my mother being able to take an afternoon off to go to the movie or visit a friend. When Abuela Martínez became so feeble that she needed a full-time nurse, Nena finally relented and put her in a convalescent home, but only after being persuaded to do so by her confessor. She visited her mother almost daily, returning home in tears. Even today, when she talks about having put her mother in a home, she starts to cry. I should be ashamed to say this, and I am, but I don't know whether I would be able to do for my mother all that she did for hers.

No family survives exile intact, and in spite of Nena's extraordinary exertions, things happened that undermined ours. As decade succeeded decade, the extended family distended. Taking care of her mother was an ordeal but an expected one. Other things were tougher to countenance. Siblings who had been raised to be *uña y carne*, as close as fingernails and flesh, hardly talked to each other. Relatives who in Cuba would have been living nearby, died in distant places. Children whose children she expected to raise moved away. Today, the older Nena gets, the more alone she is, the fewer people she has to care for. To her, a woman's work is cyclical mothering. In her youth, a woman mothers her children; in her middle age, she mothers her children and her parents; in her old age, she mothers her children and her grandchildren. By sundering the family, exile broke this cycle, and eventually Nena had to confront what she regards as American problems—separations, loneliness, divorces, family strife. Contented for many years in Miami, she has in the end come to bear the brunt of exile as fully as my father. My mother knows that those Nochebuenas of old will not return.

In all the years I have resided away from Miami, I've missed only one Nochebuena there, and that because one year my parents decided to spend Christmas in North Carolina, an experiment that didn't turn out well and won't be repeated. As long as Nena and Gustavo are alive and willing, I'll go to their house for Nochebuena. Although the celebration and the celebrants have changed a great deal throughout the years, more than my parents and I would have liked, Nochebuena remains for me the holiest—if no longer the happiest—night of the year. But I have no illusions. Our Miami Nochebuenas have come to resemble those skeletal Christmas trees from Cuba. I wish it were different, but the time to do anything about it may have passed. I could make a joke and say that you can't make roast pig from a sow's ear. But this is no joke. After my parents have passed away, I hope many years from now, I will celebrate Nochebuena in Chapel Hill with my American wife, my almost-American children and my American stepchildren. Instead of going to Miami, I'll be staying put. I'll be a squatter, not a roamer. But I will be squatting far from home. I know that in Chapel Hill my Nochebuena traditions will suffer a further attenuation, and when this happens I'll find myself in the position that my father occupies now—I will be the only Cuban rooster in the house. The good night, which became less than good in Miami, may well not be good enough in Chapel Hill. My reluctant but hopeful wager is that the not-so-*buena* Nochebuena will be followed by an excellent Christmas.

A Brand New Memory

Elías Miguel Muñoz

A Cuban exile and immigrant to the United States, Elías Miguel Muñoz (1954–) has been fascinated not only with the experience of uprootedness, as in his novel The Greatest Performance, *but in its opposite: complete accommodation to and internalization of the values and lifestyle of the United States. In his novel* A Brand New Memory, *Muñoz has provided a piquant satire of a Cuban-American princess in her and her family's "totally American" celebration of Christmas.*

A Brand New Memory (excerpt)

This holiday season the Princess is in the mood for sounds. She'll be listening to rock, hip-hop, Latino pop, and salsa. Yeah, she wants all kinds of music, the whole spectrum. That's the advantage of being a Nineties-kind-of-person, you have a lot to choose from: Sixties rock classics, Seventies pop oldies, Eighties New Wave, Nineties New Age and Alternative Rock. And then there's all that excellent *Rockero* stuff, bands from Mexico, Spain, Argentina. Cool. And also fab movie soundtracks. And what about rap? She loves some rap mixes! Too bad she has to play that music low; her parents hate it. They think it's disgusting and vulgar, primeval noise, and how dare those people call themselves "artists"? Luckily, though, her folks don't mess much with her listening trips. (Rap is the only exception.) She wonders why. Do they think that music isn't powerful enough to influence her? Are they naive enough to believe it can't affect her? Whatever the reasons, thank God they stay out of her sound room!

Her private trip: eclectic moods she's named *Navidad Jamming*; sessions that her mother, as usual, will crush mercilessly. "*Ca suffit!* The ceiling and the walls are vibrating. Our guests think it's an earthquake!"

Gina turns down the volume on her Quake Machine and goes through her wardrobe. Nothing too adolescent, please; the following scene requires class, sophistication. She has to play the part of a Pinos Verdes young lady, daughter of an Auxiliary Wife, the incarnation of beauty, refined taste, and good manners. *Oui oui.*

No matter how hateful the scene, she loves preparing for it. The wardrobe fittings are exciting. Makeup, hair, anticipation. Actors have to change all the time; they're always undergoing a—what was the title of that creepy Kafka story she read in English Lit? Ah, yes: metamorphosis. (That's if they're good. Because some actors can only play the same old part—basically, themselves!—movie after movie.)

She dons a pretty little dress and, displaying her most dazzling smile, goes to greet the holiday company. *Chez Les Domingos*, TAKE 15. Roll 'em! "Merry Christmas, dear ladies! Feliz Navidad. Joyeux Noel. How are you all doing?" The company invariably consists of Maman's friends: overdressed, overdone-in-tanning parlors and surgically enhanced matrons who feed Gina the same lines every year. "Look at that child, how she's grown! Why, you're a lady already. How old are you now, fourteen, sixteen?" Or: "My my, you are beginning to resemble your mother so much! Soon we won't be able to tell the two of you apart."

Exhausting. It's so totally exhausting to perform in front of a live audience. Multicamera takes are absolute killers! She rushes back to her dressing room (careful to dodge the reporters and the fans who crowd the hallways asking for autographs) and there she comes up with her own share of comments for the addle-brained visitors: "Seeing you is revolting and I'm not a lady and I never want to be a lady. I haven't grown an inch in two years and if you're referring to the way I'm growing, widthwise, then you can take your Xmas tree and shove it, you hear? Oh, and one more thing: I LOOK NOTHING LIKE MY MOTHER!!"

Like Gina, Daddy, too, gets grumpy around Christmas. But for different reasons. He complains about the crowds and the TV specials and the jingles and the funny-looking fat men with white beards who sit outside the stores and ask for money. "Ho ho ho to you, too!" Daddy snaps at poor Santa who's only doing his jolly job.

"They dress up their houses with lights two months before Christmas!" he says of his neighbors. "Their roofs, windows, porches full of ridiculous lights. We're barely finished with Thanksgiving and they're already putting up their trees!" Daddy never dreams of a White Christmas, and has never believed in a Winter Wonderland. However, he doesn't mind that during the holidays his flower sales always increase. *Ho ho ho!*

Maman ignores Benito Scrooge and dives into the holiday spirit with zest. No other collective ritual gives her greater joy than Joyeux Noel. She spends days trimming the tree and plastering the walls with decorations. But she doesn't follow any of the native Cuban traditions, certainly not when planning the menu. She has Guadalupe prepare gallons of eggnog using a renowned *Golden Hill* recipe. There is to be no pork roast and no black beans and no fried plantains. The family will savor thin, tender slices of turkey carefully cooked in Swiss honey, dressed with rose petals and windflowers. (A feast to be consumed with the proper silver cutlery, *mais oui*.) For dessert the Domingos will be served "tartalisa," a lemon tart invented and personally baked by Maman. And as an after-dinner drink they will sip herbal tea, their pinkies pointing up as they bring the cups to their lips. *Oui oui*.

Mr. and Mrs. Domingo will exchange presents, as required by Anglo-Saxon culture, on December 25, Christmas morning. The last few years he's been giving her jewelry—no fakes— and she buys him clothes: classic suits and sport coats and ties. Normally, they thank each other with a kiss and soon thereafter focus their attention on Gina. They love to see her opening her presents; her reaction is one aspect of the holidays they both look forward to. Her effusive hugs, her excitement and joy are all the Domingos expect from their daughter by way of gifts. The true meaning of Christmas.

———

Gina's list for Santa is long this year, but it always is. Heck, better to give Mr. Claus-Domingo lots of possibilities. In any case, she doesn't expect to get everything (four CDs, three movies recently released on video, shoes, and a bunch of clothes). As last Christmas, this year she'll ask for one expensive item. Just in case she gets lucky. Last December it was a video camera; on this year's list it's a computer.

She usually includes, as well, an out-of-the-question thing, something she knows she won't get, like a pet. Yeah, a Chow with a shiny black tongue and big, clumsy paws. *Jamais*, as Maman would say. Madame Elisa would never allow one of those "beasts" in the house. She had a horrible experience back in Cuba with a "fierce canine," and as a result developed an acute case of dog phobia. Even little poodles scare the hell out of her.

Santa Domingo was magnanimous. Gina was presented with not four but six compact discs, not three but five movies, and a powerful laptop computer with a laser printer. Initially, she used the machine to do fancy graphics and prepare class assignments. Then she started to write her thoughts into a personal file named YOU, sort of like a computer log, an electronic diary. In the old days young women wrote their journals in longhand, carefully crafted feminine letters. Not anymore, thank God. Now human beings had fabulous machines that did all the dirty work. These objects helped you when you needed them but didn't force you to spend time listening to *their* problems. Ideal pals.

She liked the tweeting sound the laptop made when you turned it on and she loved the screen-saver, which was a night full of stars. Her machine kept up with the images that ran through her head. It did it all so fast! Using the computer was like talking to herself, only better. Thoughts looked sharper on the screen, for some reason. And she also loved not having to use paper until she was ready to print and have a hard copy. No waste of precious trees. But the most amazing thing about this hardware was that it allowed Gina to keep a record of her life, of who she was. The real "You," magically stored in files and hidden. Saved.

Daddy had gone to a lot of trouble to get this machine for his princess. There were many varieties of hardware on the market, most of them relatively affordable. But Benito knew little about computers so he must've done his homework. (He was partly motivated by his own need to computerize his business, which he did after this holiday season.) Daddy was such a smart shopper, well-informed, never fooled nor distracted by salespeople. All Gina had told him was that she wanted a computer to write her compositions and organize her class notes. Nothing snazzy. He didn't even need to get a CD-ROM drive; she could use the school computers for that. But when Gina opened the box she found state-of-the-art equipment, pretty expensive stuff, and gobs of info about programs available to her; programs she was expected to download and use, just *had* to use according to the manufacturers.

She hadn't taken the computer class at school because she didn't like the types it attracted: pitiful-looking boys fluent in Computerese but lacking in basic communication skills. Total nerds. So, being computer-illiterate, she spent a few hours sifting through the printed data before she could begin to play with her toy. She learned more than she needed to, but such seemed to be the goal of computer makers: overloading—and overwhelming!—users.

Gina learned that cyberspace was dense space, packed with voices and dialog chambers, exclusive clubs, shopping rooms. People communicated within a time that was faster and more linear than actual time. Letters, urgent messages, secret codes, confessions, fantasies were transmitted within the invisible walls of a space which was considered more real than real.

Did she wish to plug into the Net? It was the cool thing to do, the way most of her classmates were now communicating with the world and with each other. Didn't she just *have* to get E-mail and access to the Info Highway? Maybe. If she did, she'd never need to go to the library again, probably. She'd have a monumental library available to her in cyberspace. Doing homework would be a breeze. And by signing onto one of those real-time lines, she might meet other young people like her. There might even be a club or a dialog chamber for Cuban Americans obsessed with Cuba! No, she didn't want to share her thoughts and words with strangers, anonymous voices disguised as friends. Weirdos.

Even so, E-mail would be fun. Everyone at school was using it. She was the only one out of the loop. So what? She didn't mind being the odd man out. Odd *girl*, that is. The world within reach through the computer was vast, tempting, but she was neither ready nor willing to enter it fully yet. First she had to master the art of filmmaking, which required all her energy and talent and concentration. Besides, she thought, life is wild and weird enough already. Why add more layers to it?

The only voice she'd hear occasionally in her machine was Daddy's. More than hearing his voice, it was his handsome face she saw peeking in, snooping around the screen, checking up on her. Daddy making sure she hadn't been swallowed up, turned into an android, or infected with a technology virus. Daddy who gave her this Christmas gift on the tacit condition that he be its gatekeeper, the savior of this daughter's mind. It was Benito's presence that stopped Gina from becoming completely dependent on her computer programs and files, unable to think without them.

He was always there, offering an imaginary hand during those times when the machine shut her out because of a glitch; when it enveloped her thoughts without her knowing it; when it gave her no access to its memory bank, which, after all, was meant to be *her* memory. Daddy brought her back around to a space without which there would be no cyber-realities: the tangible world of her room. Home.

◄ IV ►

Los Pastores

The Shepherds

Anonymous

The following is a translation of one of the many versions of "Los Pastores." It was encountered in performance in Rio Grande City, Texas, by folklorist M. R. Cole, who persuaded the owner of the script (also the teacher/director of the annual performances) to make a hand-written copy in 1891. Cole then translated the work into English and published it for the American Folk-Lore Society in 1907. Besides representing an important historical text, the extra-literary circumstances of the dictation and memorization of the play make clear how immense an undertaking it was for semiliterate, rural folk to learn the antiquated diction and baroque poetry that has survived in this community pageant. Of all the collections and studies of Hispanic theater and drama in the United States, no other subject has garnered so much attention as our very own cycle of miracle plays in the Southwest.

Further reading: M. R. Cole, *Los Pastores. A Mexican Play of the Nativity*, trans. M. R. Cole (Boston: Houghton Mifflin and Company, 1907); Lily Litvak, ed., *El nacimiento del Niño Dios: A Pastorela from Tarimoro, Guanajuato* (Austin: University of Texas Center for Intercultural Studies in Folklore, 1973); Juan Bautista Rael, *The Sources and Diffusion of the Mexican Shepherd's Play* (Guadalajara: 1965); Richard Flores, *Los Pastores. History and Performance in the Mexican Shepherd's Play of South Texas* (Washington, D.C.: Smithsonian Institution Press, 1995).

Los Pastores

Argument

The play opens with a Christmas hymn, after which Lucifer appears, soliloquizing. He is uneasy at the portents, and determines by some device to ascertain from the shepherds the truth about the Messiah's coming. He hides as they approach, singing. The Hermit joins the shepherds to learn what they know about the Messiah, and journeys on with them to their night camp. Parrado goes to inspect the flocks, and the others are about to go to sleep when an angel appears. No one notices the apparition except Tebano, but Parrado rushes in, demanding a boon for some joyful news. All promise something, and he describes the vision of an angel, singing Glory to God on High! All but Tebano refuse to believe the tale, but the angel reappears, and warns them against Lucifer. The angel vanishes, and Lucifer comes in as a traveller, asking shelter for the night. The shepherds refuse, and the Hermit demands the stranger's name. Lucifer replies by giving an account of his fall, in veiled language, and declares that he will pursue the King and his followers to the death. The angel returns as the shepherds are running off, and after a fiery dialogue drives Lucifer out before him. The next scene shows the shepherds preparing for supper. Bartolo sends the lad Cucharón off to see if the flocks are safe. Lucifer intercepts the boy, and endeavors to learn from him about the Messiah's coming. Cucharón thinks he says Matías, and tells a story about a man of that name, answering all Lucifer's questions at cross purposes. Lucifer is about to consume him in flames when Cucharón calls on God for aid, and Lucifer retires discomfited. Cucharón rushes back to camp, declaring that he has seen the Devil. Nabal immediately follows with news of an angelic vision, and heavenly music is heard. Lucifer, still lingering about, hears the music, and sees the radiance which heralds the coming of Michael. The angel arrives announcing that he is come to protect the shepherds, and after a long argument subdues Lucifer, who is dismissed to everlasting punishment. The shepherds then set out for the manger. Each one sings an appropriate verse as he approaches, recites a prayer, offers a gift, and then retires, after calling on the next shepherd by name. When all but Bartolo have adored the Babe, they urge him to perform that duty. He prefers to sleep in his blanket, and makes jocular excuses until, out of patience, they carry him off by force. After his prayer, they sing a lullaby, and begin a prolonged farewell. Bato brings the performance to a close by invoking blessings on the whole company, and on his Majesty the King.

The Shepherds

[Chorus of Shepherds behind the scenes]

SONG

En el por- tal de Be - lén Hay
muy gran cla - ri - dad, Por- que a-llá na-ció el Me -
cí - as, Y el nos pon-drá en li - ber - tad.

In Bethlehem's holy manger
  There shines a wondrous light;
To save our souls from danger
  The Saviour's born tonight.

In Bethlehem the ox's stall
  Shows us a happy sight;
Where Jesus, come to save us all,
  Was born of Mary bright.

March on together joyfully,
  While the angels sing;
For our Lord's Nativity
  We tamales bring.

To Holy Mary thanks we raise,
  And Joseph, for their grace;

Mere shepherd lads, we now may gaze
On the Redeemer's face.

Angels and seraphs by the throne,
Joyfully on high,
The names of Mary, and her son
And Joseph glorify.

The guilt of Adam in his fall
Our Saviour prophesied,
Will wash away, and loose us all
From bonds of sin and pride.

A branch sprang from a sturdy tree,
A flower from the bough,
And Jesse's trunk is fair to see, —
The Babe its blossom now.

A bitter contest ours to wage,
The evil power to quell;
To match the cunning, dare the rage
Of Satan, Prince of Hell.

[Enter LUCIFER as music dies away]

LUCIFER   Driven out from heaven by Michael's, arm,
I left my august home on high,—'
Ambition was my cursed sin.
Disgraced, cast out, I own my fault!
What are these songs that pierce my ears?
What means this sacred sphere? These chants
Of praise, these sounds of joy to-day
That fill me with despair? I hear
The heavenly host, with dulcet voice
Sing: "Victory to the Lord of all,
Creator of the heaven and earth!"

Now fear is added to my rage
When to the earth the Star declares:
In New Arabia He is born!
Swell, stifling rage, till every man
Has perished by my flaming sword!
What ho! Ye ministers of Hell,
To earth! Give aid to sow the seeds
Of countless ills! If to the winds
I look, I find them whispering joy,
Attentive in their bliss to catch
And echo back the angels' songs.
If to the earth I turn, all there
Tumultuous seems, and feeds my woe.
Deeper to probe my sorrow's cause
The elder Scriptures I consult,
See here the prophecy declares:
"The ox shall know his Master, warm
Him in the manger with his breath."
The very words! this is no dream.
Daniel's space of seventy weeks
Which should elapse before He came,
Is filled exactly. Here I see
Ezekiel's prophecy foretell
The tender Babe in Bethlehem,
Born while a royal hand holds fast
Judea. For Atajer says:
"When earth is filled with prodigies,
And sea with portents, then shall come
The long-desired Prince of Peace.
Victorious He shall appear,
And fill the earth with glory." These
Three suns that beam with rosy light
Proclaim the news; whence I infer

Already has the Lamb come down
To the proud earth, in human flesh.
Out, science, I will read no more,
The labor frets my patience! Why
Should I thus wear my heart away
When man is a disloyal knave?
Daniel the stranger preached it, when
He came to save Belshazzar, show
Eternal punishment to those
Approaching fast the gates of hell.
Saul, too, proclaimed it, 'spite his hours
Of frenzy, and the crazied king,
Nebuchadnezzar, when the two
Confessed their guilt and pride; whereon
Came holy Michael to convince
Them of their madness. Did not I
Then rule a realm apart? Once, in
The time of Benedict, not all
His people had the skill to rear
The walls of their razed church. Did I
Not build them up? Past doubt. Then why
Probe deeper,—fear? I know that man
Shall conquer by his strength and art.
What else is man, or this wild beast,
But just a handful of dead clay
Created by the Omnipotent
From naught, by sovereign wisdom? I
Will make this monster fall
Prostrate, from that God-given height!
Forth from the eternal gloomy cave
All ye who dwell therein! Lend aid
With bold and skilful artifice

Vengeance to wreck on man, my foe!
Are not my sufferings caused by him?
And is he not my enemy?
Beyond a doubt. Then who forbids
The rigor of my punishment?
With artful wiles, in sable clad,
I hasten to tempt him. War on man,
Unending war, and death to all!
But here come shepherds up the hill,—
A means to learn of the events
Passing in Galilee. My wrath
Has thirst to know. I hide myself.

[LUCIFER *retires*]

[*Enter* HERMIT, *who sees the* Shepherds *approaching. He stands aside until after their entrance and first songs*]

HERMIT   Shepherds are climbing these wild hills.

ALL   They go to greet him born to save.

TEBANO   The time has come to celebrate
            This sacred sacrifice of love.

PARRADO   Give the chorus; we are ready.

TEBANO   As soon as thou didst send me forth
            Like vigilant apostle I
            Searched every nook, looked high and low.
            Outside the walls of Bethlehem
            An angel band to me appeared.
            With humble mien the spirits fair
            Gave us glad tidings of a Maid,
            A miracle of loveliness;
            Then sang a sweet strange melody.

The actors in full costume, except that the devils are without their masks.

SONG

Es-ta no-che con la lu-na, Y ma-ña-na con el sol, Co-je-re-mos pa-ja-ri-tos Pa-ra la i-gle-sia ma-llor.

At night, when the moon shines bright,
And by day, 'neath the sun's hot ray,
Snare the birds, snare the finch and the sparrow,
To sing in the great church to-morrow.

PARRADO   Had I a little store of wealth,
How gladly would I build the church
A noble choir; a column raise
Of virgin gold, circled with lights,
That all might catch its yellow gleam,
At night, when the moon shines bright.

TEBANO   I would make the sconces flash
With carbuncles and diamonds,
And many another precious stone,—
With jewels bright, and butterflies.
Two splendid organs, richly carved,
Should tower aloft; a stately arch
In honor of our Lord should span
The altar; there in vigil I
Would kneel and pray the live-long night,
And by day, in the sun's hot ray.

PARRADO   My fervent love would take delight
To make the church-bells all of gold,
The belfry-tower of silver too,
The incensory, missals, stands,
The sacred vessels, one and all,
Of purest, finest virgin gold.
And for sweet singers in the choir,
Snare the birds, snare the finch and the sparrow.

TEBANO   I would make the holy vestments
Out of cloth of gold and silver.
The chalice and the paten both
Of filigree; a golden lamp
To light up all should hang above,
And candelabra like the sun,—
My offering to deck the church!

And we should go, a happy band,
To sing in the great church to-morrow.

PARRADO   Sing on without a pause, O thou
Clear voice whose accents ring with joy,
As shines the lovely countenance!
Shepherds, sing on, I love your songs,
But haste your steps, time runs apace.

GILA   Shepherds, at last the day has dawned
When we should joyfully depart
For Bethlehem. The miracle
Awaits us in the manger there.
Get ready packs with what we need
Upon the journey; strap up all,
And then trudge briskly o'er the hills,
Cheering our hearts with hopeful song.

PARRADO   Gila says well. Come, brothers, take
Our way across the flowery fields.

SONG

1. En ri-sue-ños can-tos De los rui-se-ño-res,
2. Her-ma-nos pas-to-res, Her-ma-nos que-ri-dos,

Ca-mi-nen a-le-gres, Her-ma-nos pas-to-res.
Tran-si-tan-do va-mos, Por e-sos ca-mi-nos.

To the song
Of nightingales
March along
Across the vales.

Shepherds kind,
Brothers dear,
Look not behind,
Rest is near.

Gaily run
O'er stone and stock;
As you come
Count the flock.

The lambkins wander
Off alone,

Look well under
Bush and stone.

Gila dearest,
Struggle up;
On the nearest
Hill we sup.

Gila, friend,
The night grows chill,
Our journey's end
Is yonder hill.

Tebano, yonder,
Shining bright,
What a wonder,
See, a light!

Mount of Olives
Sad and steep,
Where the shepherds
Feed their sheep!

The mountain crest
We wind about;
Dear Gila, rest,
Thou'rt tired out.

O heavens drear!
Have pity now,
We cannot bear
The falling snow.

The sheep are bleating,
And lambkins all,

To see the fleeting
Snowflakes fall.

The stars amazed
Stand still to see,
The snowdrifts raised
On Calvary.

On yonder mount
With ledges steep,
By the clear fount
We mean to sleep.

In yonder wood,
Comrades dear,
Pasture's good,
The spring flows near.

A fire light,
Let Gila braize
Tamales right
Before the blaze.

The kid is done,
'T is time to sup;
Come, Gila, run,
And serve it up.

BATO   Come, brothers, let us sup e'er dawn.

PARRADO   Brother, thou sayest well, for here
Is pasture, and a spring hard by.

CUCHARÓN   Let us sit down and fall to meat,
I'm fairly famished,—stiff with cold.

[HERMIT *approaches, soliloquizing*]

HERMIT   When, cruel fate, will cease the pains
Which rack me ever here alone
In this rude desert, where I see
No living things but rats and snakes,—
And dainty song-birds sure are they!
From day to day my woes increase,
Nor find I who might give me news
Of the expected Saviour's birth.
But here are shepherds, and they seem
Preparing for their evening meal.
In hope of tidings I draw near.

[*To* Shepherds]

Heaven guard you, shepherds!

TEBANO   Who so late
Breaks the repose of peaceful men?

HERMIT   Listen a moment, thou shalt know.
'T is nearly now a century
That I dwell in this desert drear,
A living skeleton, a soul
In a dead body. O'er the hills
In loud lament I give the winds
My sorrows. Late I heard the pipe
Of shepherds, with the bleat of sheep,
And came to learn the mystery.
Know ye it, brothers? Tell me straight
Pour balm into this wounded heart.

TEBANO   If thou wouldst journey on with us,
Come, and thy doubts may shortly cease.

HERMIT   With all my heart, but give me food;
With hunger I am like to swoon.

CUCHARÓN   Nay, eat thy fill, for here thou seest
Tamales, kid, and all the rest.
Once satisfied, we take the road.

HERMIT   Wait not for me, for I am one
Can eat and journey both at once.

GILA   Shepherds, the kid is ready now,
Let Bato bring the sauce-pans in
That I may serve it hot to all.

BARTOLO   O clever girl! where didst thou learn
Such phrases? Hast thou been to school
In noble mansion, that thou speak'st
So airily? By thy good leave,
A mouthful now I dare to take!

HERMIT   A good girl, Gila, by my faith,
She always suited me because
She cooks so well, and any dish,
Or veal or lamb, she seasons hot,
Makes omelets light, pinole thick,
And browns tamales to my taste.

MELISO   Listen to what I heard last night
Down in the village. There they say
Gerardo's daughter's to be wed.

GERARDO   They have not asked me for the girl,
Just talked of it among themselves;
But if she were provided for,
'T would take a great load off my mind.

PARRADO   Now heaven forbid! For when I can,
[aside]   I mean to marry her myself.

BARTOLO   Gila, good girl, I'm dead with sleep;
                Watch thou; I'm weak, and need to rest.

GILA   A pretty pass it's come to now!
                Unlucky girl! And did I wed
                For this,—to wake and watch the sheep?
                How happy was I when a maid!
                I cannot think what foolish whim
                Induced a girl so young as I
                To wed a sickly, cross old man.
                This is my grief,—a heavy load!

BARTOLO   Come, no complaints. Is supper o'er?
                Then bring the gourd, 'tis time to drink
                My night-cap. But what sound is this,
                What melody begins to swell?
                Bah! it is gone. To sleep, my friends,
                The sounds have ceased.

PARRADO   To sleep, while I
                Give a last look to all the flocks.

                                    [*Exit* PARRADO]

ALL   Till he returns let us be gay.
                Strike up the music, dance and sing!

SONG

Es - ta sí que es no - che bue - na,
Es - ta sí que es no - che bue - na,

sí que las o - tras no , Por - que di - sen
De re - go - ci- jo y a - mor, Por - que di - sen

que na - ci - ó El Di- vi- no Re - den - tor.
que na - ci - ó El Di- vi- no Re - den - tor.

This is the holy, holiest eve,
None other half so bright,
For Jesus, powerful to save,
Is born for us to-night.

This is the holy, holiest eve
Of love and pure delight,
For Jesus, powerful to save,
Is born for us to-night.

BATO   A virgin bore the tender Babe,
For heavenly His conception was.
A tiny Child, He came disguised
In human flesh, prepared for death,
Trembling, suffering, giving life,
Becoming man. The angels sang:
"The Prince of Peace is born to-day!"

BARTOLO   The Child was born in winter's chill,
After so many weary years.

The mighty sea was once a fount,
The eternal sun grew from a star.
Thou tender Child, thou infant God,
Thou incarnation of our joy,
New man, strong Sampson, Solomon
Rich and wise! Thou, Joseph, Jonas,
David! Of thee the angels sang:
"The Prince of Peace is born to-day."

BATO   Kneeling before their infant God,
They formed a joyous circle round.
Tremontón amid the straw
Laughed and gamboled for the Babe!
Mengo, to sound of tambourine,
Danced and capered high for joy;
And over all the angels sang:
"The Prince of Peace is born to-day!"

BARTOLO   How rich the voices swell the air!
The angel bands are bearing flowers,
And singing humble songs of praise.
Ah! me, how sweet the mighty tones!
They sing: "Glory to God on High!"

SONG

Glo - ria   á Dios en   las   al . . . . .
De   la   mas pu - ra   don . . . .

tu - ras   Paz al   hom - bre   en   la
ce - lla   Na - ció el cla - vel   en - cen -

tie - rra,   al   hom - bre   en la tie - rra.
di - do,   el   cla - vel   en - cen - di - do.

"Glory to God," the angel said,
"And peace to man." Behold within
The stable, in a manger laid,
Jesus, the conqueror of sin.

Of Mary, Maid Immaculate,
Was born this flower of Jesse's tree;
To free mankind from Adam's fate
The Saviour came, by God's decree.

Sweet Mary, Maid Immaculate,
Has borne a son of high renown;
To save mankind from Adam's fate,
Jesus in human form came down.

Swift, happy Michael, run,
Leave the host on high!

> *To greet the bléssed Son,*
> *Haste thy footsteps, fly!*

[*The* ANGEL (Michael) *appears, but vanishes so quickly that the Shepherds scarcely realize what the vision is*]

ANGEL   *Gloria en excelsi Deus,*
            Shepherds of earth, be not afraid,
            For God himself has sent me down
            To tell you of the Saviour's birth,—
            Your fond desire! The holy men
            Of yore foretold it; mine the task
            To give you joy of this great gift
            Our Lord permits you to receive.

[*Enter* PARRADO]

PARRADO   Asleep, my brothers?

ALL   Wide awake!

PARRADO   Give me a present for my news,
            And I will tell you what I saw
            A moment since on yon hill-top.

TEBANO   What dost thou ask?

PARRADO   Nay, offer each.

TEBANO   Pilio, my ox.

NAVAL   My ox, Palomo.

TORINGO   My spotted steer.

TULIO   To please thee I
            Will pipe a tune.

MELISO   And I will dance.

HERMIT	I will dance too with all my heart.
BARTOLO	I promise thee a snow-white lamb.
BATO	My gift thou shalt not know until Thou dost declare thy news.
PARRADO	Come say, What wilt thou give?
BATO	I promise thee Gold, most welcome sure to thee.
PARRADO	I like the gifts, and chiefly thine, But e'er I speak, give me the gold; We're wasting time.
BATO	Thou lik'st the gifts?
PARRADO	Indeed, indeed they suit me well.
BATO	Then e'er thou dost pretend to them, Tell us thy news.
PARRADO	Listen, and I Will tell you all. There by the hill, In yonder field, the wonder came. An angel, or a seraph fair, A gleaming star in birdlike flight I saw, while gath'ring in my flock. I know not what it was; it seemed To shoot forth radiance like the sun. With strange sweet voice that thrilled my ear, It sang: "Glory to God on high."
ALL	Who would believe a tale like this?
PARRADO	Believe it, for by Heaven above I seem to see it now!

TEBANO   And well
Thou mayst. The heavenly vision flashed
Before me here a moment since.
It said: "Shepherd, be not afraid,
You soon shall see in Bethlehem
A manger-cradled miracle."
You doubt me? Look! For now again
It comes. How beautiful! A star,
A planet shines less bright!

[ANGEL appears]

PARRADO   The same
Rare prodigy of which I spoke!
I saw it yonder, but amazed
Marked not it came from heaven!

ANGEL   But now
I saw thee gathering in thy flock
Beside the wood, but spoke not then.
Time lacked, for Lucifer drew near,
Furious, eager to destroy
Thy brothers, rob them of their souls!
Shepherds, beware, the demon comes;
Resist him all, and trust in God!

[ANGEL disappears]
[LUCIFER enters]

LUCIFER   Grouped on these hills the shepherds lie
[aside]   Sleeping. I summon all my craft
To steal their souls. All Hell assist!

[To Shepherds]

Shepherds, be not afraid of me.
I am a man, no savage beast,

And all I ask is shelter, food,
And fire,—a stranger's right.

TEBANO
Good sir,
Most gladly would I grant thy wish,
Did I not fear . . . just wait a bit.

[*Aside to the other* Shepherds]

As quick as maybe, let's away!

LUCIFER
[*aside*]
That timid answer suits my pride!
But I abandon force, and try
What cunning may to trap this boor.

[*To* TEBANO]

Tell me, my friend, what frightens thee?
I dress in black, the hour is late,
But what of that? In very truth
I am the richest man alive!
Come thou with me, my fortune's thine!
Dost thou refuse? Then woe betide!

MELISO
Hearest thou, Mengo, the reply
Of this black lion's mug?

MENGO
Take care!
If I get angry, I may pitch
This stranger in the fire!

LUCIFER
[*aside*]
Thou knave,
I'll tear thy heart out first! I come
From murky dungeons, horrid caves,
A roaring lion, breathing flames!
And what enrages me? A dream!
A vision of a new-born babe,
Destined to vanquish Lucifer!

The hermit and two devils.

Well, be it so! In Bethlehem
No shepherd, great or small, I swear,
But shall fall victim to my wrath!
For I am Lucifer! I come
To scour the valley, seeking out
This God, my foe! All Hell I bring
With me, to make a hell of earth!
In hunter's garb I take the field
To chase the souls of each and all!

[*To* Shepherds]

Health to you all, good people!

TEBANO   Thou art welcome.

What wouldst thou among
These rugged cliffs, in such a plight?

LUCIFER   By evil chance I lost my road
Among the moors. A stranger's right
To food and rest I claim.

TEBANO   My heart
Warns me this stranger's like to prove
Some thief.

HERMIT   Who art thou, say? I shake
With fear!

LUCIFER   Thou askest who I am?
Know me that lordly favorite
Of the invincible King, whose might
Holds earth, sea, heaven in his hand.
His vassals served me—god-like host,
But I gazed scornful at the sun,
And swelled with futile pride . . . I learned
That I must bow before a boy,
A babe in Virgin Mother's arms!
What shame to yield my pride to her!
Wonder not, shepherds, seeing me
Enter your country. I pursue
My tyrant foes, give blow for blow,
And seek their death at cost of life!

HERMIT   Flee, brothers, 't is Apollyon!

[They run off]

[Enter ANGEL]

ANGEL   Nay,
Flee not, good shepherds! Neither thou,

Wily serpent, venomous beast!
Thou 'rt not content, infernal snake,
With thy past crime of making Eve
And Adam sin against God's law?
Out of my presence, lest my sword
Of flame consume thee! Did it fail,
With Mary's name I'd cast thee down!
Knowest thou not that even now
The seraphs two by two write down:
"Jesus is born to conquer sin!"

LUCIFER   Michael, among these rustic louts
Let me prepare my traps, extend
My nets, wound with my deadly ire
Those who have wounded me! May I
Not burn the world, since with it I
Should perish too?

ANGEL   No, traitor, no!
Behold me to protect them here!

LUCIFER   Thou, Michael, to protect them com'st!
If once in Heaven thou didst prevail,
On earth thou canst not! I am king
Of earth! Perish beneath my brand!

ANGEL   What power like God's!

[*Exit* ANGEL, *driving* LUCIFER *before him*]
[*Enter* Shepherds]

CUCHARÓN   Come, shepherds all,
Since here we're safe and sound arrived,
Let us sit down and sup in peace.

BATO   Brothers, how long the day has seemed!
                 I'm faint with hunger.

CUCHARÓN   As for me,
                 I'd make no bones of eating nails.

BARTOLO   Dear wife, get supper quickly. Hear
                 What Cucharón and Bato say.

GILA   Barely arrived, I'm out of breath;
                 I wish they would not bother me.
                 I have not made the salad, come,
                 Make it thyself, if such thy haste!

[*Enter* LISARDO]

LISARDO   Last night in secret I set forth
  [*aside*]   Alone, across the dreary moors,
                 Looking for Uncle Bartolo,
                 For Gila, Nabal, Bato,—then
                 My cattle strayed on every side.
                 Let me but find the beasts, their hides
                 Shall stretch beneath my whip!

GILA   There, there,
                 Don't worry me to death. If they
                 Are famished, let them come and eat
                 At once!

HERMIT   For my part I draw near
                 Without twice asking. Give me part
                 Of what is ready, for the cold
                 Is cruel on this height, and I
                 Assure thee hunger makes me faint.

LISARDO   Attention, brothers, pious men,
                 See grandee Don Toringo take

A morsel from the spit! Are there
Fritters? Then listen to the tale
Tebano told me. First I bless
The mouthful, as the Fathers use
When they eat sitting: *"Nominis
Santi adentro abiscum, cantis
Pastores contiflores!"* Know,
My faithful flock, that when I stood
With Bartolo beneath the bays,
We heard sweet viols sound! A light
Rosy as dawn played o'er the sky.

BARTOLO   To finish off my supper well,
Give me a pot of wine. Then warm
Wrapped up in shawls, I'll sleep till dawn.

CUCHARÓN   Friend Bartolo, how cold it is!
The marrow's frozen in my bones.

BARTOLO   Quick Cucharón, run guard the flock,
Lest wolves devour the little lambs.

CUCHARÓN   No use complaining! Though my feet
Ache still with running. Tell me, friends,
Where are the lambs?

HERMIT   Poor Cucharón
I wager they have not strayed far.

CUCHARÓN   I freeze afield, while here in camp
Bartolo shivers,—by the fire!
Well, friends, I'm off!

> [*The* Shepherds *all lie down to sleep*]
> [*Enter* LUCIFER, *meeting* CUCHARÓN]

LUCIFER   From these rude hinds
[*aside*]   The truth despairing fury seeks.

Seven devils and shepherd lad.

[*To* CUCHARÓN]

Whence com'st thou, shepherd?

CUCHARÓN   From the camp,
Good sir.

LUCIFER   I ask thy country, fool.

CUCHARÓN   My cousin's dead, God rest his soul!

LUCIFER   Knave, how darest thou jest with me?

CUCHARÓN   Nay, I spake true. Now let me pass.

LUCIFER   Later, mayhap, if so I choose.

CUCHARÓN   Woe's me, what meanest thou, my Lord?

LUCIFER   Thou shalt know later.

CUCHARÓN Why not now?

LUCIFER Soon shalt thou know! But fear me not.

CUCHARÓN Thou 'rt clothed in black! Perchance I'm dead,
And this a carrion crow, well taught
By scent, come straight to bury me!

LUCIFER This simpleton may serve my turn,
[aside] Reveal what heaven hides from me;
For oft God grants these innocents
Grace to perceive His high designs.

           [To CUCHARÓN]

Look thou, shepherd, answer truly,
And naught of harm shall come to thee;
But palter with me, and thy flesh,
To quiv'ring morsels torn, shall bleed
A warning to the world!

CUCHARÓN This is
A fearful threat! Ah! how my teeth
Do chatter! God grant some good end!

LUCIFER Say then, hast heard the gossips tell
Of the Messiah's birth, or that
He soon shall come?

CUCHARÓN O sir, kind sir,
Matías is my cousin, sir!
Two years ago, by accident
He slew a man, was banished for 't,
But some days since they pardoned him.
Had he come home with lightning speed
He might be here,—or near at least.

LUCIFER   Matías, fool! I said not so!
               Again, good shepherd, answer me.
               The true Messiah's born, or no?

CUCHARÓN   There is no True Matías! I
               By the same token now recall
               I saw him circumcised, and stood
               For him at baptism. Him we named
               "Matías" plain, no hint of "True."
               'T was for his father, Matthew, sir,
               First cousin to my father, and
               Akin to my old Grandpa, who
               Married his cousin german. See,
               Good sir, these Mats descend each one
               From old Mathusalem; and he
               They say was grandson of Matán.
               Matthew who killed his ma-in-law
               Descended, by my uncle's side,
               From Aaron. I believe, kind sir,
               My grandfather must be the True
               Matías!

LUCIFER   Cease thy chatter, fool!
               Must flames burn truth from thee?

CUCHARÓN   What, flames!
               Ah! no, kind sir, I recollect
               Here in this very village I
               Knew one Matías, smith by trade.
               An *honest* man, still I'll not swear
               He is the *True* Matías.

LUCIFER   Now
               By the fierce fire that tortures me,
               Thy heart I'll tear from out thy breast!

Slave! Ass! Thy family pedigree
Thou dar'st recite, while I consume
In helpless rage!

[Seizes CUCHARÓN]

CUCHARÓN   O God! I burn!

LUCIFER   That name affronts me!

CUCHARÓN   In God's name!
I burn!

LUCIFER   At that name's power
I loose my hold; but saving it
I should have swallowed thee in flames.

CUCHARÓN   Down to the depths! If now I fail
To rout thee, Cucharón is lost
For aye!

LUCIFER   Lie not to him who comes,
He is my enemy, and I,
Devil, Torment, Hell, o'erthrown,
Seek nor encounter aid. Here end
My words! I go, in blackest Hell
To suffer everlasting pain!

[LUCIFER *disappears, and* CUCHARÓN *rushes off the stage. The* Shepherds *wake]*

MELISO   Now to speak of something else,
What has become of Cucharón?

BARTOLO   Perhaps he's frozen with the cold,
And these his funeral chants, for hark!
The music sounds! Nay, here comes he,
Flying!

BATO Bartolo frightens me!
     He's talking in his sleep mayhap,
     Or else the cold has turned his brain!
     Here comes the fellow; look at him,
     Good brother Hermit! One would say
     The man with fright had lost his wits!

  [Enter CUCHARÓN *in great fright and confusion]*

HERMIT Cucharón, my good fellow, tell
     What has occurred. Thou frighten'st me.
     Hast thou been dreaming, or hast lost
     The sheep?

CUCHARÓN The sheep! I would 't were that!
     Friends, I have met the Devil!

       [Enter NABAL]

NABAL Ah!
     Let me, though with a rustic tongue,
     Describe the wondrous vision seen
     But now within this wood. Yet stay,
     Celestial music fills the air!
     Listen all, 't is heaven's message.

SONG

   To-day I am immortal made.
   By a heavenly prodigy, —
   The Son in human flesh arrayed,
   Sent by God to set us free.

     [Enter LUCIFER]

LUCIFER Hark how the voices chant the words
 [aside] I read; declare the day is come
     'Spite of my wiles! Again they sing!

SONG

Ve - nid Mi - guel di - cho - so,

Del Ar - ca ce - les - ti - al, A - pre - su - rad el

pa - so, Ve - nid co - rred vo - lar. De

Da - niel y de Y - sai - as Se

cum - plen los ba - ti - si - nios . Que

hoy su cuer - po . sus - ten - ta La

u - nión del Ver - bo Di - vi - no.

Behold your prophecies come true,
Seers of the holy line!
A tender babe unites the two —
The human and divine.

LUCIFER　　What ringing voices join the song,
　　　　　　Flooding the air! I cannot choose
　　　　　　But listen, though I burst with rage!

SONG

Swift, happy Michael, run,
　Leave the host on high!
To greet the Holy Son
　Haste thy footsteps, fly!

LUCIFER　　What sound of rushing in the wind!
[*aside*]　　What rosy gleams across the night!
　　　　　　Michael, perchance? Well, let him come,
　　　　　　I care not now!

　　　　　　[*The* ANGEL *appears*]

ANGEL　　　Before I give
　　　　　　This waiting band the joyful news,
　　　　　　To endless exile must I hurl
　　　　　　Prince Lucifer. Speak, crafty snake,
　　　　　　What mean thy threats? Wouldst thou deceive
　　　　　　These shepherds? Then behold me come
　　　　　　Swift to their rescue! Haughty prince,
　　　　　　My mission is to humble thee,
　　　　　　Soon shalt thou writhe beneath my foot,
　　　　　　There vanquished for eternity!

LUCIFER　　Then long live Hell! Thy rigor here
　　　　　　Were death indeed! I will away
　　　　　　To the volcanoes of my realm!
　　　　　　Defiance to the will that craves
　　　　　　This vile submission! Answer me,
　　　　　　Ye shepherds, I will speak at length.

Plainly, I am the Devil! God
Himself has ordered me to kill
You all! Wouldst thou escape? Then come,
Follow me, brother. Jewels, gold,
Pearls,—riches of the Emperor
My father,—all are thine! [*to Michael*] Scorner,
Wherefore dost seek me here on earth?
Did not suffice my banishment
From heaven, and must the Holy Writ,
And these celestial harmonies,
And messengers announcing peace,
Still deeper render my despair,—
Bring fresh confusion on my head?
Ah! woe is me! Art thou indeed
Commissioned by Almighty God
To crush my power? Then man as well
Shall perish in the sight of God!

ANGEL   For this vain menace thou shalt feel
An added pang, although the boast
Is but thy ancient pride, I know.
Why linger'st thou? What dost thou seek?
How to retract, or dost thou weigh
Thy peril, shouldst thou challenge me
To combat? Nay, the remedy
Lies in thy hand! Cease raving, fiend,
Thy little strength is useless now.

LUCIFER   Michael, I know thee well. Thou think'st
To conquer me with arrogance,
Trumpet thy triumph, matching thee
With Lucifer! Although thou didst
In our first contest vanquish me,

The second count not, therefore, gained.
The agile foe wounds first, but oft
Presuming, falls in later strife.
One right my fury claims,—to kill
This woman.

ANGEL   Hellish beast, thy wish
Must leap divinest barriers. Round
About her circle hosts to guard
'Gainst perils, most of all 'gainst thee!

LUCIFER   'Tis she Isaiah promised! Here
Blooms Joseph's staff with mystic flower!
Woman, at last thou conquerest me.
Nay, words, stay on my lips! Open,
Ye fiery depths, Michael must pay
The treason which offends me!

ANGEL   Wretch,
What sayest thou?

LUCIFER   Thou owest me,
Michael, revenge for my defeat.
Proudly I claim this woman.—No?
Then Hell assist me! These her guards,
In bloody fragments will I hew,
A warning to affright the world!

ANGEL   Proud spirit, thou shalt see fulfilled
The prophecy of David,—truth
Made evident by this event:
"Under thy feet the dragon thou
Shalt trample!" Yield thy neck, accursed!

LUCIFER   Yield!

ANGEL   Thou canst no longer choose.

LUCIFER   Michael, what power on earth like mine?

ANGEL   Monster, what power like God's?

LUCIFER   That name
                 Again, my master torment! I
                 Must turn and hear my sentence. Thou
                 Didst conquer me.

ANGEL   Thou knowest well
                 For thy mad crime I chased thee forth
                 By word of God from heaven's seat.
                 But tell me, wherefore didst thou sin?
                 Come hither first; beneath my foot
                 Bow low thy stubborn neck.

LUCIFER   Michael,
                 The measure of my strength this day,
                 No later, thou shalt know! Thyself
                 In pieces straight I'll hew to show
                 My mettle.

ANGEL   Vanquished at my feet
                 Art thou, and shalt behold thyself,
                 For greater punishment, bound down
                 Forever with this chain.

                      [The ANGEL binds LUCIFER with a chain]

LUCIFER   Ah me,
                 Could pain be greater? Shame and rage,
                 Why burst ye not my heart? My wrath
                 Shall fright the elements! Alas!
                 The sudden malice, ruthless force
                 That crushes me! I must endure

The most atrocious torment! Thou
Descendedst at the word of God
From heaven, whence I fell, to prove
A carpet for thy feet! Michael,
My spirit yields; that name alone
Could vanquish me, subdue my will.

SONG

I grieve not for my fall,
   Nor mourn my perished state,
   But sorrow to await
This fiercest pain of all.

LUCIFER   Michael, thou hold'st me captive here,
But for my war on man I call
The bands of hell; and to inspire
Terror, this mount, this dusky cave
Shall vomit out the murky host.

SONG

Inferno, what a tyrant thief
   Thou hast laid in cruel pain.
   See what shackles now restrain
Acccurséd Lucifer, thy chief.

LUCIFER   Here at my cry of anguish haste,
At valor's call, ye troops of Hell!
Infernal legions, aid me now
In hour of need! Come, minions, come!
They gather, will not linger! Ah!
Why should he still breathe air whose birth
Was marked for evil from the first?

SONG

1. A - pren - ded flo - res de
2. Que a - yer ma - ra - vi - llas

mí, . Lo que va de a - yer á hoy,
fuí, . Y hoy som - bra de mí no soy.

Ye blossoms, learn your fate from me,
　　How unlike morrow follows morrow;
　At eve an angel I, and free,
　　At dawn this captive shade of sorrow.

LUCIFER　　　Ye planets, stars and elements,
From northern to the western sky,
From southern bound to orient,
Give ear unto my bitter cry!
Now all my glory's growth is o'er,
The heavens I ne'er again shall see,
For pride is an ill counsellor,—
Ye blossoms, learn your fate from me!

SONG

Ye blossoms, learn your fate from me!

LUCIFER   Since now thou hast usurped my place,
Thou doest despise my ancient worth;
To render deeper my disgrace
Thou com'st to hail the Saviour's birth.
O fortune, turn thy scornful face,
Mark not the grief that tortures me!
O'er that bright dream of sovereignty,—
Mine e'er I learned this depth of sorrow,—
Let memory hang, and anguished sigh:
How unlike morrow follows morrow!

SONG

How unlike morrow follows morrow!

LUCIFER   God reared me midst his shining host,
But though excess of lust and pride,
My godlike beauty soon was lost,
My envious spirit mortified;
My power became an empty boast,
The Prophets' words were justified.
But though the throne be lost to me,
Know, Daniel, where I took my stand!
Isaiah, great was my degree!
Though now a slave in Michael's hand,
At eve an angel I, and free!

SONG

At eve an angel I, and free!

LUCIFER   Ah! second, deadlier hour of pain,
               Redemption dawns in Jesus' eyes;
               My schemes for Adam's fall were vain,
               Father of Sin, I lose my prize!
               The abysses gape to swallow me,
               My torment ne'er shall know a morrow!
               At eve, that form of majesty,
               At dawn, this captive shade of sorrow!

SONG

At dawn, this captive shade of sorrow!

LUCIFER   Ah, Michael, was I not a chief
               In yon celestial court on high?
               Yes, now that folly's work is wrought,
               I scarcely know myself, so lost!

ANGEL   Well, dragon, since thou knowest all,
               And seest all, how dar'st presume
               To steal their faith from Christian breasts,
               From these who pray thy very Lord?
               How, fool, audacious, found thy wrath
               Courage to wage a frenzied war
               On those whom God was pleased to bless?
               Haste thee away, serpent, lest I
               To thy just torment add of woe
               A double part, to 'quit the crime
               I frustrate, 'gainst these simple souls!

LUCIFER   All thy commands I will obey,
               But Lucifer will not depart
               And leave unfinished his last work.

ANGEL   What, Lucifer, thou lingerest still?

Begone! and let these shepherds haste
To see the Word made human flesh.
Arise, thou loathsome beast, plunge down
The yawning chasm, where damning sin
Will prove itself thy sharpest pain.
Gird up thy loins, since from the earth
Thy Maker exiles thee for aye,
While man receives through sovereign grace
The gift of love which conquers sin.

LUCIFER A crater, belching poisonous fire,
I fain would bury rescued man
Beneath the lava of my hate!
Hopeless with thee my further strife;
Man must I tempt, and should I fail,
Eternal enemies we rest,
And all will follow in God's plan
When I, engulfed, embitter Hell.

ANGEL To thy abode, Demon! Depart,
Iniquitous phantom, I command!
Plunge in the abyss, well-earned thy pain!

LUCIFER How, Michael, thou pursuest me still!
Then know me wrathful foe to all,—
Aspid, gad-fly, raging lion,
Thunderbolt charged with deadly fire!
For man has sorely wounded me.
I sigh and groan and weep with rage,
Calling for surcease,—since to speak
One's sorrow dulls its sharpest pang.
Now all will follow in God's plan
When I engulfed embitter Hell.

[SATAN *vanishes, and the* Shepherds *sing their song of victory*]

SONG

1. Vic - to - ria cla - men los
2. Co - rri - do va Lu - ci -

cie . los, por - que ha ven-ci - do Mi - guel.
fer . á pe - sar de sus des - ve - los.

The heavens are chanting "Victory,
Saint Michael has prevailed!"
Watch Lucifer crestfallen flee,
His baneful schemes unveiled!

ALL   *Together let us joyful sing*
In Lucifer's despite;
Confusion to th' infernal king,
Glory to Michael's might.

ANGEL   This song of triumph celebrates
Submission of the rebel prince.
Now hear, ye shepherds, gladdest news,

The greatest joy to-day on earth.
Fear not to listen. Grace is yours,
For God is born this holy night,
In humble manger, 'mid the straw
Of two dumb beasts,—His wond'ring hosts.
Have done with trembling, seek Him out,
Close following my guiding light,
That you may know His gracious face.

SONG

Sing Parrado and Bato still,
Brothers, we reach the sacred hill.

Shepherds, sing our blissful lay,
Now the night shines bright as day.

Shepherds, across the mountains steep,
Climb on, sing on, driving our sheep.

Shepherds, the joyful notes rise wild,
We soon shall greet the Holy Child.

PARRADO   Beloved brothers, day has dawned,
Haste to the manger, off'ring each
His humble gift to immortal God.

[The manger is unveiled, and the Shepherds *approach slowly]*

TEBANO   Approach and view the Sacred Babe.

PARRADO   Divine in beauty as in might!
But friends, whom see I by the Child?
Is she not Mary, called the Fair?

HERMIT   The purest Mother of Our Lord,—
Virgin and sacred Rose of heaven!

PARRADO Ah me! who could have dreamed last eve
     So fair a face would greet us, here?
     In truth, good fortune guided us!
     God chose her out of all to be
     His mother; would that she were mine!

MELISO Bridle thy tongue, for this is God.

PARRADO O what a pretty little Babe!
     Were he but grown a bit, I'd steal
     Him off to play with nephew Jim.

MELISO Brother, thou speakest like a fool!

PARRADO Now by our gracious Lord, I swear
     I'm like to lose my wits for joy!

GILA What, art thou swearing at the Babe!

PARRADO Enough, dear Gila, let's approach,
     Adore the Child, and lay our gifts
     Before this miracle of love,
     And look with wondering awe on God.

TEBANO Quick, let us go, in Heaven's name.

PARRADO This night, miraculously fair,
     Is our long-wished-for Holy Night.

ALL Yes, brothers, this is Holy Night.

PARRADO Beauteous angels hover round
     Singing the peace of God on earth.
     See the manger ringed with light
     Brighter than earthly radiance far!
     Draw near in peace and offer prayer.

TEBANO Thou shouldst go first, that art the chief.

PARRADO   Tebano, Nabal, Mengo, come;
Gila, Hermit, Don Bartolo.—
Listen, thus you all shall go.
Tebano, thou as eldest, first
Must say thy prayer, and humbly bring
Thy offering to the infant God.

TEBANO   Since as the eldest I begin,
I must approach the Child with awe,
To teach you all due reverence.

[Tebano *approaches singing*]

How tender is the mother,
    Rosy bright Aurora;
Jesus smiles her lover,
    A Zephyr for this Flora.

PRAYER

To-day when graced by favors high
Joy fills my heart at sight of thee,
Thou holy Maid Immaculate!
Take my poor basket, heaped with flowers.
(Would I had lands to offer thee!)
And give us—sinners all—thy prayers!
Come nearer, shepherds, say with me
Ave Maria! at her feet!
Farewell in peace, thou holy Rose,
Parrado comes to greet thee now.
Approach, Parrado, and adore
The tender Babe in manger laid.

PARRADO
[*singing*]   *To Bethlehem I take my way,*
    With joy and reverent awe,

To see the Saviour, born to-day,
Low laid in humble straw.

PRAYER

Heaven save thee, daughter of the Lord,
Mary, the sinners' constant friend,
Mary, the mother pure of Christ.
Princess, lovely flower of Spain,
I greet thee! for the spotless Lamb
Hath made thee mistress of the world.
Parrado bows to kiss thy feet,
And humbly craves thy blessing. Grant
The boon, with mercy infinite.
On thee be peace, thou holy Rose,
Gilita comes to greet thee now.
Approach, Gilita, and adore
The tender Babe in manger laid.

GILA   Bartolo, hear him ask me now
To go with him, and see the Child.
I fain would go; dost thou consent?

BARTOLO   Well, since Parrado wishes it
I give thee leave, but first thou must
Dance us a round to earn the boon.

GILA   I long to see the shining face
Of this most gracious holy child,
And so for once I will obey.
Come, piper, blow a jolly tune!

[Singing]

Rosy little treasure,
Joy of saints above,

Gabriel and Gila.

Star from heaven's azure,
  Pure as snow-winged dove.

PRAYER

Jesus, see me, a mere woman,
Humble, prostrate, here before thee,
Gazing at my high Creator
Shivering on the wretched straw.

His humility incites me,
Faith emboldens me to offer
This poor linen, Virgin Mother,
Praying Thou wilt shape Him garments.
And for the joy which I profess
At Thy heavenly grace to me,
O Lord who comest down to earth,—
Whom I confess,—receive these gifts,
These toys and linen,—all I have.
Now this poor shepherdess retires,
Gila by Thy leave withdraws,
Bless her, O Master of my heart.
Farewell, farewell, thou holy Rose,
The hermit comes to kiss thy feet.
Approach, dear Hermit, and adore
The tender Child in manger laid.

HERMIT   As I was telling o'er my beads,
Thou cam'st to lead me to the Child.
But, Gila, hast thou really seen
The Babe? Ah! how my heart leaps up!
To joyous music I draw near.

[Singing]

From my desert cell,
   I hastened forth to greet
The Infant God, and swell
   The crowd about His feet.

Jesus, Lord, I bring
   A necklace fair for Thee,
And this pretty string
   Of beads, my rosary.

Last of all I urge,
  Thou take my book of prayers,
And the well-worn scourge
  That speeds my soul's affairs.

PRAYER

All slept, none watched for Thy advent,
But I alone, alert and glad,
I urged them on, I brought them here,
Vouchsafe us welcome, gracious Lord.
A silversmith of Mexico,
Our glorious country! made me this,
A reliquary richly wrought.
Take it, dear Mother, for thy Son,
Behold on it the holy cross.
'T will hush the Baby when He cries!
O my sweet Jesus, Lord of Hosts,
Thy creatures' lover,—*Dominus,*
Momentus Deus! How Thy flock
Is freed from Satan and his wiles!
I fain would shelter Thee from cold.
Accept this cloak, Thy hermit's gift,
For naught but a recluse am I,
My dwelling in yon rugged mount.
Devotion brings me, wonder not,
For who should love Thee more than I,
Or sooner strive to see Thy face?
Dear Virgin, look, this rosemary
I bring thee for thy Babe. When thou
Dost dress him, rub the healing herb
Upon his navel. Fare thee well,

Peace be on thee, thou holy Rose,
Here Nabal comes to kiss thy feet.

NABAL   *To Bethlehem I take my way*
[*singing*]   *Led by love within;*
O'erjoyed I seek my Lord to-day,
      And bring the ox to Him.

PRAYER

Although poor Nabal weary comes,
He feel not fatigue, his wish
To reach the manger winged the miles.
Zounds! What unequalled prodigy!
The dearest little angel Child,
Lies in the manger! Well he said,
The stranger with the shining wings,
When he announced the miracle,
That Glory in the manger lay!
Receive my gift, thou loving Maid.
The ox to warm Him every morn,
And patient watch Him while He sleeps,
With pious joy, Virgin, I give
Thy heaven-sent Son, fruit of thy womb.
Now will I send Meliso here,
Farewell, farewell, thou Holy Rose,
Meliso comes to kiss thy feet.

MELISO   And hast thou seen Him? Now's my turn!
Strike up, fandango, beat the drum!

SONG

Above the shouting multitude
      As I lay thinking dreamily,

I heard a voice from out the wood
Chanting, chanting joyfully.

PARRADO   What listening, friend? a merry way
To earn thy wage, the while my sheep
Stray herdless? greater sheep's-head thou!

MELISO   Hear me, Master, 't was the music,
'T was the dancing made me leave them!

SONG

Above the shouting multitude
    As I lay thinking dreamily,
I heard a voice from out the wood,
    Chanting, chanting joyfully:
"Ye shepherds sleeping night away
    In mountain pasture wild,
Seek Bethlehem, make no delay,
    Adore the Holy Child."

PRAYER

Here see the Saviour of the world
Low lying on the stable straw;
He who to save mankind from sin
Was born of Mary, Anna's child,
The gracious, prophet-promised Maid,
Saint Joseph's blessed, spotless wife.
My heart beats high to see His face!
What glory have the chosen pair,
Mary and Joseph, in their Son!

[*To* MARY]

Good woman, how dost thou to-day?
And how thy husband? Has he work

In plenty? See, my milking pail
Is broken; he shall mend it straight.
Last eve, as my good woman milked,
The black cow beat her vicious hoof
Sharp on the pail, and crash it went!
Angry I cried, "Good mother, faith,
If thus thou carest for my goods,
I'm like to barter goods for care!"
I have a sister widowed late,
She begs to tend thy little one.
She'd feed Him well on dun cow's milk,
The same's made brother Gabe so stout.

Parrado   Listen how he importunes her!
How darest thou speak to Mary thus?

MELISO   Who is 't thou callest Mary, say?

PARRADO   Daughter of Anne and Joaquin, faith,
The Virgin bright, Saint Joseph's wife!

MELISO   Might princess, heavenly queen,
Mother! Vouchsafe to pardon me,
A foolish shepherd and thy slave.
No costly gift I bring thy child,
But be thou pleased to share with Him
My rustic offering of a cheese.
Heaven's peace be on thee, Holy Rose,
Toringo comes to kiss thy feet.

TORINGO   *Now at last I'm able,*
[*singing*]   *By fortune's kind behavior,*
To bring a pretty cradle
And rock the Infant Saviour.

PRAYER

Weary and footsore, still I come
Before I rest, to see the Child.
It is my privilege to give
Thee, Lord, this cock,—Thy Passion's bird,—
To wake Thee when Thou slumberest deep.
Accept it, gracious Child, and hear
How loud it crows! It chants at dawn,
Again at prayer-time. Cockerel dear,
This morn thy clarion heralded
Our glorious Lord's Nativity!
Trumpeting: "Christ is born to-day!"
Heaven's peace be on thee, Holy Rose,
Gerardo comes to kiss they feet.

GERARDO   *Baby born amid the straw,*
[*singing*]   *Laid with cattle in the stall,*
        Suffering winter's cruel law,
            The ox thy warmth, thy comfort all!

PRAYER

How Thou art trembling, lovely Child,
Chilled with extremity of cold.
These quivering limbs show human frame,—
High pledge of God, redeeming man.
Adam rejoicing shows himself,
His voice in loving accents sounds,
Praising the Child-Restorer,—He
Who bears for all the weight of sin.
To Thee, O child, with pleading eyes
And piteous voice, couched on straw,

I bring an humble gift. Accept
These little baskets. Virgin sweet,
Thy constant lover offers thee
These lengths of linen for thy Babe.
Heaven's peace be on thee, Holy Rose,
Here Mengo comes to kiss thy feet.

MENGO
[singing]

I drive my sheep, I do not tarry,
 Bethlehem I enter soon;
To the Child of Grace I carry
 As a gift this baby-spoon.

PRAYER

Mengo am I, a shepherd lad
Who loving brings these rustic spoons.
And were the wide world mine, I'd lay
It at Thy feet, with life and soul.
Thou art my God, and Lord of all,
The Universe lies in Thy hand!
Heaven's peace be on thee, Holy Rose,
Here Tulio comes to kiss thy feet.
Approach, my brother, and adore
This tender babe in manger laid.

TULIO

If I'm to sing, why thou must dance,
Gila and thou,—for well thou know'st
My feet are lead when music sounds.

PARRADO

Shepherds, disputes are out of place,
Strike up, and after let him pray.

SONG

Tulio thrummed his lute and chanted,
Capered as he ran

To see the infant God, the vaunted
Grandson of Saint Anne.

1. Pas - to - res con re - go - ci - jo
2. Es - ta es la cau - sa que á to - dos

a - llu-den me á fes-te - jar . . . A un ni-ño Diós que ha
nos es pre-ci-so el de-jar . . . La ca - ba - ña don-

na - ci - do, En Be-lén en un por - tal.
de a-bit-amos Por ve-nir-te a - do - rar.

TULIO   *Kind brother shepherds, lend your aid,*
[*singing*]   *To praise the God in manger laid.*
               Our homes we left behind us far,
               To worship 'neath the guiding star.

PRAYER

As we have sung, my errand here
Is to adore my infant Lord.

I did not think to bring a gift,
Not even a tamal for Thee;
But were I owner of a lamb,
How gladly would I offer it!
Rich Bartolo supplies my lack.
O Light of heaven, Thou art the Son
Of virginal Aurora bright!
Nothing have I to offer Thee,
Unless it be this lute of mine.
Take it, my fair Aurora, since
'Tis all I have. Should Jesus cry,
Why sound the strings, and straight
    He'll smile!
Heaven's peace be on thee, Holy Rose,
Lisardo comes to kiss thy feet.

LISARDO   *Though I'm but a little boy,*
[*singing*]   *I long to see Thy face,*
     To thank Thee for Thy gift of joy
      And marvel at Thy grace.

PRAYER

Along rough paths in regions wild,
See Mary climbs among the cliffs.
My voice I raise in praise of Thee,
I offer Thee a homely gift,
Two ribbons, and these Holland strips.
Dear mother, use them for thy Babe;
Make for Him little shirts and bands,
And what thou pleasest else. Farewell,
Peace be on thee, thou Holy Rose,
Here Bato comes to kiss thy feet.

SONG

Se le - van-tó her-ma - no Ba - to, De
don - de es -ta - ba sen - ta - do, Ca -
mi - na pa-ra Be-lén, Ver un Dios hu-ma-na-do. .

Our brother Bato rose in haste,
From where he sat, in great surprise;
He journeyed o'er the dreary waste
To greet his God in human guise.

BATO   *I rose, I donned my cloak in haste,*
[*singing*]   *I sallied forth in great surprise;*
              I journeyed o'er the dreary waste
                 To greet my God in human guise.

PRAYER

I did not bring an offering
To this high Deity, but I
Will give him a wild honeycomb.
I climbed the mountain yesterday,
(Ah! what clear celestial music,
More sweet than strains that usher in

Aurora and the God of Day!)
I climbed and uttered my lament,
Calling the heavens to pity me.

SONG

Brother Bato leaves his home,
Leaves his sheep to pasture wild,
Leaves his cattle free to roam,
Leaves his all to seek the Child.

BATO   Ye little birds, the sun is up,
Cease your chatter, hear my woes.
Beloved scenes that day and night
Ring with my sorrows, hear once more!
O'er hill I sigh, o'er dale I moan,
And when the sun's red rays shoot up
Like bloody arrows, still I weep.
The wildest beasts that roam the woods
Listen to me, tamed by my grief.
How ignorant, how lost was I
Back in my hamlet yesterday,
Unthinking of this morn's event!
Then said my father: "Mount away,
Andrew, nor stop to eat or drink.
Go learn the truth, fetch me the news."
Then called I to my brother: "Quick,
My dapple gray, my graceful steed!"
I mounted, and by dint of spurs
I reached the spot, I found the child.
How still He lies, the pretty Babe,
And what a mighty power is this!
O Mary, give thy Boy to me,
Trust me to rear Him brave and strong;

I'll give Him for His daily needs
Thirty reales every month,—
A goodly sum it seems to me.
Oh! what a darling little Babe,
I'd never tire of watching Him!
Nor was I half so stout and trim
When I lay on my mother's knee.
O new-made mother, beautiful,
More lovely than the evening star,
A pair of wonders are ye twain!
No longer would I tend my sheep,
Thy Infant's page I fain would be,
And follow Him to win thy grace.

GILA Bato, thou ramblest in thy talk,
    Thou makest us ashamed of thee.

BATO In God's name, Gila, let me be.
    You all bring Jesus offerings,
    And I alone find naught but words.

GILA Offer thy heart.

BATO Ah! yes, my heart,
    And nothing more. But wait a bit,
    Let's see if I, though half a fool,
    Can't find a way to show my love.
    Among the trifles in my pouch
    I carry something sure to please
    The Babe. O sorrow, O mischance!
    All else I find but only that!
    Ha! Ha! at last! Now give me joy!
    Joy, brothers, joy! Gila, a kiss!
    At last I find the pretty toy.
    See the little perinola!

Now, Jesus, thou and I can play.
This game concerns me, brothers, see,
And all ye lookers-on as well.
His eyelids droop, they almost close,
The Love! He wants to take a nap!
No, look, He's opening His eyes,
He beckons, sighs,—the little dear!
See, Baby Master, Goldenlocks,
Behold thy Bato on his knees.
Look, pretty, here's a toy for Thee,
See what a dainty game to play;
Bato will teach Thee how to play!
For I have faith that if I win
Thou'll grant me what I ask. Look here,
Grasp it and spin it,—so, buzz! buzz!
Then as the different letters fall
Bato will keep the count for Thee.
The L means: leave it; and the P,
Put in; the S, sustain Thou me;
The T, that I take all from Thee.
Now I begin to dance the round.
Watch, dearest Child, the game Thou know'st
Concerns me and the others here.
Strike music, while I dance the round!

SONG

1. A la som - bra de mi ar - bol fron -
2. A bre - via - da en su som - bra des -

do - so, Es - tá la ma - dre del gran Re - den - tor.
can - sa, Fa - ti - ga - da del gran - de do - lor. .

(*bis.*)

Underneath a leafy tree
  Rest the Mother and her Son;
In its grateful shadow, she
  Lies with suff'ring overcome.

The birds caress Him with their wings,
  Twitt'ring to one another,
But Jesus sobs (the while one sings),
  "How cold the snow is, Mother!"

Journey on, Mary, be not afraid,
Bethlehem's near, thou blesséd Maid.

SPOKEN

The L has fallen (Jesus, hush!),
And L means, leave me at Thy feet;

Let arrogance be overcome
By loyal courage, virtue's sword.
Since death cuts short deception's arts,
Let him who will not praise thy name
Learn his great peril e'er too late.
Now let the second dance begin.

SONG

Underneath a leafy tree. . . .

SPOKEN

The P falls this time, rightly too,—
A highly favored letter 't is.
Pluck, Lord, the scales from sinners' eyes;
Permit them to enjoy Thy love,
Thy aid and comfort, till they climb
The path that leads them to Thy throne

SONG

Underneath a leafy tree . . .

SPOKEN

The S comes now. By Thy sweet peace
Save, Lord, our souls from error's bond;
Save the apostate, who would die
In blindness; save him from despair;
Save him from cruel sin and shame;
Save by Thy voice, unseal his eyes,
That he may hear and see the truth

Now the last twirl, for that decides
If Jesus, or if I gain all.

SONG

Underneath a leafy tree . . .

SPOKEN

T means take all, and all I ask,—
Thy care to grant it. Show the strength
Of Thy great power, that all may praise
Thy holy name; and error, war,
And schism vanish from the earth,
So men may rise from earth to heaven
As freely as the wild birds soar!
Thou hast won the perinola,
Take it, belovéd Child, from me;
Remember Bato on this day
Of Thy most glad Nativity.
I praise Thy mercy, offer free
Myself, to serve Thee evermore.
Remember me, Thou Rosy Babe,
God of the Manger, heaven's Lord.
See, I bring this honeycomb.
Take it, sweet Child, pure flower of Heaven.
When next I come, I promise Thee
A dish of fritters crisp and hot.
Peace be on thee, thou Holy Rose,
Cucharón comes to kiss thy feet.

CUCHARÓN   *Dancing and singing*
[*singing*]   *Like bird on a tree,*

Joyfully bringing
Tamales to thee.

PRAYER

At Thy feet with grateful heart,
This shepherd boy in perfect love
Adores Thy great Nativity,
I sorrow that I may not bring
Rich gifts as merits Thy great love.
I offer these poor cakes, and gaze
Unworthy on Thy splendor. Now
Farewell, farewell, thou holy Rose,
Bartolo comes to kiss thy feet.
Bartolo, thou canst understand
What draws us on to Bethlehem;
What thou wouldst take to give the Child
Thou shouldst prepare; the time has come.

BARTOLO   Why take Him gifts? The rather I
Will ask that He relieve these pains
Which keep me wretched, cold, and weak.

TEBANO AND PARRADO   Haste to arrive before the Kings.

BARTOLO   Better arrive at fall of night,
When supper time is drawing on.

GILA   Rise, Bartolito, rise, 't is time
To start.

BARTOLO   Nay, Gila, go thy ways,
Bartolo me no Bartolitos.

HERMIT   To holy ground, Jerusalem,
Come, Bartolo, with joyful heart.

Shepherds urging Bartolo to rise.

BARTOLO	Go thou, and give the Saviour thanks.
NABAL	O come and see the kindly ox, Warming his guest and Infant Lord.
BARTOLO	Indeed not I; he might prove fierce And gore me sadly with his horns.
MELISO	Come, thou shalt see the friendly ass Munching his hay beside the ox.
BARTOLO	Not I, I hate to watch a feast When I get neither bite nor sup.
TORINGO	Come now, the Pleiades ride high; Thou shouldst arise.

BARTOLO   Nay, go thy ways,
           Nor bother me.

GERARDO   Come, Bartolito,
           The morning star is shining bright.

BARTOLO   Oh, what a tale, the vesper bell
           Has scarcely rung!

MENGO   Arise, Bartolo,
           Be not so lazy, waspish friend!

BARTOLO   Arise? I'm tired on this side,
           Let's try the other.

TULIO   Bartolo,
           Come look on Him with eyes of love.

BARTOLO   If thou 'rt so anxious, bring Him here.

LISARDO   In Bethlehem's a baptism feast;
           Let's thither.

BARTOLO   I'm not god-father,
           Why go then? Bring me, one of you,
           The baptism gift which falls to me.

BATO   Bartolo, rise, for honor's sake.

BARTOLO   Take care thou dost not make me rise,
           And break thy jaw!

CUCHARÓN   Rise, Bartolo,
           Let us be off to Bethlehem.

BARTOLO   Away, thou needst not plague me too.

ALL   Stubborn fellow, we must carry
           Thee to greet the Son of Mary.

BARTOLO   A minute then to wrap me up,
                In this sharp wind I might catch cold.

[*Enter* LUCIFER *unperceived by the* Shepherds]

LUCIFER   How I tormented yonder lout,
                But now he sees me conquered quite.
                Bowed down with shame, the battle lost!
                Condemned to endless punishment,
                I take my way to darkest hell,
                In cursed gloom to burn for aye!

[*Exit* LUCIFER]

BARTOLO   *To Bethlehem I take the road*
[*singing*]   *With joy my Lord to know;*
                I offer to the Infant God
                This lambkin white as snow.

PRAYER

        Behold Bartolo weak and ill,
        He brings but few tamales now
        For Gila is not well. Indeed,
        A wonder is this tender Child!
        Ungrateful mother, who dost use
        Severity with this dear Babe!
        The fragrant "Bed of Flowers" thou,
        While He lies stretched upon the straw!
        I bring Thee milk, and honey wild,
        Poor gifts! O would that wealth were mine
        To offer! Now for song and dance.
        I must arrange the serenade,
        So pardon, all, for any faults
        You may have noted in my part.

PARRADO   Right, Bartolo, while Mary sleeps
           And Joseph rests, with joyful tone,—
           But softly not to wake the Child,
           Rather to soothe His slumber light,—
           Chant Him a tender lullaby.

SONG

A la ru - ru, ni - ño lin - do,
Duér - me - te gra - ni - to de o - ro,
Ya se dur - mió el ni - ño lin - do,

A la ru - ru, vi - da mí - a,
Que la no - che es - tá muy frí - a.
Ya se dur - mió el a - gra - cia - do.

Mien - tras que duer - me des - can - za

La pe - na de mi cui - da - do.

Duér - me - te, ni - ño chi - qui - to,
Sien - do tú la her - mo - su - ra

A - ma - ble, tier - no y güe - ri - to.
Te mues - tras tan po - bre - ci - to.

Hush-a-bye, my little son,
   Hush-a-bye, my heart of gold;
Softly slumber, little one,
   Night is dark and wind blows cold.

Hush-a-bye, my pretty nestling,
   Safe in mother's bosom warmed;
While he slumbers, peace my wrestling
   Heart, thy anxious sorrow's charmed.

PARRADO   Straight when we knew of this new light
Our bonfires blazed to greet the sky,
And Christendom arose in joy.
Tulio struck his lute; Toringo
Sang (though badly out of tune);
Meliso fain would dance, but Uncle
John forbade the silly fellow.
Now all the other shepherds here
Have chosen me to speak for them,
Thinking me most discreet (my age
Is thirty-five). So in their name
I wish you all the season's peace.
But first of all to this dear Child
I wish to bow, and kiss His feet,—
Nay kiss Him all from head to foot,
This Infant God so beautiful!
One who resembled a great bird,
But bore a face of man, a youth,
A wizard, very like, came by
Singing Peace! Peace! He left us dazed,
Then joyful that we were alive.
Then came Meliso who had seen
The Child. With joy in eyes and voice
He cried: "Run quick, Parrado, run

To Bethlehem, a wonder's there,
A Child—God, born between two beasts.
Divinely beautiful He is,
And loving. Hasten to adore,
Delay not on the road; let all
Accompany thee, adore with thee
In reverence and love. There thou
Shalt see the little God whose love
Has wrought this miracle. His years
Are countless, yet an hour-old babe
He seems, there in the manger. Round
About Him hosts of angels stand,
A thousand stars shine o'er His head,
All kindly spirits wait on Him
To mark His rank with honors due.
A jar of honey and a chain
I bring,—a cross hangs from it, sign
Of safety for thy trusting flock.
This crown of laurel I put on.
Farewell, thou Bread of Shepherds, here
The distraught shepherd's praise ends.
To all the noble company
We wish a Merry Christmas.

TEBANO   Nay,
To whom shall we address our prayers
For pardon?

PARRADO   Sure, to all these friends,
Long life to them! With song and dance
We beg their grace for all our faults,—
Too many to escape their sight!

SONG

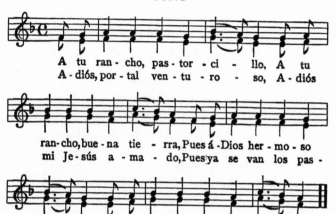

A tu ran - cho, pas - tor - ci - llo, A tu
A - diós, por - tal ven - tu - ro - so, A - diós

ran-cho, bue - na tie - rra, Pues á -Dios her - mo - so
mi Je - sús a - ma - do, Pues ya se van los pas -

ni - ño, A-quí en el por - tal te que - das.
to - res, A re - co - jer sus ga - na - dos.

To the cabin, shepherd brother,
    Home across the mountains wild!
Farewell, Baby, farewell, Mother,
    In Thy manger rest, sweet Child.

Onward, brother, see our master
    Angry looks; make haste to drive
Sheep and lambkins fast and faster;
    Night may fall e'er we arrive.

We left our flocks to pasture free,
    Forsaking all to see Thy face;
Since Thou dost guide our footsteps, we
    Shall trust to find them by Thy grace.

The Star of Bethlehem stood still
    Above the manger, as a sign;
The shepherds followed, by Thy will,
    To greet the human Child divine.

Happy manger, Jesus loving,
Now farewell, Thy shepherds haste
To gather far and near their roving
Sheep, and drive them o'er the waste.

O manger blest, we must not stay;
O loving Jesus, time constrains
The shepherds now to speed away
From Bethlehem's consecrated plains.

O happy manger, mercy-seat,
Farewell! True Saviour, loving, dear,
The shepherds humbly kiss Thy feet,
And leave Thee, till another year.

Bless all the shepherds, mighty Lord,
Our Hermit, too. Let grace abound;
And grant us life to praise Thy word,
Until another year comes round.

PARRADO	Farewell, Aunt Mary!
GILA	Uncle Joe, Farewell!
MELISO	Farewell, clear light of heaven!
TORINGO	Farewell, dear Jesus!
GERARDO	Thee I give My heart!
HERMIT	I offer Thee my soul!
PARRADO	On Thee I hang my hopes. My heart Is cheered; I offer Thee my life, My sheep as well, fifty in all,— Fifty when we set out, at least:

They all are Thine,—would they were more!
Sovereign Father, Thou whose mercy
Grants us to know Thy heavenly power,
And that we are Thy children all,
Let not wrong our senses snare,
Nor sin creep in to kill our souls.
We ask with faith, since Thou permit'st
This humble service in Thy praise.

SONG

Now with heavy heart,
Witness ye stars above,
Poor shepherd, I depart,
I leave the spot I love.

SPOKEN

I pray you, brother shepherds all,
Sorrow with me, for I must leave
The center of my dearest love.
This is cruel anguish, yes;
My life may pay for such a pang,—
Leaving behind me what I leave!
To-day with tears and bleeding hearts,
We turn away who glad approached.

PARRADO The hour has come. Without delay
We must depart. Dear Mary, thou
And Joseph, too, thy servants bless.
Humbly kneeling, see this shepherd,
Waiting joyfully the blessing.
Friends, raise your voices one and all
To say farewell, we must depart!

CUCHARÓN   To our beloved priest who strives
            So fervently to guide his flock
            Whither they may enjoy God's love,
            We fain would go, and offer up
            Our thanks on yonder hill,—now see,
            Cucharón's off! The sheep are lost,
            And we must find them, Bato else
            Will scold!

BATO   It only needs to bless,
            Great Lord, our priest, the country
            Where dwells our King, and our dear church
            Where he doth glorify Thy Son.
            Long may he live secure from sin
            To praise Thy name unceasingly!

END

Bibliography

Altamirano, Ignacio Manuel. *Christmas in the Mountains*. Trans. Harvey L. Johnson. Gainesville: University of Florida Press, 1961.

Arroyo, Anthony S., and Gilbert Cadena, eds. *Old Masks, New Faces: Religion and Latino Identities*. 3 vols. New York: City University of New York, Bildner Center, 1995.

Babín, María Teresa. *Panorama de la cultura a puertorriqueña*. New York: Las Americas Publishing Company, 1958.

Barker, George C., ed. and trans. *The Shepherds' Play of the Prodigal Son (Coloquio de los pastores del hijo pródigo). A Folk Drama of Old Mexico*. Berkeley: University of California Press, 1953.

Campa, Arthur L. *Hispanic Culture in the Southwest*. Norman: University of Oklahoma Press, 1979.

———. *Spanish Religious Folktheatre in the Spanish Southwest*. Albuquerque: University of New Mexico Bulletin Language Series, 1934.

Canino Salgado, Marcelino. *El cantar folklórico de Puerto Rico*. Río Piedras: University of Puerto Rico Press, 1974.

Castañeda, Carlos. *Our Catholic Heritage in Texas, 1519–1936*. New York: Arno Press, 1976.

Chipman, Donald E. *Spanish Texas, 1519–1821*. Austin: University of Texas Press, 1992.

Cole, M. R. *Los Pastores. A Mexican Play of the Nativity*. Trans. M. R. Cole. Boston: Houghton Mifflin, 1907.

Delacre, Lulu. *Las navidades: Popular Christmas Songs from Latin America*. Book and cassette. New York: Scholastic, 1991.

Dolan, Jay P., and Allan Figueroa Deck. *Hispanic Catholic Culture in the United States: Issues and Concerns*. Notre Dame, Ind.: University of Notre Dame, 1994.

Espinosa, Aurelio M., Jr. "The Field of Spanish Folklore in America." *Southern Folklore Quarterly* 5 (1941): 29–35.

Flores, Richard. *Los Pastores. History and Performance in the Mexican Shepherd's Play of South Texas.* Washington, D.C.: Smithsonian Institution Press, 1995.

Florit, Eugenio. *La estrella: auto de Navidad.* Havana: García Ucar, 1947.

Fontana, Bernard L. *Entrada: The Legacy of Spain and Mexico in the United States.* Albuquerque: University of New Mexico Press, 1994.

Galilea, Segundo. *Religiosidad popular y pastoral hispanoamericana.* New York: Northeast Pastoral Institute, 1981.

García, María Cristina. *Havana USA: Cuban Exiles and Cuban Americans in South Florida, 1959–1994.* Berkeley: University of California Press, 1996.

Kanellos, Nicolás. *The Hispanic American Almanac.* Detroit: Gale Research Inc., 1993.

Kanellos, Nicolás and Claudio Esteva Fabregat, eds. *Handbook of Hispanic Culture in the United States.* 4 vols. Houston: Arte Público Press, 1994–1995.

Knippling, Alpana Sharma, ed. *New Immigrant Literatures in the United States: A Sourcebook to Our Multicultural Heritage.* Westport, Conn.: Greenwood Press, 1996.

Limón, José. *Dancing with the Devil: Society and Cultural Politics in Mexican American South Texas.* Madison: University of Wisconsin Press, 1994.

Litvak, Lily, ed. *El nacimiento del Niño Dios: A Pastorela from Tarimoro, Guanajuato.* Austin: University of Texas Center for Intercultural Studies in Folklore, 1973.

López Cruz, Francisco. *El aguinaldo en Puerto Rico.* San Juan: Instituto de Cultura Puertorriqueña, 1972.

Lucero-White, Aurora, ed. *Coloquios de pastores.* Santa Fe: Santa Fe Press, 1940.

Jaramillo, Cleofas M. *Shadows of the Past; Sombras del Pasado.* Santa Fe: Seton Village, 1941.

María y Campos, Armando de. *Pastorelas mexicanas. Su origen, historia y tradición.* Mexico City: Diana, 1985.

Meléndez, Gabriel. *So All Is Not Lost: The Poetics of Print in Nuevomexicano Communities, 1834–1958.* Albuquerque: University of New Mexico Press, 1997.

Meyer, Doris. *Speaking for Themselves: Neomexicano Cultural Identity and the Spanish-Language Press, 1880–1920.* Albuquerque: University of New Mexico Press, 1996.

Moreno Villa, José. *Navidad, villancicos, pastorelas, posadas, piñatas.* Mexico City: Isla, 1945.

Otero, Nina. *Old Spain in Our Southwest.* New York: Harcourt, Brace, 1936.

Pacheco, Ferdie. *The Christmas Eve Cookbook: With Tales of Noche Buena and Chanukah.* Gainesville: University of Florida Press, 1998.

Pitt, Harriett Philmus. *Land of Two Christmases*. New York: Oxford University Press, 1965.

Rael, Juan Bautista. *The Sources and Diffusion of the Mexican Shepherd's Play*. Guadalajara, 1965.

Ramírez, Guillermo. *El arte popular en Puerto Rico*. New York: Colección Montaña, 1974.

Ribera Ortega, Pedro. *Christmas in Old Santa Fe*. Santa Fe: Sunstone Press, 1973.

Rodríguez, Jeanette. *Our Lady of Guadalupe: Faith and Empowerment among Mexican-American Women*. Austin: University of Texas Press, 1994.

Sánchez Korrol, Virginia. *From Colonia to Community: The History of Puerto Ricans in New York City, 1917–1948*. Westport, Conn.: Greenwood Press, 1983.

Santiago, Esmeralda and Joie Davidow, eds. *Las Christmas: Favorite Latino Authors Share Their Holiday Memories*. New York: Knopf, 1998.

Zavala, Adina de. *History and Legends of the Alamo*. Houston: Arte Público Press, 1996.

Credits

Alfaro, Abelardo Díaz. "Santo Clo to La Cuchilla," trans. Nicolás Kanellos. Reprinted and translated with permission of Mrs. Gladys Díaz Alfaro.

Anonymous. "The Arandelas"/ "A las Arandelas," trans. Nicolás Kanellos. Printed with permission of the translator.

Anonymous. "Christmas is a-coming"/ "El año nuevo se viene," trans. Nicolás Kanellos. Printed with permission of the translator.

Anonymous. "Down from the Mountains"/ "De las Montañas," trans. Nicolás Kanellos. Printed with permission of the translator.

Anonymous. "If You Give Me Meat Pies"/ "Si Me Dan Pasteles," trans. Nicolás Kanellos. Printed with permission of the translator.

Anonymous. "The Magi Kings"/ "Los Reyes Magos," trans. Nicolás Kanellos. Printed with permission of the translator.

Anonymous. "New Year's Eve"/ "Víspera de Año Nuevo," trans. Nicolás Kanellos. Printed with permission of the translator.

Anonymous. "Los Pastores," trans. M. R. Cole. Reprinted from *Los Pastores: A Mexican Play of the Nativity* (Boston: Houghton, Mifflin and Company, 1907).

Bernardo, Anilú. "Loves Me, Loves Me Not." Reprinted from *Loves Me, Loves Me Not* (Houston: Arte Público Press, 1988) with permission of the publisher.

Bustillos, José Maria. "Christmas Carols"/ "Cantares de Navidad," trans. Nicolás Kanellos. Printed with permission of the translator.

Calderón, Salvador. "A Sad Christmas Eve," trans. Nicolás Kanellos. Printed with permission of the translator.

Carrillo, Adolfo. "The Phantoms at San Luis Rey," trans. Nicolás Kanellos. Printed with permission of the translator.

Chacón, Felipe Maximiliano. "Christmas"/ "La Navidad," trans. Nicolás Kanellos. Printed with permission of the translator.

Chacón, Herminia. "Samuel's Christmas Eve," trans. Nicolás Kanellos. Printed with permission of the translator.

de Acevedo, S. R. "Little Christmas Candles"/ "Velitas de Navidad," trans. Nicolás Kanellos. Printed with permission of the translator.

de Anda, Diane. "The Christmas Spirit Tree." Reprinted from *The Ice Dove and Other Stories* (Houston: Arte Público Press, 1997) with permission of the publisher.

de los Santos, J. N. "The Star of Bethlehem"/ "El Astro de Belén," trans. Nicolás Kanellos. Printed with permission of the translator.

de Zavala, Adina. "Legend of the First Christmas at the Alamo." Reprinted from *History and Legends of the Alamo and Other Missions in and around San Antonio,* ed. Richard Flores (Houston: Arte Público Press, 1996) with permission of the publisher.

Fernández, Roberto G. "The Good Night." Reprinted from *Raining Backwards* (Houston: Arte Público Press, 1988) with permission of the publisher.

Flores, Jesús María. "Christmas Night"/ "Noche de Navidad," trans. Nicolás Kanellos. Printed with permission of the translator.

Gallardo, Aurelio Luis. "Christmas Eve," trans. Nicolás Kanellos. Printed with permission of the translator.

González, Jovita. "The Good Eve." Reprinted from *Dew on the Thorn*, ed. José Limón (Houston: Arte Pdblico Press, 1997) with permission of the publisher.

Hinojosa, Rolando. "The Gulf Oil Can Santa Claus." Reprinted with permission of the author.

Huyke, Juan B. "A Story about Santa Claus," trans. Nicolás Kanellos. Printed with permission of the translator.

Jaramillo, Cleofas. "Noche Buena and Religious Drama" (an excerpt). *Shadows of the Past* (Santa Fe: Seton Village, 1941).

Luján, E. "Christmas Eve," trans. Nicolás Kanellos. Printed with permission of the translator.

Mohr, Nicholasa. "Christmas Was a Time of Plenty." Reprinted with permission of the author.

Mora, Pat, and Charles Ramírez Berg. "The Legend of the Poinsettia." Reprinted from *Tun-ta-ca-tun,* ed. Sylvia Peña (Houston: Arte Público Press, 1988) with permission of the publisher.

Muñoz, Elías Miguel. "Brand New Memory," by Elías Miguel Muñoz. Reprinted from *Brand New Memory* (Houston: Arte Público Press, 1998) with permission of the publisher.

Otero, Nina. "The Márgil Vine." *Old Spain in Our Southwest* (New York: Harcourt, Brace and Company, 1936).

Paredes, Américo. "A Cold Night." Reprinted from *The Hammon and The*

Beans and Other Stories (Houston: Arte Público Press, 1994) with permission of the publisher.

Pérez-Firmat, Gustavo. "The Ghosts of Nochebuenas Past. Reprinted from *Next Year in Cuba* by Gustavo Pérez-Firmat, copyright © 1995 by Gustavo Pérez-Firmat. Used by permission of Doubleday, a division of Random House, Inc.

Reina, Manuel. "Christmas Eve"/ "Noche Buena," trans. Nicolás Kanellos. Printed with permission of the translator.

Rivera, Tomás. "The Night before Christmas," trans. Evangelina Vigil-Piñón. Reprinted from . . . *y no se lo tragó la tierra/And the Earth Did Not Devour Him* (Houston: Arte Público Press, 1995) with permission of the publisher.

Thomas, Piri. "Those with Less Shared More." Reprinted with permission of the author.

Villanueva-Collado, Alfredo. "The Day We Went to See the Snow," trans. Nicolás Kanellos. Reprinted from *Cuentos hispanos de los Estados Unidos,* ed. Julián Olivares (Houston: Arte Público Press, 1998) with permission of the publisher.

Yglesias, Jose. "The Good Night." Reprinted with permission of Rafael Yglesias.